Hiking Waterfalls Georgia and South Carolina

A Guide to the States' Best Waterfall Hikes

Second Edition

Melissa Watson

FALCONGUIDES

GUILFORD, CONNECTICUT

FALCONGUIDES®

An imprint of Globe Pequot, the trade division of
The Rowman & Littlefield Publishing Group, Inc.
4501 Forbes Blvd., Ste. 200
Lanham, MD 20706
www.rowman.com

Falcon and FalconGuides are registered trademarks and Make Adventure Your Story is a trademark of The Rowman & Littlefield Publishing Group, Inc.

Distributed by NATIONAL BOOK NETWORK

Photos by Melissa Watson unless otherwise noted
Maps updated by Melissa Baker, The Rowman & Littlefield Publishing Group, Inc.

British Library Cataloguing in Publication Information available

Library of Congress Cataloging-in-Publication Data
Names: Watson, Melissa, author.
Title: Hiking waterfalls Georgia and South Carolina : a guide to the states' best waterfall hikes / Melissa Watson.
Description: Second edition. | Guilford, CT : FalconGuides, 2022. | Includes index. | Summary: "A guide to nearly 100 of the best waterfall hikes in Georgia and South Carolina. Many of the hikes and waterfalls are located along the border between the two states, within easy access of each other" — Provided by publisher.
Identifiers: LCCN 2021039086 (print) | LCCN 2021039087 (ebook) | ISBN 9781493052042 (paperback) | ISBN 9781493052059 (epub)
Subjects: LCSH: Hiking—Georgia—Guidebooks. | Hiking—South Carolina—Guidebooks. | Waterfalls—Georgia—Guidebooks. | Waterfalls—South Carolina—Guidebooks. | Georgia— Guidebooks. | South Carolina—Guidebooks.
Classification: LCC GV199.42.G46 W38 2022 (print) | LCC GV199.42.G46 (ebook) | DDC 917.5—dc23
LC record available at https://lccn.loc.gov/2021039086
LC ebook record available at https://lccn.loc.gov/2021039087

♾️™ The paper used in this publication meets the minimum requirements of American National Standard for Information Sciences—Permanence of Paper for Printed Library Materials, ANSI/NISO Z39.48-1992.

For Mom: You are the most amazing person I know! You're my best friend, my mentor, and my inspiration. I love you beyond the earth, the sky, the mountains, and the creeks! You have been an unending influence on me, and I will be thankful for you for as long as I live. Thank you for being you! My "MAMA."

Contents

Georgia Waterfalls

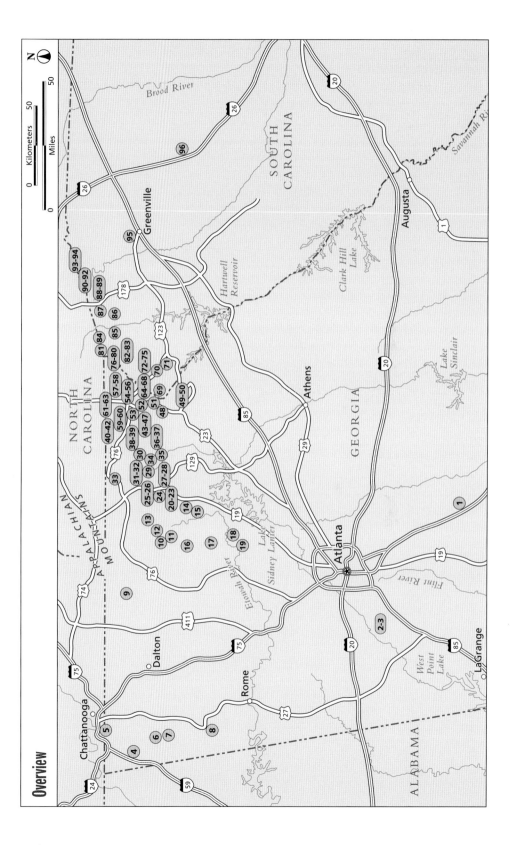

Overview

Acknowledgments

I'd like to thank my family for their love, patience, and support: Terri Sansonetti; Maria, Frazier, Christina, and Cory Payton; Doug, Romy, Johann, and Watson; Sue, Tom, Frank, Thomas, Luanna, Joe, Kristen, Rebekah, Nathaniel, Katilee, Mark, Jonathon, Joshua, Silas, Micah, and Giulia Strazza; Michelle, Roland, Lucas, and Zackary Arisolo; and Natlie and Beni Pajoga. I love you all!

To my partner, Cheryl Arcand: I know it isn't always easy standing by while I document the details, take photos, talk into a tape recorder, and then spend hours on the computer putting it all together. Thank you for your love, patience, and understanding, and for carrying all the extra weight around the house. It does not go unnoticed. I love you!

To my closest friends, for always bringing joy to my life: Dawn McKinney, Shari Santos, and Maris Herold. Whether near or far, you are always dear to my heart and always bring a smile to my face. Thank you!

Many people were helpful in confirming the accuracy of the hikes contained within. I'd like to thank all of the people working in the parks and forests for their investment of time, their wealth of knowledge, and their dedication to the precious nature described in this book. Thank you all!

Introduction

In this the second edition of *Hiking Waterfalls in Georgia and South Carolina*, I have spread my wings and branched out to the western portion of Georgia. My explorations were well worth the effort, as I have added nearly fifty wonderful waterfalls to the Georgia portion of this book. South Carolina has proven itself a formidable friend as well, showcasing an additional thirty new waterfalls across the upcountry of the state.

As I enhance my explorations, I continue to be entranced by the magic of waterfalls. From small cascades to tall, free-falling water, each has a character and beauty of its own. They are truly magical, mysterious wonders of nature. After 30 years of research, it is my pleasure to share with you the fruits of my labor and the abundant passion that I have for nature. Over these past decades I have spent months at a time camping, hiking, and reveling in the waterfalls of Georgia and South Carolina. Some of that time was spent in frustration, due to inaccurate trail or driving directions. And so I began writing the first edition of this book with one goal in mind—accuracy. I continue to carry on with that goal in the second edition, and strive to guide you with ease to the most amazing parks, forests, treks, and trails.

My big boy Mikey has since passed, but his little brother Bandit is rapidly learning the ropes of life on the road. Together we hiked and re-hiked each trail in this book while documenting every detail along the way. Those details have now been put to the pen and shine through these pages. I've provided specific trail directions and thorough driving directions. I've also included GPS coordinates and the appropriate *DeLorme: Atlas & Gazetteer* map page and coordinates to assist you on your quest to find the falls.

I hope you find this book entertaining as well as accurate as you delve in to the descriptions of nearly one hundred hikes. From roadside beauties to those set deep in the forest, the waterfalls await. Enjoy this user-friendly guide as it leads you to the most magnificent waterfalls in Georgia and South Carolina. Don your hiking boots and grab your camera—a world of discovery lies ahead.

How to Use This Guide

The waterfalls in this guide have been divided into geographic areas. This way, when you plan to visit a certain town, you can easily see which waterfalls are nearby. A detailed map of the trails and their surroundings is provided for each area.

Along with each map you'll find the featured hikes shown on that map. Each hike in this guide is presented in the same format, which begins with a brief description of the waterfall, from the author's perspective.

Next come the hike "specs": important information starting off with waterfall height, and my personal beauty rating for each waterfall. Next is the trail distance, always listed as the out-and-back total distance for the recommended hike. In some instances it's not necessarily a hike. Some waterfalls are so easily accessible that you can view the waterfall from the roadside or parking area. Then you'll find difficulty (how much exertion the trail will require), trail surface, approximate hiking time, other trail users you might encounter, and blaze color. I have also noted the county in which the waterfall is located, land status (national forest/park, private owner, etc.), trail contacts, and FYI (for your information) where applicable for additional information on the area or any other important information, such as park hours and whether a fee is charged.

Lastly you'll find the relevant *DeLorme: Georgia Atlas & Gazetteer* (2010, 6th Edition) and *DeLorme: South Carolina Atlas & Gazetteer* (2006, 3rd Edition) page and coordinates to supplement the maps provided in this guide. I highly recommend getting the *DeLorme: Atlas & Gazetteer* for any state in which you plan to hike. They've been of great help to me on my explorations. The National Geographic Trails Illustrated topographic maps are another useful tool and an invaluable resource when navigating through the mountains of the Chattahoochee, Sumter, and Nantahala National Forests.

Following the hike specs you'll see "Finding the trailhead." Because you can't enjoy the hike if you can't find the trailhead, I have provided explicit driving directions, usually from two points of reference, using either a main intersection or a state line as your starting point.

Many of the trailheads are located along USDA Forest Service roads. Most of these are unmarked dirt roads, and there may be several of these in a given area.

For this reason, I have given specific driving distances in mileage rounded to the nearest 0.1 mile. I've also tried to give you the best route to the trailhead. So if you see what appears to be a shortcut on the map, chances are there's a good reason I didn't send you that way. (**Note:** When parking near a Forest Service gate, be sure not to block the gate, and try to leave room for others when parking in pull-offs.)

While I prefer a good old-fashioned map and compass, more and more people are becoming adept at using the Global Positioning System. I therefore have provided GPS coordinates for the trailheads and waterfalls.

"The Hike" is where you'll find a general description of what to expect along the trail. I've also included a

You'll be amazed at the places a country road can take you.

brief history for each waterfall, perhaps how the waterfall got its name or some interesting information about the area. I personally learned quite a bit while researching this portion of the book and found some of the folklore to be thoroughly entertaining. I hope you do as well.

The "Miles and Directions" provide thorough hiking directions. Any questionable turn, every fork, and every T junction have been documented. I've given you the distance at which you'll reach them and provide left/right directions with corresponding compass direction.

I have worked very hard to keep you from getting lost, but please remember that trails do change over time, as do the waterfalls. The appearance of a waterfall may change with each rainfall, or lack thereof, and with every season. This is the reason I return to the same waterfalls time and time again, and yet I'm always greeted with a new experience.

For Your Safety

Before you hit the trails, there's some important information you should know to help keep you safe and sound.

Know your limits. If I say that a trail or portion of trail is for experienced hikers only, I mean it. This means no children. Some of the trails presented in this book are extremely steep and potentially dangerous. Please heed all warnings and hike within your limits.

Carry the essentials. There are "10 Essential Items" every hiker should carry: map, compass, flashlight, first-aid kit, knife, waterproof matches, candle/fire starter, extra clothing, food, and lots of water. Better to have these things and not need them than to need them and not have them. You'll find every one of these items (plus some others) in my day pack at all times.

Give someone your itinerary. Whether you hike in a group or hike by yourself, always tell someone where you'll be hiking and when you expect to return. If there's a place to sign in at the trailhead, please do so prior to hiking. And don't forget to sign out when you return.

Watch for the blazes. For those of you new to hiking, blazes are colored markers on a tree or natural surface that indicate where the trail goes. Not all trails have blazes, but for those

Blazes help keep you on track.

that do I have listed the blaze color in the hike specs. Be aware that blazes on some trails may be few and far between. Additionally, two blazes together on the same surface indicate that there's a sharp turn in the trail ahead.

Dress in layers, and always bring rain gear. It can protect you from rain, wind, and cold. Weather conditions can change rapidly and drastically in the mountains, check the weather prior to hiking. It pays to be prepared.

Wear the right footwear. It's extremely easy to twist an ankle or stub a toe while hiking. Hiking boots are a simple way to prevent this. Wear good hiking boots or trail runners, and break them in prior to hiking—you don't want to ruin your hike with blisters.

Carry a towel in your pack. Some trails call for fording creeks, and you don't want to hike with cold, wet feet. Not to mention you may want to take a dip. I swear by chamois-style pack towels, available at local outfitters or REI. They're lightweight, compact, and dry quickly.

Know where you've been. Here's a helpful hint when hiking on unfamiliar trails: Make it a habit to turn around and look at the trail from the other direction after taking a fork or T. This way, when you're hiking back out, it will look familiar and you won't miss any crucial turns.

Be careful at the brink. Don't play at, around, or near the brink of any waterfall! I cannot stress this enough. Every year people die at waterfalls, and I guarantee they never thought it would happen to them.

Don't climb the face of any waterfall. Countless injuries, even deaths, have been attributed to this as well. Always remember that the rocks and terrain around any waterfall are dangerously slippery, regardless of how surefooted you may be. Not to mention the environmental impact.

Respect the water. Water currents are extremely strong at both the brink and the base of waterfalls. Never cross at the brink of a waterfall; and if you choose to take a dip at the base, look before you leap. Rocks and trees might lie beneath the surface, and currents are likely strong. Choose your swimming holes wisely.

Taking Care of Mother Nature

Many creatures make their home in the forest. As you hike, remember that you're a guest on their terrain; respect them and the forest that harbors them. Try to live by the philosophy of "Take nothing but pictures; leave nothing but footprints." Every stone in the creek, every wildflower along the trail, has its purpose within the ecosystem. Please don't remove these or any items, except litter, from the forest.

A camera is an added bonus to your pack. When you see wildflowers in bloom, you can take their beauty home with you in photos while leaving them for others to appreciate as well.

Note: Federal law prohibits picking wildflowers; removing stones, feathers, or any other natural artifacts; and harassing wildlife in national parks. This is recommended for other jurisdictions as well—leave nature as you found it.

Take nothing but pictures; leave nothing but footprints.

Practice "pack it in, pack it out" hiking. If you bring food into the forest, bring a trash bag to carry the wrappers and remnants out. There's nothing worse than arriving at a stunning waterfall and finding it littered with human debris. Please don't litter the trails I have shared with you.

Last but not least, don't shortcut the trails. If you see a shortcut between switchbacks, I implore you to resist the temptation to take it. Stay on the main trail. Shortcutting destroys valuable vegetation, creates erosion, and makes the trails harder to follow.

Happy trails!

Trail Finder

Author's Favorite Waterfalls

5. Glen Falls
7. Lost Wall Falls (Dickson Falls)
11. First Falls on Long Creek
25. Helton Creek Falls
27. Raven Cliffs Falls (Georgia)
30. High Shoals Falls
39. Hemlock Falls
44. Upper Crow Creek Falls
46. Haven Falls
48. Panther Creek Falls
50. Toccoa Falls
51. Waterfalls of Tallulah Gorge
55. Martin Creek Falls
61. Darnell Creek Falls
63. Mud Creek Falls
67. Opossum Creek Falls
68. Long Creek Falls
69. Upper, Middle, and Lower Brasstown Falls and Falls on Little Brasstown Creek
70. Riley Moore Falls
72. Yellow Branch Falls
83. Lee Falls
87. Twin Falls
93. Falls off Jones Gap Trail

Best Swimming Holes

13. Sea Creek Falls
19. Poole's Mill Falls
20. Falls on Waters Creek
25. Upper Helton Creek Falls
30. Blue Hole Falls (High Shoals Trail)
38. Sliding Rock on Wildcat Creek
48. Panther Creek Falls
51. Bridal Veil Falls (Waterfalls of Tallulah Gorge Trail)
53. Stonewall Falls
70. Riley Moore Falls

86. Long Shoals
89. Carrick Creek Falls
92. Lower Wildcat Branch Falls

Most Crowded Waterfalls

1. High Falls
2. Cochran Mill Falls
4. Waterfalls of Cloudland Canyon: First, Second, West Rim, Hemlock, and Cherokee
5. Glen Falls
11. Long Creek Falls
16. Amicalola Falls
19. Poole's Mill Falls
24. DeSoto Falls
25. Helton Creek Falls
27. Raven Cliffs Falls (Georgia)
28. Dukes Creek Falls
29. Horse Trough Falls
34. Anna Ruby Falls
45. Minnehaha Falls
48. Panther Creek Falls
49. Henderson Falls
50. Toccoa Falls
51. Waterfalls of Tallulah Gorge
57. Sarahs Creek Falls
59. Ada-Hi Falls
70. Riley Moore Falls
71. Chau Ram Falls
73. Issaqueena Falls
85. Oconee Bells Trail
86. Long Shoals
87. Twin Falls
89. Carrick Creek Falls
90. Raven Cliff Falls (South Carolina)
92. Lower Wildcat Branch Falls
93. Falls off Jones Gap Trail
95. Reedy River Falls
96. Horseshoe Falls

Least Crowded Waterfalls

6. Pocket Falls
7. Lost Wall Falls (Dickson Falls)
9. Shadow Falls
18. Barefoot Falls
21. Crow Mountain Creek Falls
37. Raper Creek Falls
40. Denton Branch Falls
41. Bull Cove Falls (North Carolina)
52. Mill Shoals on Stekoa Creek
56. Dick's Creek Falls
58. Holcomb and Ammons Falls
66. Falls on Reedy Branch
74. Cedar Creek Falls
77. Miuka and Secret Falls

Roadside Waterfalls

10. Noontootla Falls
15. Clay Creek Falls
20. Falls on Waters Creek
23. Upper Falls on Dicks Creek
26. Trahlyta Falls

33. Cupid Falls
35. Bean Creek Falls
36. Soque River Falls
38. Sliding Rock on Wildcat Creek
53. Stonewall Falls
60. Sylvan Mill Falls
62. Eastatoah Falls
63. Mud Creek Falls
71. Chau Ram Falls
86. Long Shoals
92. Lower Wildcat Branch Falls

Best Waterfall Hikes for Backcountry Camping

27. Raven Cliffs Falls (Georgia)
41. Bull Cove Falls (North Carolina)
48. Panther Creek Falls
52. Mill Shoals on Stekoa Creek
55. Martin Creek Falls
67. Opossum Creek Falls
76. Pigpen and Licklog Falls

Map Legend

Municipal

≡(75)≡ Interstate Highway

≡(178)≡ US Highway

≡(154)≡ State Road

≡[457]≡ County/Forest Road

= = = = Unpaved Road

--·--·-- State Boundary

Trails

------- Featured Trail

- - - - - Trail

Water Features

Lake/Reservoir

River/Creek

Intermittent Stream

Waterfall

Rapid

Spring

Land Management

National Forest/
National Military Park

Wildlife Management Area

State/Local Park/
State Historic Site

Symbols

∧ Arch/Cave

||||| Boardwalk

Boat Ramp

≍ Bridge

▲ Campground

⊛ Capital

† Cemetery

•—• Gate

Lodging

P Parking

Picnic Area

■ Point of Interest/Structure

Ranger Station

Restrooms

○ Town

① Trailhead

Viewpoint/Overlook

? Visitor/Information Center

♿ Wheelchair Accessible

Georgia Waterfalls

Central Region

Macon to Atlanta

1 High Falls

Ethereal! Your spirit's instantly lifted when you gaze upon the perfection that is High Falls. The hike is short and easy, and the reward is out of this world.

Height: 30 feet
Beauty rating: Excellent
Distance: 0.2 mile
Difficulty: Easy
Surface: Stairs and wide gravel path
Hiking time: 10 minutes
Other trail users: None
Blazes: None

County: Monroe
Land status: High Falls State Park
Contacts: (478) 993-3053; www.gastateparks .org/HighFalls
FYI: Fee required; 7 a.m.–10 p.m.
Maps: *DeLorme: Georgia Atlas & Gazetteer:* Page 34 B2

Finding the trailhead: *From I-75 near Forsyth,* get off at exit 198. Drive east on High Falls Road for approximately 1.5 miles. Turn left into the main entrance to the park (just after crossing the bridge). The trailhead is directly across the street from the park entrance on the south side of High Falls Road. **GPS:** N33°10.754'/W84°01.041'

The Hike

Standing at the trailhead you'll see a trail leading left and another that heads right. The direct route to the falls as described below is to head right (south) down the steps and follow the footpath quickly to an overlook of High Falls. A red wooden fence separates you from the Towaliga River. Although comparatively it's not that "high," this is the tallest waterfall in Georgia that sits south of Atlanta, and they are just as worthy as any waterfall that you'll find in the mountainous upcountry of the state. If you'd like to extend the hike, the Nature Trail continues past the falls and the trail forms a figure-eight-style double loop that covers 1.2 miles.

This lovely state park has open grassy fields, large rolling hills, and as a bonus you can view the Towaliga River Dam from several points in the park. There are picnic tables and barbecue grills scattered here and there under the shade of tall pine trees. Picnic shelters and playgrounds accompany them, making this a very pleasant place to gather with family or meet up with friends. If this wasn't enough, the park also offers canoe and kayak rentals and has a campground. It's no wonder that it stays busy

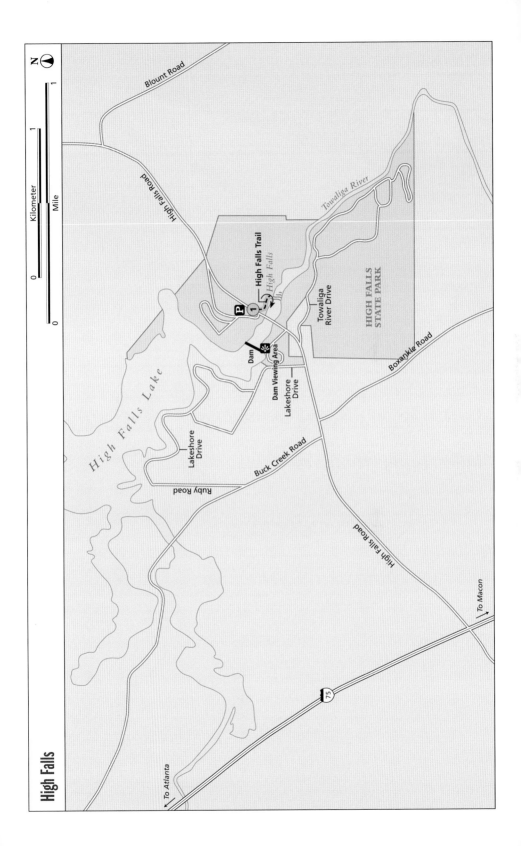

High Falls

A short easy hike leads to High Falls.

year-round, especially in spring and summer. Arrive early or you may have to wait in line to make entry.

Miles and Directions

0.0 Hike south down the stairs.

0.1 Arrive at High Falls (N33°10.712'/W84°00.984'). Backtrack to trailhead. (***Option:*** Continue hiking past the falls on the Nature Trail.)

0.2 Arrive at trailhead.

2 Cochran Mill Falls, Lower Bear Creek Falls, Bear Creek Dam, and Bear Creek Falls

Remnants of the past! From an old stone structure to a defunct dam to a well-preserved mill wheel, this hike leads you on a historical journey with roots dating back over a century deep. If that isn't intriguing enough, each of these fabulous features is accompanied by a wonderful waterfall.

Height: Cochran Mill Falls: 25 feet; Lower Bear Creek: 10 feet; Bear Creek Dam: 20 feet; Bear Creek Falls: 30 feet

Beauty rating: Cochran Mill Falls: very good; Lower Bear Creek: fair; Bear Creek Dam: good; Bear Creek Falls: good

Distance: Cochran Mill Falls: 0.16 mile; Lower Bear Creek: 1.04 miles; Bear Creek Dam: 1.6 miles; Bear Creek Falls: 1.88 miles

Difficulty: Easy

Surface: Wide gravel road, hard-packed dirt, smooth stone

Hiking time: 1 hour

Other trail users: None

Blazes: None

County: Fulton

Land status: Cochran Mill Park

Contacts: (770) 306-0914; www.cochranmill park.com

FYI: Fee required; open 30 minutes before sunrise to 30 minutes after sunset

Maps: DeLorme: Georgia Atlas & Gazetteer: Page 25 E9-E10

Finding the trailhead: *From the junction of South Fulton Parkway and GA 70 near Rico*, drive east on South Fulton Parkway for 4.4 miles. Turn left onto Cochran Mill Road. Drive 0.4 mile. Turn left onto Upper Wooten Road at the entrance to the park. *From the junction of South Fulton Parkway and GA 154 near Palmetto*, drive west on South Fulton Parkway for 2.6 miles. Turn right onto Cochran Mill Road. Follow directions above. The trailhead is the gate across the street from Upper Wooten Road on the north side of Cochran Mill Road. **GPS:** N33°34.281'/W84°42.775'

The Hike

This 800-acre park has an extensive trail system open for hiking, mountain biking, and equestrian use. Although the park is big, the parking area is not, so visit on a weekday whenever possible. As you pay the day-use fee, there are two things you notice right off the bat. First is how wonderfully wooded this park is. Second is how poorly marked the trailheads are. Be sure to print the official park map along with this text to help navigate as needed.

Go around the gate and hike downhill on the wide gravel road. You'll quickly come to a well-built bridge that crosses the creek downstream from Cochran Mill

Bear Creek Dam is small but smashing.

Falls. Nearby, a large grassy area has picnic tables and the trees offer plenty of shade. A large pool rests at the base of the falls, and the stone remnants from the old Cochran Mill oversee it all. After crossing the bridge, follow the path left (north) through the populated picnic area. A quarter-mile from the trailhead you'll go right (north) at the first of several upcoming forks and Ts. The next fork has you bypassing the Cochran Mill Loop Trail on your right. Just past this trail you will cross a footbridge and reach a T. Go right here, following the lively Bear Creek upstream. Until now you were hiking on a gravel road. From here forth the trail becomes a narrow singletrack that stays with the creek for the remainder of the hike. Near the half-mile mark you'll reach Lower Bear Creek Falls, which forms a large rockslide. When you reach the next T, again go right (east) crossing a footbridge and staying with the creek. The hike continues upstream leading you to the final two falls. First you'll come to Bear Creek Dam, where a small waterfall is formed by the man-made structure. Although it's not tall, the flow is smooth, and there's something pacifying about it. At 0.1 mile from the dam a side path leads to an old millstone sitting on the ground. After taking a peek at the past, return to the main trail and hike uphill over smooth stone to the brink of Bear Creek Falls. From this vantage point you can view the falls and see the sparse remains of another mill that stood here over a century ago.

This hike offers a lot of bang for your buck. You get four waterfalls in less than 1 mile, and a chance to see some of the historical foundations of Chattahoochee Hills. For more information on the mills, visit www.chatthillshistory.com/owen-cochran-mill.html.

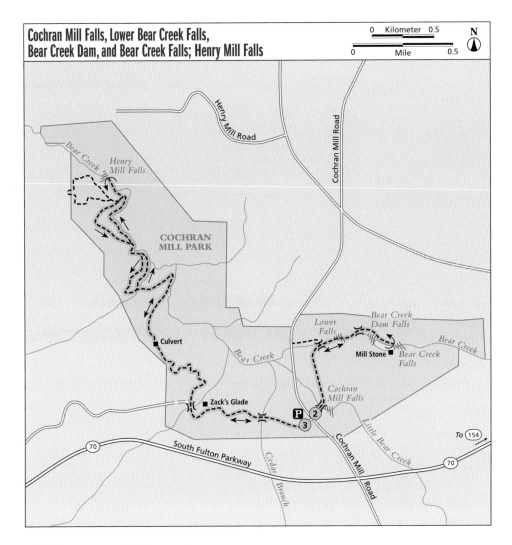

Cochran Mill Falls, Lower Bear Creek Falls, Bear Creek Dam, and Bear Creek Falls; Henry Mill Falls

Miles and Directions

0.0 Hike northwest down the wide gravel roadlike trail.

0.08 Cross a footbridge near the base of Cochran Mill Falls (N33°34.342'/W84°42.724'). Follow the trail north through the picnic area.

0.25 Come to a fork. Left leads west toward the road; go right (north).

0.38 Come to a fork. Right (east) is the Cochran Mill Loop Trail. Go straight (north).

0.4 Cross a footbridge and immediately come to a T. Left (west) is the red trail. Go right (east) on the green Cascades Trail following the creek upstream.

0.52 Arrive at Lower Bear Creek Falls (N33°34.616'/W84°42.659'). Continue hiking generally east. (*Option:* Return to the trailhead.)

A lone cow enjoys the passive sunset.

0.65 Come to a T where the Nature Center Trail forms a large loop. Go right (east) and immediately cross a footbridge.

0.8 A side trail leads to Bear Creek Dam (N33°34.626'/W84°42.438'). Continue hiking upstream.

0.9 Follow the side path toward the millstone.

0.92 Arrive at the millstone. Backtrack to the main trail.

0.94 Arrive back at the main trail, go right (east) and uphill over smooth stone.

0.96 Arrive alongside Bear Creek Falls (N33°34.598'/W84°42.352'). Backtrack to trailhead.

1.88 Arrive at trailhead.

3 Henry Mill Falls

Soulful! Although it's only 15 feet tall, the tan stone bed and crystal-clear water meld together to create a picture-perfect setting. Bring a towel and spend some time basking in and out of the water as you cleanse your soul with an endless bounty that only Mother Nature can provide.

See map on p. 15.
Height: 15 feet
Beauty rating: Very good
Distance: 5.68 miles
Difficulty: Easy to moderate
Surface: Gravel road, hard-packed dirt
Hiking time: 3 hours
Other trail users: Horses, mountain bikes
Blazes: Yellow, blue

County: Fulton
Land status: Cochran Mill Park
Contacts: (770) 306-0914; www.cochranmill park.com
FYI: Fee required; open 30 minutes before sunrise to 30 minutes after sunset
Maps: *DeLorme: Georgia Atlas & Gazetteer:* Page 25 E9–E10

Finding the trailhead: *From the junction of South Fulton Parkway and GA 70 near Rico,* drive east on South Fulton Parkway for 4.4 miles. Turn left onto Cochran Mill Road. Drive 0.4 mile. Turn left onto Upper Wooten Road at the entrance to the park. *From the junction of South Fulton Parkway and GA 154 near Palmetto,* drive west on South Fulton Parkway for 2.6 miles. Turn right onto Cochran Mill Road. Follow directions above. The trailhead is the gate that you saw directly in front of you when you turned left onto Wooten Road to enter the park. **GPS:** N33°34.267'/ W84°42.790'

The Hike

The city of Chattahoochee Hills has outdone themselves. Before you even reach the park, you're in awe at the large magnolia trees lining the roadway. When you reach the park, you find it's wonderfully wooded with an extensive trail system for hiking, mountain biking, and equestrian use.

From the trailhead, follow the wide gravel road southwest. You'll bypass a yellow-blazed trail on the right before crossing a footbridge over Cedar Branch. As you delve deeper into the lush forest the sights, scents, and sounds heighten the pleasure. Beyond the footbridge you'll hike past Zack's Glade, a large open grassy area surrounded by forest. A tenth of a mile from here you'll come to a fork. Go right, following the wide gravel yellow-blazed trail northwest. After crossing a bridge, the trail splits again. Go right again, now hiking north on a traditional narrow dirt path. This is the Henry Mill Falls trail. When you reach the next fork at 0.88 mile the yellow-blazed trail splits again. Horses are welcome to the right (northeast), but you want to go left (northwest), which is open to bike and foot traffic only. The path is smooth singletrack that gently rolls up and down. It's premier for mountain biking, but can

Multicolored rock forms the face of Henry Mill Falls.

get muddy after heavy rains. Lush greenery surrounds the trail and a variety of birds serenade you. In such a beautiful setting it's easy to let your mind wander. Don't drift too far; this trail can be a bit confusing. Many routes crisscross, so follow the trail map and Miles and Directions to stay on course. The park map shows this trail as a single loop, but in reality it splits and rejoins twice forming a double loop. As you follow Bear Creek downstream, it widens and comes to life the farther you go. Tall pines and oaks stand side by side pleasantly shading the trail while large rock formations enhance the entertainment. When you reach the brink of the falls, the water is delightful. An intriguing blue-green hue is formed from the vegetation beneath it. A sandy beach sits downstream from the falls, and a fantastic swim hole is ready and waiting. As you backtrack to the trailhead, follow the other legs of the loops to see more of this fabulous forest.

Miles and Directions

0.0 Go around the gate and follow the wide gravel road southwest.

0.2 Bypass the yellow-blazed Pete's Single Track Trail on the right; it leads to the parking area. Stay straight (west).

0.25 Cross a footbridge over Cedar Branch. Continue hiking west.

0.55 Hike past Zack's Glade on your right (north) and stay straight (southwest) on the gravel road.

0.65 Come to a fork. The yellow-blazed Cedar Branch trail leads left (south). Go right (northwest) on the wide gravel yellow-blazed trail.

0.7 Cross a bridge and the trail immediately splits. Go right (north) on the Henry Mill Falls trail.

0.88 Reach a fork where the yellow-blazed trail splits. Right (northeast) is for horses. Go left (northwest).

1.3 Cross a culvert over a tiny stream.

1.95 Rock-hop a creek and come to a fork. A blue-blazed trail leads straight (west). Go right (north) following yellow blazes.

1.96 Come to another fork where the yellow trail splits. Left is west; you'll return on that path. Go right (north).

2.15 Come to a T. Left leads south back to the last fork. Go right (north) following Bear Creek downstream.

2.28 Come to another fork where the trail splits again, forming the second loop. Left leads west. Go right (northwest) on the horse trail following blue blazes.

Turkeytail is known for its cancer-fighting properties.

2.6 Come to a T. Left (southwest) leads back to the last fork. Go right (northwest).

2.75 Arrive at Henry Mills Falls (N33°35.298'/W84°43.823'). Backtrack to the T.

2.9 Reach the T and go right (southwest).

2.93 Come to a fork. Right leads around another loop. Go left (southwest) toward the trailhead.

3.3 Arrive back at the fork where the loop began (see 2.28). Go right (south).

3.42 Reach the T (see 2.15). Go right (south).

3.72 Come to a T where the loop began at 1.96 miles above. Go right and backtrack to the trailhead.

5.68 Arrive at trailhead.

Northwest Region

Trenton

4 Waterfalls of Cloudland Canyon: First, Second, West Rim, Hemlock, and Cherokee

Exhilarating! This hike gives you five fantastic waterfalls in less than 2 miles of trail. You'll be thrilled as your senses take in the fabulous sights, sounds, and scents this diverse forest has to offer. Although it's a strenuous hike, it's worth every step. As you head down into Cloudland Canyon, don't think of the climb back out. Instead, live in the now and enjoy the magnificent nature surrounding you.

Height: First: 75 feet; Second: 100 feet; West Rim: 180 feet; Hemlock: 100 feet; Cherokee: 65 feet
Beauty rating: First: excellent; Second: good; West Rim: good; Hemlock: excellent; Cherokee: excellent
Distance: 1.96 miles
Difficulty: Strenuous
Surface: Man-made stairs, hard-packed dirt
Hiking time: Spend the day

Other trail users: None
Blazes: Blue, yellow
County: Dade
Land status: Cloudland Canyon State Park
Contacts: (706) 657-4050; www.gastateparks .org/CloudlandCanyon
FYI: Fee required; 7 a.m.–10 p.m.
Maps: *DeLorme: Georgia Atlas & Gazetteer:* Page 12 C2

Finding the trailhead: *From the junction of GA 136 and GA 157 near Cooper Heights,* drive west on GA 136 for 3.2 miles. Turn right into Cloudland Canyon State Park. Follow the main park road for 1.3 miles to a stop sign. Go straight down the hill and park. *From the junction of GA 136 and US 11 in Trenton,* drive east on GA 136 for 6.0 miles. Turn left into Cloudland Canyon State Park. Follow directions above. The trailhead is at the Interpretive Center on the left less than 0.1 mile from the stop sign. **GPS:** N34°50.146'/W85°28.784'

The Hike

First off, it's important to know this is an insanely busy park. If you want even an ounce of solitude, go early. Or better yet, spend the night camping or in one of the park's cabin rentals. Next, if you're not fit, this isn't the hike for you. Plain and simple, it's a strenuous trek. Lastly, don't bother bringing a hiking stick; the steps are metal grates and the stick goes right through, rendering it more of a hazard than help.

The trail begins to the left (southwest) of the Interpretive Center (IC). Before you start the hike, enjoy the view from the main overlook directly behind the IC. This vantage point offers long-range views of Cloudland Canyon and the full expanse of West Rim Falls. It's quite a different perspective than the one you'll have when you hike into the canyon and stand at the base of this behemoth beauty. From the IC (facing the entrance), go left following the blue blazes southwest along the east rim of the canyon.

You soon transition to yellow blazes following the Waterfalls Trail past the park cabins. Beyond the cabins you begin a gradual descent into the canyon until you reach a T. Left (south) is the West Rim Loop Trail; go right (north) staying on the Waterfalls Trail. The gradual part

A perfect green pool forms at the base of Cherokee Falls.

of this descent is now gone, and you begin steeply climbing down many steps into the canyon. At the bottom of the steps you'll come to a T. Again, left (south) is the West Rim Loop Trail; go right (north). As you pause from the concentration of your steps, you're taken aback by large rocky outcroppings. When you reach the third T, left leads west to Cherokee Falls, while right leads east to all of the other waterfalls on this fabulous hike. Go right for now making your way down many more steps until you reach another T. Left leads generally east to Hemlock Falls. For now, go right hiking downstream on the Sitton's Gulch Trail. You'll cross a footbridge and hike down one last set of steps, which leads directly to the base of First Falls on Daniel Creek. The water is thunderous and powerful, and you can see the remnants of an old structure sitting above the falls. Continue hiking downstream passing one impressive cascade after another. In less than 0.1 mile, a short muddy path leads to Second Falls on Daniel Creek. As you continue hiking downstream, you'll reach a rock hop across a swiftly moving tributary that flows into Daniel Creek. Look up. This is the base of West Rim Falls, the same waterfall you viewed from the main overlook behind the IC.

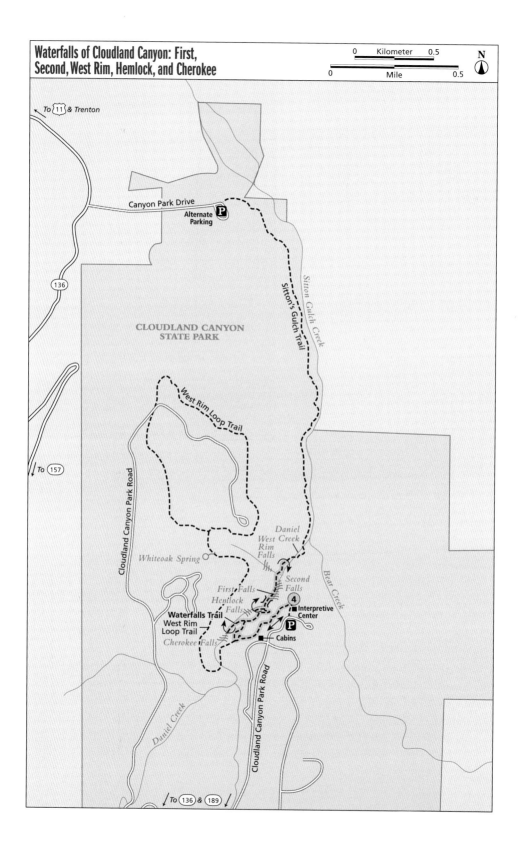

Beyond West Rim Falls the trail continues another 2.75 miles to an alternate trailhead and parking lot. Backtrack to the T where you began the Sitton's Gulch Trail. You'll find the sights, sounds, and smells of this diverse forest scintillating. Daniel Creek tumbles over large boulders, while petals from the tulip trees blanket the trail with color.

When you reach the T, hike toward Hemlock Falls. In less than 0.1 mile you're sitting at an overlook of this spectacular waterfall. The water makes a freefall into a plunge pool where a large boulder is dwarfed by the 100-foot falls. Backtrack to the T, climb up the stairs, and make your way to Cherokee Falls. Although it's not as tall as Hemlock Falls, it has a similar appearance. The water makes a clean freefall into a pristine, inviting swim hole at the base. Backtrack to the trailhead to finish the hike.

Cloudland Canyon State Park, established in 1938, is located in the northwest corner of Georgia on the western edge of Lookout Mountain. This 3,538-acre park includes rugged canyons, dense forest, abundant wildlife, waterfalls, wild caves, and numerous recreational opportunities. On top of all this, the park straddles a 1,000-foot-deep gorge cut into the mountain by the combined waters of Bear and Daniel Creeks. If you've never been, it's certainly worth a visit.

Miles and Directions

0.0 Hike southwest along the rim of the canyon following signs toward the falls.

0.27 Come to a T. Go right following the Waterfalls Trail north.

0.3 Come to a T at the bottom of the steps. Go right following the Waterfalls Trail north.

0.4 Reach another T. Left leads west to Cherokee Falls. Go right (east) hiking down more stairs. (*Option:* Go left to see Cherokee Falls.)

0.55 Come to another T. Left leads west to Hemlock Falls. Go right hiking north on the blue-blazed Sitton's Gulch Trail. (*Option:* Go left to see Hemlock Falls.)

0.6 Cross a footbridge and hike down the steps.

0.63 Arrive at First Falls (N34°50.171'/W85°28.869'). Continue hiking downstream on the Sitton's Gulch Trail.

0.67 Follow the short path toward the creek.

0.71 Arrive at the base of Second Falls (N34°50.197'/W85°28.849'). Return to the main trail.

0.75 Back on the Sitton's Gulch Trail, continue hiking downstream.

0.81 Reach a rock hop at the base of West Rim Falls (N34°50.279'/W85°28.824'). Backtrack to the T at 0.55 mile above.

1.07 Arrive at the T. Go right (west) toward Hemlock Falls.

1.14 Arrive at an overlook of Hemlock Falls (N34°50.130'/W85°28.943'). Backtrack to the T.

1.21 Arrive at the T. Hike up the stairs toward the T at 0.4 mile above.

1.36 Arrive at the T. Go right (west) toward Cherokee Falls.

1.46 Arrive at Cherokee Falls (N34°50.043'/W85°29.048'). Backtrack to trailhead.

1.96 Arrive at trailhead.

5 Glen Falls

Unbeatable! The Glen Falls trail leads to two exceptional waterfalls. Each is very different from the other, yet each will grab your attention and send your imagination reeling with delight.

Height: 30 feet, 12 feet
Beauty rating: Excellent
Distance: 0.95 mile
Difficulty: Moderate
Surface: Hard-packed dirt
Hiking time: 30 minutes
Other trail users: None
Blazes: None

County: Walker
Land status: Chickamauga and Chattanooga National Military Park
Contacts: (706) 866-9241; www.nps.gov/chch
FYI: 6 a.m.–sunset
Maps: *DeLorme: Georgia Atlas & Gazetteer:* Page 12 A3

Finding the trailhead: *From the junction of GA 157 (Red Ridinghood Lane) and Lula Lake Road in Lookout Mountain,* drive east on GA 157 for 1.8 miles to the parking area on the right. **Note:** GA 157 becomes TN 58 (Ochs Highway) when you enter Tennessee. The marked trailhead is on the same side of the road as the pull-off. Near the parking area you'll see a sign reading "Ruby Falls Left 100 Yds." **GPS:** N34°59.529'/W85°20.444'

The Hike

Although the trailhead and much of the trail is located in Tennessee, the falls reside inside the Georgia state line. The roadway where you parked is extremely busy; use caution near the trailhead, especially if you have small children or dogs. The trail is equally as populated, so don't expect to have this to yourself. Although you can't hear any moving water, you're in for a treat. Follow the rocky dirt path due south on a steady descent into the forest. Wildflowers are abundant, and in springtime it's a fiesta of flowers blooming with color.

Near the halfway point you'll rock-hop a pair of wet-weather tributaries and begin to climb. At 0.4 mile a steep side path leads down to the creek alongside Lower Glen Falls. This part of the falls is multifaceted and the water twists, turns, and drops from all different directions as gravity takes hold. The Glen Falls trail continues west and uphill to a footbridge over the creek near the base of Upper Glen Falls. Water shoots out between two stone walls, forming a shallow pool at the base before flowing under the footbridge.

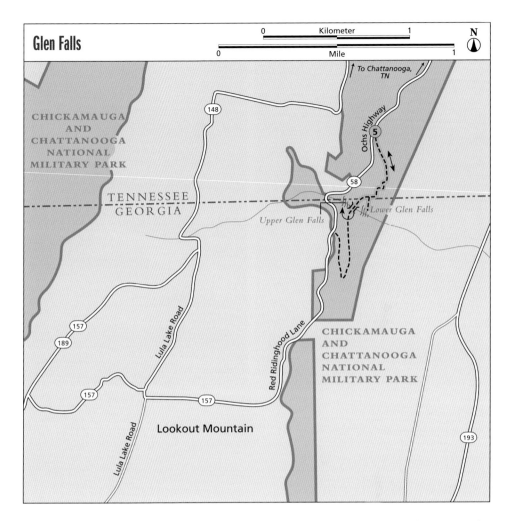

0   Kilometer   1

0   Mile   1

N

To Chattanooga, TN

148

CHICKAMAUGA
AND
CHATTANOOGA
NATIONAL
MILITARY PARK

Ochs Highway

5

58

TENNESSEE
GEORGIA

Upper Glen Falls

Lower Glen Falls

Red Ridinghood Lane

Lula Lake Road

157

189

157

157

CHICKAMAUGA
AND
CHATTANOOGA
NATIONAL
MILITARY PARK

Lookout Mountain

Lula Lake Road

193

These two waterfalls are polar opposites. Upper Glen Falls is a single stream of water that plummets cleanly out between two large rock walls. Lower Glen Falls is layered and three dimensional. If the beautiful waterfalls and wildflowers aren't enough, this trail also boasts some very impressive trees and rock formations. Despite its proximity to a very busy road, this is a peaceful and enjoyable hike. While in the area you may want to visit Ruby Falls. It's not detailed here because it's located in Tennessee, but wow, what a dreamscape! This dramatic waterfall flows inside a large cavern, and colored lights accentuate the scenery. Although it's a "tourist trap," the waterfall is unique and worth a visit.

Another tourist attraction that's worth a trip is the famed Rock City, located in Lookout Mountain, Georgia. Perhaps you've seen a barn with the words "See Rock City" splayed across the roof. Well, you're not far from this wonderland. Rock City

Left: Lower Glen Falls is full of character. Right: Upper Glen Falls cutting through a crevice in the stone

has caverns, gardens, rock formations, an overlook, and a waterfall that flows from an area known as Lover's Leap.

Miles and Directions

0.0 Follow the trail south and downhill into the forest.

0.3 Rock-hop a tiny tributary.

0.35 Step over a second wet-weather tributary.

0.4 Follow the steep side path south toward the creek.

0.425 Arrive alongside Lower Glen Falls (N34°59.259'/W85°20.528'). Backtrack to the main trail.

0.45 Arrive at the main trail, continue hiking east.

0.5 Cross a footbridge near the base of Upper Glen Falls (N34°59.249'/W85°20.554'). Backtrack to trailhead.

0.95 Arrive at trailhead.

LaFayette

6 Pocket Falls

Surreal! Nooks, crannies, and crevices cover the tall stone that forms the face of Pocket Falls. That combined with a multitude of green moss gives this one a prehistoric look about it. Mother Nature really painted a surreal and spectacular landscape here.

Height: 50 feet
Beauty rating: Excellent
Distance: 0.7 mile
Difficulty: Easy
Surface: Boardwalk, hard-packed dirt
Hiking time: 20 minutes
Other trail users: None
Blazes: None

County: Walker
Land status: Crockford-Pigeon Mountain Wildlife Management Area
Contacts: (706) 295-6041; www.georgiawildlife.com/crockford-pigeon-mountain-wma
FYI: Sunrise–sunset
Maps: DeLorme: Georgia Atlas & Gazetteer: Page 12 E3

Finding the trailhead: *From the junction of GA 193 and GA 341 (Davis Crossroads) near LaFayette, drive south on Hog Jowl Road for 2.7 miles. Turn left onto Pocket Road. Travel 1.2 miles to the parking area at the end of the road. The trail is the gravel road to the right leading south on the Pocket Wildflower Trail.* **GPS:** N34°42.742'/W85°22.794'

The Hike

Ignore the gravel road leading southeast from the trailhead kiosk. Instead take the wide gravel path to the right following the Pocket Wildflower Trail south. This path ends at the Shirley Miller Wildflower trailhead where a web of wooden boardwalks weaves through the forest. You'll immediately cross a footbridge and come to a fork. Go either way as the two legs quickly reunite. The shade of the forest and cool damp air are refreshing, but it can be a little buggy in the warmer months. You'll enjoy abundant birdlife singing, chirping, and flitting about. When the boardwalk ends, a narrow dirt path follows the creek upstream. You'll pass a colorful cascade before reaching the base of Pocket Falls. The falls are spectacular! Two streams of water are separated by a large cliff wall. Brilliant green vegetation covers some of the stone, adding character to an already alluring waterfall.

The Crockford-Pigeon Mountain WMA is extraordinary, enticing a variety of outdoor enthusiasts. It boasts over 20,000 acres and is popular for hiking, hunting, fishing, rappelling, and spelunking. Among the natural wonders you'll find creeks,

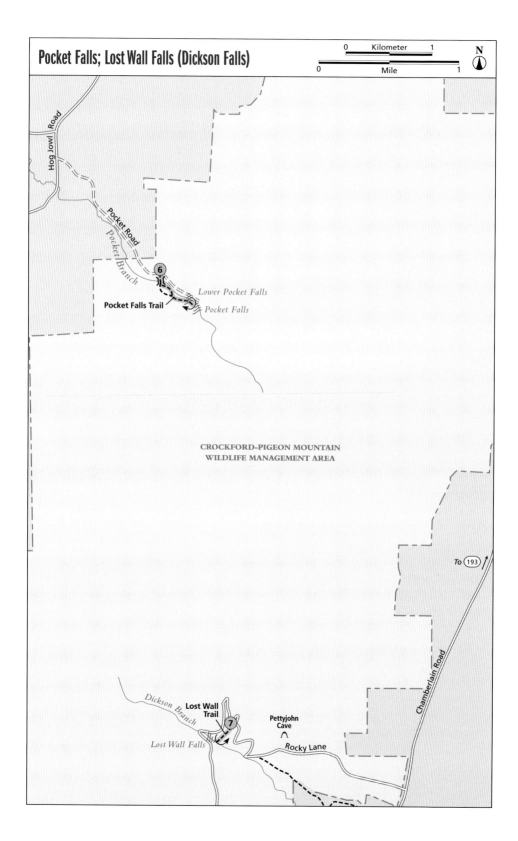

Pocket Falls; Lost Wall Falls (Dickson Falls)

Hog Jowl Road

Pocket Road

Pocket Branch

6

Lower Pocket Falls

Pocket Falls Trail

Pocket Falls

CROCKFORD-PIGEON MOUNTAIN
WILDLIFE MANAGEMENT AREA

To (193)

Chamberlain Road

Dickson Branch

**Lost Wall
Trail**

7

Pettyjohn
Cave

Lost Wall Falls

Rocky Lane

Left: Follow the yellow brick road of the forest. Right: Pocket Falls found a perfect pocket to flow through.

lakes, springs, waterfalls, rock formations, and caves. They also have several designated camping areas so you can take your time exploring nature's bounty.

Miles and Directions

0.0 Hike south on the wide gravel Pocket Wildflower Trail.

0.05 Reach the trailhead for Shirley Miller Wildflower Trail. Cross a footbridge onto the boardwalk.

0.06 Come to a fork with a trail map posted. You can go either way, but for mileage sake go left hiking east and upstream.

0.16 The two legs of the loop reunite. Go straight (southeast).

0.2 The boardwalk ends. Continue hiking south upstream.

0.4 Arrive at Pocket Falls (N34°42.558'/W85°22.546'). Backtrack to the fork where the boardwalk splits.

0.64 Reach the fork where the loop begins. Go left (northwest) following the other leg of the loop.

0.7 Arrive at trailhead.

7 Lost Wall Falls (Dickson Falls)

Clean! A wall of stone stands before you as you hike toward Lost Wall Falls. These rocky bluffs are just part of the adventure. The waterfall makes a clean freefall over the cliffs, and an intriguing large cavern sits behind the wash of white water.

See map on p. 28.
Height: 70 feet
Beauty rating: Excellent
Distance: 0.25 mile
Difficulty: Easy
Surface: Hard-packed dirt
Hiking time: 10 minutes
Other trail users: None

Blazes: None
County: Walker
Land status: Crockford-Pigeon Mountain Wildlife Management Area
Contacts: (706) 295-6041; www.georgiawildlife.com/crockford-pigeon-mountain-wma
Maps: *DeLorme: Georgia Atlas & Gazetteer:* Page 12 F3

Finding the trailhead: *From the junction of GA 193 and US 27 Business (Main Street) in LaFayette,* drive west on GA 193 for 2.8 miles. Turn left onto Chamberlain Road. Drive 3.4 miles. Turn right onto unmarked Rocky Lane at the WMA sign. Travel 1.8 miles and park on the left as the road makes a big bend to the right. *From the junction of GA 193 and GA 341,* drive east on GA 193 for 5.3 miles. Turn right onto Chamberlain Road. Follow directions above. **GPS:** N34°40.019'/W85°22.257'

The Hike

What once was an unofficial rock climber's path is now a well-trodden trail shared by waterfall enthusiasts with a kiosk at the trailhead. Although there are no blazes, it's easy to follow. An obvious narrow footpath leads south into the forest. You'll have to briefly scramble over some rocks, but otherwise it's a straightforward hike to the falls. As you approach the "Lost Wall," you'll stand in awe by the impressive wall of cliffs before you. The trail follows the cliffs to where the waterfall plummets down over the stone face. A large cavern is formed in the middle of this rock wall, and the water makes a freefall right in front of it. If you're lucky, you may see some locals rappelling down the face of the falls, as this is a popular place for rock hounds. The falls flow on Dickson Creek, explaining the obvious alias Dickson Falls.

The surrounding WMA covers over 20,000 acres and is full of adventure. There are miles of hiking

The multitude of mushroom species are always intriguing.

CANYONEERING

Canyoneering is a sport that entails traveling through canyons and often following the creeks and rivers that run through them. So what makes this different from hiking?

Canyoneers actually hike down the creek or river itself, not alongside it. Whether jumping from rock to rock, trudging through chilling water, or rappelling down the face of a waterfall, these brave explorers use whatever means of travel necessary. It's quite common to see them with climbing harnesses, rope bags, and even a wet suit as they make their way through the icy mountain waters around us.

trails, wildlife and wildflowers are abundant, and there are many natural features worth exploring. The WMA houses several springs, waterfalls, and cave systems. As a matter of fact, you passed one such cave system, Pettyjohn's Cave (N34°39.896'/ W85°21.823'), en route to the trailhead. This underground labyrinth boasts 6.5 miles of subterranean trails. Within it there are several large caverns including Entrance Room, Echo Room, and Bridge Room.

While you're in the area, I highly recommend visiting Pocket Falls as well (Hike 6).

Miles and Directions

0.0 Follow the dirt path south into the forest.

0.05 Scramble over a rocky area and continue southwest.

0.125 Arrive at Lost Wall Falls (N34°39.926'/ W85°22.345'). Backtrack to trailhead.

0.25 Arrive at trailhead.

Lost Wall Falls is best known among rock climbers and rappelers.

8 Marble Mine Falls

Intriguing! The color of the water, and the fact that you can go behind the freefall of this low-flow waterfall, makes this one unique. Adding to the surreal scenery is a pair of caves carved out of the stone on either side of the waterfall. Intriguing indeed.

Height: 20 feet
Beauty rating: Good
Distance: 2.0 miles
Difficulty: Easy to moderate
Surface: Wide gravel footpath
Hiking time: 1 hour
Other trail users: None
Blazes: Orange

County: Chattooga
Land status: James H. (Sloppy) Floyd State Park
Contacts: (706) 857-0826; www.gastateparks.org/JamesHFloyd
FYI: Fee required; 7 a.m.–10 p.m.
Maps: *DeLorme: Georgia Atlas & Gazetteer:* Page 18 A3

Finding the trailhead: *From junction of US 27 and GA 156 in Armuchee,* drive north on US 27 for 10.5 miles. Turn left onto Sloppy Floyd Lake Road. Drive 2.7 miles to the ranger station on the right. Park here. *From junction of US 27 and GA 48 in Summerville,* drive south on US 27 for 1.3 miles. Turn right onto Marble Springs Road. Drive 0.9 mile. Turn right onto Sloppy Floyd Lake Road. Travel 1.4 miles to the ranger station on the right. The trailhead is the bridge over the lake on the south side of the road. **GPS:** N34°26.358'/W85°20.263'

The Hike

Park at the visitor center and pay at the self-pay kiosk where you can also grab a trail map. The hike begins by crossing the long footbridge over the Upper Lake. As you cross you see they rent paddle boats elevated on pontoons. They also have a small boat ramp where you can drop your own vessel into this lovely lake and spend the day. When you reach the opposite shore, go right loosely following the water's edge southeast. By 0.2 you'll come to the official Marble Mine trailhead and immediately cross a footbridge. The trail enters the forest and brings you to a fork. Right (west) is the purple-blazed Upper Lake Trail, which loops around the southern part of the lake. You want to go left, staying with the orange blazes as you begin to climb. You almost immediately come to a T. Right leads toward the lake; go left following the wide gravel trail south as it climbs. You'll hike past some old metal bins and structures and bypass a yellow-blazed trail on the right that leads to the Jenkins Gap Trail. Continue following the wide, clay, roadlike route generally south. You'll cross a culvert and quickly come to a marked fork. To the right (west) a wide gravel road again leads to the Jenkins Gap

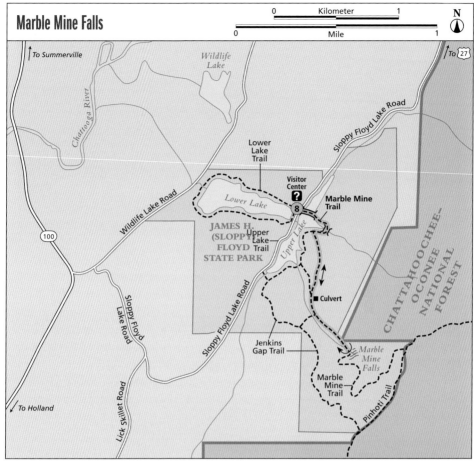

0   Kilometer   1

0   Mile   1

N

To Summerville

Wildlife Lake

To 27

Chattooga River

Sloppy Floyd Lake Road

Lower Lake Trail

Visitor Center

Wildlife Lake Road

Lower Lake

Marble Mine Trail

100

JAMES H. (SLOPPY) FLOYD STATE PARK

Upper Lake Trail

Upper Lake

CHATTAHOOCHEE– OCONEE NATIONAL FOREST

Sloppy Floyd Lake Road

Culvert

Sloppy Floyd Lake Road

Jenkins Gap Trail

Marble Mine Falls

Marble Mine Trail

Lick Skillet Road

To Holland

Pinhoti Trail

Trail. Stay straight ahead (south) on the Marble Mine trail. You'll bypass another spur trail on the left that looks like it would be ideal for ATVs, but they are not allowed here. Despite the fact that you're following a roadlike trail, it's very peaceful. Woodpeckers drum on the trees, keeping beat for a variety of other birds that serenade you while you hike. Deer are abundant too, so bring binoculars and try to catch a glimpse. After hiking 1.0 mile you'll arrive at Marble Mine Falls. This is a unique waterfall. Water flows over a rock ledge, dropping into a small pool of milky blue-green water. A duo of deep holes carved out of the stone sit on opposite sides of the waterfall, and a wooden walkway leads behind the falls to give you a closer

These goats were just as curious about me as I was them.

You'll cross this lovely lake on the way to Marble Mine Falls.

look. The striations in the stone and the duet of damp caves are quite intriguing. As is the mysterious milky color of the water, gleaming with hints of green and blue.

If you want to extend the hike, the Marble Mine Trail continues south to the right of the falls and ends at the Pinhoti Trail. The Pinhoti Trail trail spans over 300 miles across Georgia and Alabama, and passes through this delightful park. The park has a pair of lovely lakes that are certainly a highlight here. The Upper Lake, which you crossed on your way to the falls, is surrounded by small foothills and open grassy fields. Lower Lake also graces the park. Each lake has a hiking trail that loops around it, and whether you're here to hike, fish, picnic, or simply soak in the sun, you're sure to enjoy the serene setting.

You may also enjoy a visit to the nearby Summerville Fish Hatchery. Trout, wall-eye, and sturgeon are among the fish produced here.

Miles and Directions

0.0 Cross the footbridge over the lake.

0.08 Reach the opposite shore and head right (southeast) loosely following the water's edge.

0.2 Begin the official trail hiking south over a footbridge.

0.29 Come to a fork. Right is the Upper Lake Trail. Go left (west) on the Marble Mine trail.

0.31 Come to a T. Go left following the wide gravel path south as it climbs.

0.63 Bypass a yellow-blazed spur trail on the right (west). Continue straight (south).

0.67 Hike over a culvert.

0.72 Come to a fork. Right leads to the Jenkins Gap Trail; go left (south) staying on the Marble Mine trail.

0.85 Bypass a spur trail on the left (east); stay straight (south).

1.0 Arrive at Marble Mine Falls (N34° 25.743' W85° 19.989'). Backtrack to trailhead.

2.0 Arrive at trailhead.

Blue Ridge

9 Shadow Falls

Boisterous! A short and easy hike leads to this little-known hidden gem. Although it's not that tall, the creek is bold, and the waterfall has an impressive flow to it. A boisterous wash of whitewater rolls down over mossy stone forming the face of these festive falls.

Height: 20 feet
Beauty rating: Very good
Distance: 0.64 mile
Difficulty: Easy
Surface: Wide logging road
Hiking time: 20 minutes
Other trail users: Mountain bikes, equestrians
Blazes: None

County: Fannin
Land status: Chattahoochee National Forest-Conasauga District
Contacts: (706) 695-6736; www.fs.usda.gov/conf
Maps: *DeLorme: Georgia Atlas & Gazetteer:* Page 14 C1

Finding the trailhead: *From the junction of GA 5 and US 76 in Blue Ridge,* drive north on GA 5 for 3.7 miles. Turn left onto Old GA 2. Travel 10.3 miles to a four-way intersection at Watson Gap. Turn left onto FS 64. Drive 3.9 miles to a pull-off on the left before crossing the bridge. (If you reach Jacks River Fields Campground you went too far.) *Note:* At 3.2 miles on FS 64 go right at the fork. *From the junction of GA 5 and GA 60 near the Tennessee border,* drive south on GA 5 for 6.5 miles. Turn right onto Old GA 2. Follow directions above. The trailhead is across the street from the pull-off. **GPS:** N34°51.886'/W84°31.145'

The Hike

The hike begins by heading north on the South Fork Trail. The trail itself is an old wide logging road that's open to horses, hikers, and mountain bikers, although you're likely to have it to yourself. In less than a tenth of a mile, you'll step over a tiny wet-weather tributary that may or may not have water in it. The greenery around you is grand, and a variety of wildflowers and ferns catch your attention. In a mere 0.3 mile, you'll arrive near the brink of the falls, which you can spy through the rhododendron. An obvious side path on the left leads to the base of Shadow Falls. A tree crosses the creek at the base, and the water swiftly falls over the nearly vertical surface of smooth stone. Potholes add character to the rock face of the falls, and the creek is crystal clear. If this wasn't enough, the mountain views en route to the trailhead are unbeatable. If you wanted to extend your stay, the primitive Jacks River Fields Campground is right around the bend.

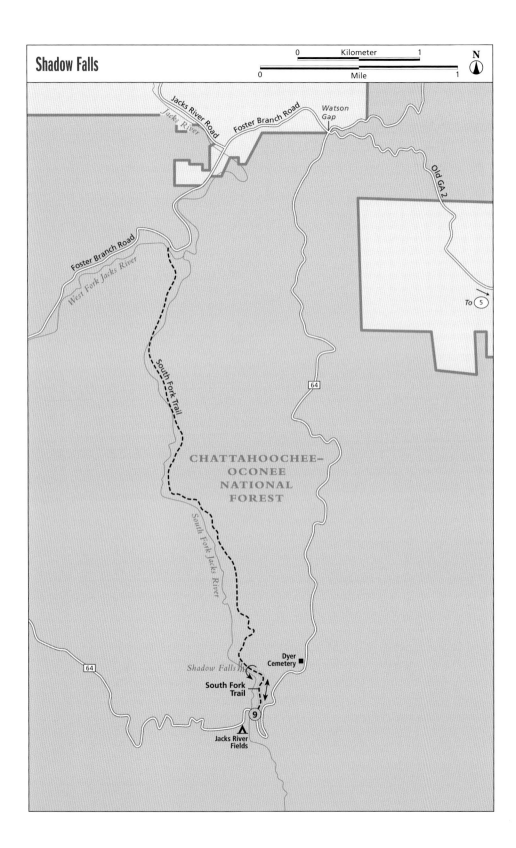

Mountain after mountain ready to explore

I also recommend a side trip to the historic Dyer Cemetery, which you passed 3.2 miles from Watson Gap. The Dyer family were early settlers and pioneers of the area. Headstones in this historic family graveyard date back to the late 1800s.

Miles and Directions

0.0 Follow the South Fork Trail uphill north.

0.07 Cross a tiny tributary.

0.3 Just after the wide logging road bends right (west), follow the side path left toward the falls.

0.32 Reach the base of Shadow Falls (N34°52.092'/W84°31.201'). Backtrack to the trailhead.

0.64 Arrive at trailhead.

10 Noontootla Falls

Challenging! Although you can view this one from the roadside, a short but challenging climb up the muddy bank gives you a more intimate appreciation of its beauty. While it's named Noontootla Falls, this one actually sits on a tributary of the spirited Noontootla Creek.

Height: 270 feet
Beauty rating: Good
Distance: Roadside or 0.13 mile
Difficulty: Strenuous
Surface: Steep dirt path
Hiking time: 30 minutes
Other trail users: None
Blazes: None

County: Fannin
Land status: Chattahoochee National Forest-Blue Ridge District
Contacts: (706) 745-6928, (706) 970-9776; www.fs.usda.gov/conf
Maps: *DeLorme: Georgia Atlas & Gazetteer:* Page 14 F5

Finding the trailhead: *From the junction of US 76 and GA 60 near Blue Ridge,* drive south on GA 60 for 13.0 miles. Turn right onto Doublehead Gap Road. Travel 5.7 miles. Turn left onto FS 58. Drive 3.1 miles to the falls on the left. Park along FS 58. *From the junction of GA 60 and GA 180 in Suches,* drive north on GA 60 for 15.5 miles. Turn left onto Doublehead Gap Road. Follow directions above. The trailhead is on the left side of the falls. **GPS:** N34°41.150'/W84°11.744'

The Hike

The forest that harbors this splendid specimen is fantastic! Tall pines are mixed with hardwoods, and a symphony of birds singing a chorus of delightful tunes keep you entertained. As you drive to the falls, FS 58 follows the energetic Noontootla Creek nearly the entire way. Cascades fill the active creek with life, and there are plenty of dispersed primitive campsites along the way. As you reach Noontootla Falls, your first impression is "oh, that's pretty." But when you look up, you realize that this thing tumbles down the entire mountain, standing hundreds of feet tall. A *steep* narrow path follows the left bank upstream from the roadway to the upper portion of the falls. Although it's short, this is a strenuous hike and is recommended for experienced hikers only: no children. As you hike you'll find yourself on all fours at times, crawling up roots and rocks as you struggle to climb. This trail has a 40 percent grade. That's right, I said 40! Bring a hiking stick to help you combat gravity, which inevitably always wins. The trail ends at a plateau alongside this steep waterslide. Ironically, the sound this waterfall makes is similar to a waterslide at an amusement park: that constant

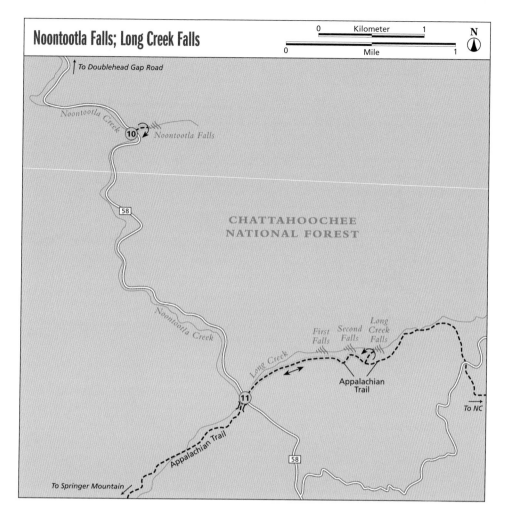

0   Kilometer   1

0   Mile   1

N

To Doublehead Gap Road

Noontootla Creek

10   Noontootla Falls

58

CHATTAHOOCHEE
NATIONAL FOREST

Noontootla Creek

Long
Creek
Falls

First   Second
Falls   Falls

Long Creek

Appalachian
Trail

To NC

11

Appalachian Trail

58

To Springer Mountain

movement of rushing water, with the occasional extra push and swoosh. If you're not sure-footed, or not up for the climb, bring binoculars to view the upper reaches from the road at the base.

Miles and Directions

0.0 Hike up the left bank of the creek.

0.065 Arrive at the upper area of Noontootla Falls (N34°41.173'/W84°11.667'). Backtrack to trailhead.

0.13 Arrive at trailhead.

11 First and Second Falls on Long Creek and Long Creek Falls

Hardy! What a wonderful treat for thru-hikers and day hikers alike. This hike leads you to three unique waterfalls and follows a portion of the world-famous Appalachian Trail. The water is crystal clear, and many of the trees are so impressively large you'll be standing in awe. But that is befitting as the trail passes through the oldest mountain range in the world.

See map on p. 39.

Height: First: 25 feet; Second: 60 feet; Long Creek: 60 feet

Beauty rating: First: excellent; Second: very good; Long Creek: very good

Distance: 1.9 miles

Difficulty: First: moderate; Second: strenuous; Long Creek: moderate

Surface: Hard-packed dirt

Hiking time: 1 hour

Other trail users: None

Blazes: White, blue

County: Fannin

Land status: Chattahoochee National Forest-Blue Ridge District

Contacts: (706) 745-6928, (706) 970-9776; www.fs.usda.gov/conf

Maps: DeLorme: Georgia Atlas & Gazetteer: Page 14 F5

Finding the trailhead: From the junction of GA 60 and US 76 near Blue Ridge, drive south on GA 60 for 13.0 miles. Turn right onto Doublehead Gap Road. Travel 5.7 miles. Turn left onto FS 58. Drive 5.3 miles and park along the roadway. From the junction of GA 60 and GA 180 in Suches, drive north on GA 60 for 15.5 miles. Turn left onto Doublehead Gap Road. Follow directions above. The trail crosses FS 58; northbound is on the northeast side of the road. **GPS:** N34°39.812'/W84°11.041'

The Hike

The trailhead for these fabulous falls is actually a junction along the famous Appalachian Trail where the trail crosses FS 58. A sign at the trailhead reads "Springer Mountain 4.5 Miles" pointing south and "Long Creek Falls 1 Mile" pointing north. This section of the AT is the final stretch for anyone thru-hiking the southbound route from Katadin, Maine, to Springer Mountain, Georgia. Although this area is populated with families and day hikers, don't be surprised if you come across some grungy thru-hikers who have literally been hiking for months. For them, this is a light at the end of the tunnel, a bittersweet end to a life-changing, soulful journey.

As you hike northbound the wide, flat path loosely follows Long Creek. This trail is a heavily used national treasure. Because it is so populated, there are many spur trails where hikers have camped, sought water, used the bathroom, etc. Avoid any spur trails that aren't specifically mentioned in this text and stay with the white blazes. The hike starts as easy

Left: You'll hike along the famed Appalachian Trail to reach Long Creek Falls in Georgia.
Right: A shallow sandy bottom is perfect for wading at the base of First Falls on Long Creek.

and flat, and then begins to climb as you delve into the rugged north Georgia wilderness. This is one of the few places on the AT that you'll see lots of children. After hiking a half-mile you'll come to an obvious side path leading down to First Falls on Long Creek. This side path follows a gentle slope and seems to dead-end at a wet, rocky area. Hike down the wet stony path and you quickly arrive at the base of First Falls. First Falls is by far a favorite. It's peaceful and soothing, and the type of waterfall that you could sit at all day long. The rock that forms the falls resembles a turtle, and a giant tree grows straight up from the "head" of the turtle. A sandy beach at the base offers a perfect place to spend time gazing at the mossy edge of the falls.

Return to the AT and continue north. Bypass the next side trail toward the creek, as this leads to the brink of First Falls. At 0.75 mile from the trailhead a side path leads steeply down to Second Falls. Unlike the gentle slope to First Falls, this is a steep, strenuous scramble that isn't suitable for children. Second Falls is multifaceted. Water

This fabulous hike gives you three amazing waterfalls and the opportunity to hike along the world-famous Appalachian Trail near its southern terminus at Springer Mountain, Georgia. The Appalachian Mountain Range is over 1.2 billion years old. It's the oldest mountain range in the world! Millions of years of erosion have worn them down to the current height of 2,000–6,000 feet, but in their glory days these mountains stood much taller. They are said to have reached heights rivaling the youthful Himalayas.

juts in and out between large boulders, and flows from many different directions. The unpredictable and inconsistent flow adds character to this fantastic wonderland of water. Again return to the AT and continue north. You'll reach a three-way fork where the Appalachian Trail heads right (south), the center trail (east-southeast) is the Benton MacKaye/Duncan Ridge Trail, and left (east) is a blue-blazed spur trail leading to Long Creek Falls. Long Creek Falls is a beautiful two-tiered waterfall. Brilliant green moss covers the face, and the water makes a clean drop over a sheer wall of smooth stone.

Miles and Directions

0.0   Hike northbound on the Appalachian Trail. (The footbridge leads southbound.)

0.5   Follow the side path toward the First Falls.

0.53 Arrive at First Falls (N34°40.050'/W84°10.568'). Backtrack to the AT and continue northbound.

0.81 A steep strenuous scramble leads north toward Second Falls.

0.83 Arrive at Second Falls (N34°40.054'/W84°10.404'). Backtrack to the AT and continue northbound.

0.95 Reach a three-way fork. Follow the trail to the left (east) to the falls.

1.05 Arrive at Long Creek Falls (N34°40.057'/W84°10.252'). Backtrack to the trailhead.

1.9   Arrive at trailhead.

Large boulders create a chaotic course for Second Falls on Long Creek.

12 Little Rock Creek Falls

Spirit-filled! This waterfall feels old but not worn. Rather, it seems wise from age, like a sage sitting atop a mountain, patiently waiting for those who come seeking knowledge.

Height: 50 feet
Beauty rating: Very good
Distance: 0.8 mile
Difficulty: Moderate
Surface: Hard-packed dirt
Hiking time: 40 minutes
Other trail users: None
Blazes: None

County: Fannin
Land status: Chattahoochee National Forest–Blue Ridge District
Contacts: (706) 745-6928, (706) 970-9776; www.fs.usda.gov/conf
Maps: *DeLorme: Georgia Atlas & Gazetteer:* Page 14 E5

Finding the trailhead: *From the junction of GA 60 and GA 180,* drive north on GA 60 for 11.7 miles. Turn left onto Rock Creek Road. Travel 3.2 miles to a small bridge. There are pull-offs on the left just before and after the bridge. ***Note:*** Rock Creek Road becomes unpaved at 1.1 miles. *From the junction of GA 60 and US 76,* drive south on GA 60 for 16.5 miles. Turn right onto Rock Creek Road. Follow directions above. The trailhead is on the left before crossing the bridge (southeast side of the bridge). **GPS:** N34°42.987'/W84°09.089'

The Hike

A narrow path heads into the forest leading southeast nearly the whole way to the falls. Although it's a short hike, you'll get a bit of a workout as the trail rises and falls repeatedly. The path loosely follows Little Rock Creek upstream, and although it's narrow, it's well-trodden. The creek presents one beautiful cascade after another, but the closer you get to the falls the thicker the brush becomes. You'll have to navigate over and around some downed trees and climb up a precipitous large boulder en route to the falls. Although it may be slow going on the trail, the final reward is worth the effort. A small plateau offers a great spot to view the falls, and the wind that this waterfall pushes out is unbelievable. I wish I could put it in these pages for you to really grasp the impressive power of Mother Nature.

While you're in the area, I recommend a visit to the nearby Chattahoochee National Forest Fish Hatchery. The hatchery proudly produces about a million rainbow trout each year. That's a lot of fish, and each one is raised with the sole purpose of restocking the streams and lakes of north Georgia. Bring your pole, cast your line, and enjoy the fresh mountain air. ***Note:*** A Georgia fishing license is required: www.georgiawildlife.com/fishing/regulations.

Little Rock Creek Falls peeking through the foliage.

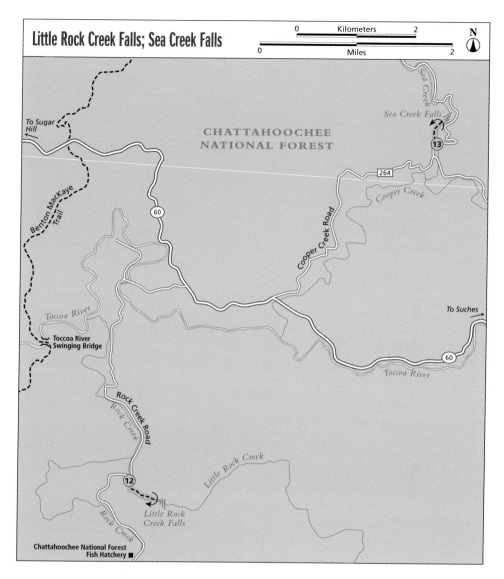

Little Rock Creek Falls; Sea Creek Falls

Kilometers
0   2
0   Miles   2

N

CHATTAHOOCHEE
NATIONAL FOREST

To Sugar Hill

Sea Creek Falls

13

264

Cooper Creek

Cooper Creek Road

Benton MacKaye Trail

60

To Suches

Toccoa River

Toccoa River Swinging Bridge

60

Toccoa River

Rock Creek Road

Rock Creek

Little Rock Creek

12

Little Rock Creek Falls

Rock Creek

Chattahoochee National Forest Fish Hatchery ■

Miles and Directions

0.0 Hike south into the forest.

0.08 Cross a wet-weather tributary.

0.4 Arrive at Little Rock Creek Falls (N34°42.842'/W84°08.782'). Backtrack to trailhead.

0.8 Arrive at trailhead.

13 Sea Creek Falls

Exceptional! Sea Creek Falls flows perfectly into its own hidden cove. Crystal-clear water exposes the multicolored rocks resting beneath the surface, and an exceptional swim hole sits snugly at the base.

See map on p. 45.
Height: 25 feet
Beauty rating: Excellent
Distance: 0.5 mile
Difficulty: Easy
Surface: Hard-packed dirt
Hiking time: 20 minutes
Other trail users: None

Blazes: None
County: Fannin
Land status: Chattahoochee National Forest–Blue Ridge District
Contacts: (706) 745-6928, (706) 970-9776; www.fs.usda.gov/conf
Maps: *DeLorme: Georgia Atlas & Gazetteer:* Page 15 D6

Finding the trailhead: *From the junction of GA 60 and GA 180,* drive north on GA 60 for 10.7 miles. Turn right onto Cooper Creek Road. (**Note:** You'll pass one Cooper Creek Road on your way north on GA 60. *Don't* take this route. Continue until you've gone the full 10.7 miles and reach the *second* Cooper Creek Road.) After turning onto Cooper Creek Road, travel 2.9 miles. Turn left onto FS 264 (along the way, Cooper Creek Road becomes FS 4). Drive 0.1 mile to a parking area on the left. *From the junction of GA 60 and US 76,* drive south on GA 60 for 16.6 miles. Turn left onto Cooper Creek Road. Follow directions above. **GPS:** N34°46.048'/W84°05.785'

The Hike

What once was an old logging road is now a narrow footpath leading north into the forest. The rich sweet smell of honeysuckle greets you with its delightful aroma, and the narrow path quickly widens. You can hear the timid power of Sea Creek, but a wall of dense brush separates you from it. This is a temporary imposition. At 0.2 mile you'll reach an open area next to the creek. Hike upstream and you soon arrive at Sea Creek Falls with the most pristine pool waiting at the base. If you're lucky enough to have this to yourself, relish in it. This is a popular swimming hole for the locals, especially in summertime.

Sea Creek Falls is located within the Cooper Creek Scenic Area. The recreation area covers over 1,200 acres and offers many opportunities for outdoor enthusiasts. There are multiple primitive campsites, miles of trails for hiking and mountain biking, and the creeks are regularly stocked making it popular for fishing as well.

If you're coming from the south, there's a nice roadside waterfall on the east side of GA 60 (N34°41.249'/W84°01.302') just across the street from Two Wheels Restaurant and Lodge. The falls have a small spillway at the top, and the bottom flows nearly sideways. Two Wheels Restaurant and Lodge is no surprise since GA 60 is a

Sea Creek Falls is tucked away in a private little cove.

popular motorcycle route with sweeping twists and turns and beautiful mountain views.

While you're in the area, you may also enjoy hiking to the Toccoa Swinging Bridge. This long suspension bridge crosses the fabulous Toccoa River approximately 0.6 mile from the trailhead, along the Benton MacKaye Trail.

Miles and Directions

0.0   Hike north and immediately stay left at the fork.

0.2   Come to an open area next to the creek. Hike upstream (north).

0.25 Arrive at Sea Creek Falls (N34°46.207'/W84°05.709'). Backtrack to trailhead.

0.5   Arrive at trailhead.

14 Cane Creek Falls

Uplifting! The true and steady waters of Cane Creek Falls flow with certainty, uplifting and inspiring the viewer. Cane Creek Falls is located on private property within Camp Glisson. The property owners have been kind enough to share this natural wonder with the public, so please follow all the rules and regulations during your visit. Check in at the gate or welcome center prior to visiting the falls, and remember: If you pack it in, pack it out!

Height: 40 feet
Beauty rating: Excellent
Distance: 0.4 mile
Difficulty: Easy
Surface: Paved road
Hiking time: 20 minutes
Other trail users: None
Blazes: None

County: Lumpkin
Land status: Private property
Contacts: Camp Glisson: (706) 864-6181; www.campglisson.org
FYI: Open 8 a.m.–5 p.m.; call ahead
Maps: *DeLorme: Georgia Atlas & Gazetteer:* Page 15 G7

Finding the trailhead: *From the junction of GA 60 Business and US 19,* drive south on GA 60 Business for 2.1 miles. Turn right onto Camp Glisson Road. Travel 0.6 mile to a fork in the road. Bear left at the fork and enter Camp Glisson. Drive up the hill and turn right onto Waightsail Henry Way. Immediately pull into the parking lot on your left at the welcome center. *From the junction of GA 60 Business and GA 52,* drive north on GA 60 Business for 2.6 miles. Turn left onto Camp Glisson Road. Follow directions above. **GPS:** N34°33.454'/W84°00.444'

The Hike

The "trail" follows Camp Glisson Road from the welcome center, around the gate, and farther into the private property of Camp Glisson. After hiking a short downhill, a trail veers off to the right leading to an observation deck at the brink of the falls. Follow the decking back out onto the paved road and continue farther. You quickly come to Fred Glisson Circle on your right. Go right here following the road steeply downhill. At the bottom of the hill, a footpath leads directly to the base of Cane Creek Falls.

Camp Glisson was founded by Reverend Fred Glisson, who held the first youth camp here in the summer of 1925. Camp sessions are still held here, and public access is prohibited when camp is in session. As you plan your visit, call ahead to confirm access is available.

Call ahead before visiting Cane Creek Falls.

This roadside smasher is north of Dahlonega off of GA 60 across from Two Wheels Restaurant and Lodge.

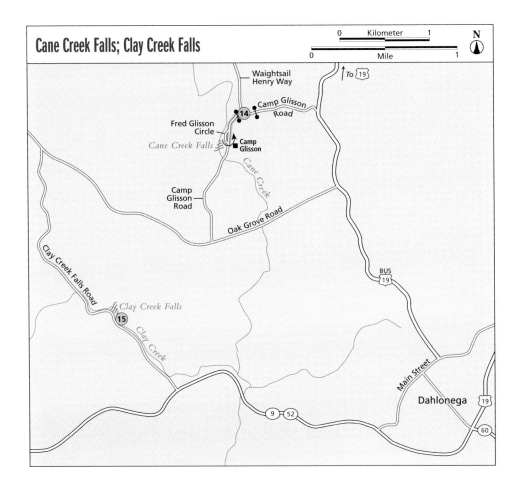

Camp Glisson Road

Waightsail Henry Way

To 19

14

Fred Glisson Circle

Cane Creek Falls

Camp Glisson

Camp Glisson Road

Cane Creek

Oak Grove Road

Clay Creek Falls Road

Clay Creek Falls

15

Clay Creek

BUS 19

Main Street

Dahlonega 19

9 52

60

Miles and Directions

0.0 Hike southwest past the gate and down the paved road.

0.1 A side road forks off to the right leading to an observation deck at the brink of the falls. Follow the decking back to the paved road. Head right hiking southwest.

0.2 Go right (west-northwest) on Fred Glisson Circle steeply downhill to the base of Cane Creek Falls (N34°33.328/W84°00.547). Backtrack to trailhead.

0.4 Arrive at trailhead.

15 Clay Creek Falls

Untouchable! This spectacular waterfall is located on private property alongside a residential road. The area is clearly marked with no trespassing signs, so you'll have to see it strictly from the roadside. Enjoy the view then move on, so as to not disturb the neighborhood.

See map on p. 50.
Height: 15 feet
Beauty rating: Very good
Distance: Roadside
Difficulty: Easy

County: Lumpkin
Land status: Private property
Maps: *DeLorme: Georgia Atlas & Gazetteer: Page 15 G6*

Finding the trailhead: *From the junction of GA 9 and US 19 in Dahlonega,* drive west on GA 9 for 2.3 miles. Turn right onto Clay Creek Falls Road. Drive 0.6 mile to the falls on the right. *From the junction of GA 9 and GA 52 where they join near Dahlonega,* drive east on GA 9/52 for 2.0 miles. Turn left onto Clay Creek Falls Road. Follow directions above. **GPS:** N34°32.257'/ W84°01.317'

The Hike

The creek splits in three as it flows over a large rock bed that forms Clay Creek Falls. As you drive along the residential road, you can't miss it. But unfortunately the falls are located on private property. When you come to visit, use caution, don't block the roadway, keep it brief, and be thankful for the opportunity to view this one at all. As Clay Creek flows through this peaceful neighborhood, the banks of the creek are covered in moss, and the natural beauty is outstanding. If you're in the area, it's worth a drive by. But don't go out of your way since you can't stay and linger here.

A drive by doesn't do the dazzling Clay Creek Falls justice.

16 Amicalola Falls

Majestic! This impressive waterfall has the claim to fame of being Georgia's tallest, falling 729 feet down the mountainside. Amicalola Falls is so tall that it's difficult to see it all at once. Each section you can view, however, is well worth the visit. The falls can be reached by climbing the many man-made steps or via an alternate route that is accessible for those in wheelchairs or with strollers.

Height: 729 feet
Beauty rating: Excellent
Distance: Hiking trail, 0.7 mile (wheelchair-accessible route, 0.5 mile)
Difficulty: Moderate to strenuous (easy to moderate for wheelchair-accessible route)
Surface: Paved path and man-made steps; crushed recycled tire material
Hiking time: 30 minutes

Other trail users: None
Blazes: None
County: Dawson
Land status: Amicalola Falls State Park
Contacts: (706) 265-4703; www.gastateparks .org/AmicalolaFalls
FYI: Fee required; 7 a.m.–10 p.m.
Maps: DeLorme: Georgia Atlas & Gazetteer: Page 14 G4

Finding the trailhead: *From the junction of GA 52 and GA 9,* drive west on GA 52 for 13.8 miles. Turn right onto Amicalola Falls State Park Road. Travel 0.7 mile to where the road dead-ends. *From the junction of GA 52 and GA 183,* drive east on GA 52 for 1.45 miles. Turn left onto Amicalola Falls State Park Road. Follow directions above. The trailhead is at the northwest end of the parking lot. **GPS:** N34°33.812'/W84°14.804' *To access the ADA parking area:* Once inside the park, turn left onto Top of the Falls Road. Travel 0.9 mile to a right into the ADA parking area. **GPS:** N34°33.921'/W84°14.931'

The Hike

This hike begins at a peaceful pond near the parking area. Walk around the pond, cross a footbridge, and the wide paved path follows the creek upstream and uphill to a lower observation area. From here you must climb 175 man-made steps to reach the upper observation area. Despite the challenging effort required to reach the premier viewing area, a footbridge over the upper portion of the falls, this trail is heavily used. People come from all over the world to visit Amicalola Falls. After all, it's the tallest waterfall east of the Mississippi River. Although it's heavily populated, it never disappoints. Every time I visit, there's a beautiful sun star gleaming off the face of the falls constantly smiling back at you. Interpretive signs along the path entertain and educate you while you hike. Rocks resting by the creek offer weary hikers a place to sit and listen to the spectacular sound of moving water. It's amazing how comforting that steady sound is. You can literally get lost in it, feeling as though you're the only one here in an isolated forest of free-flowing water. They call the paved portion of this trail wheelchair accessible, but you'd be hard pressed to push a wheelchair up the

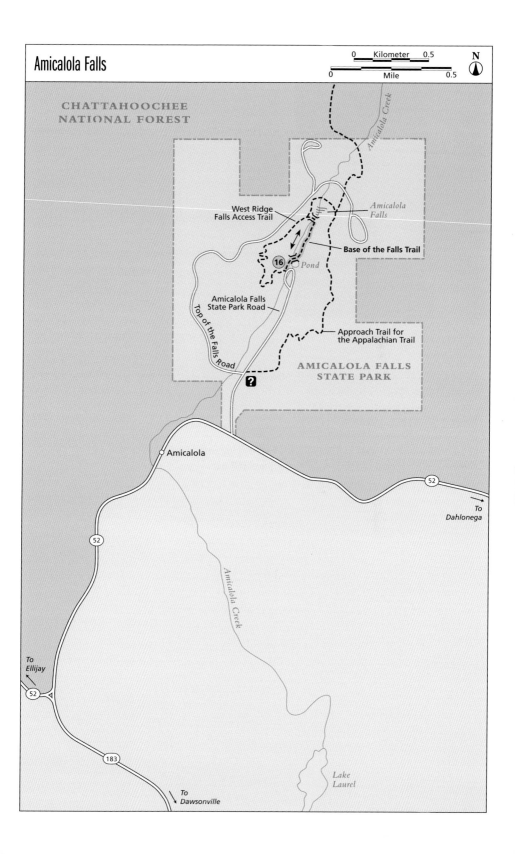

Amicalola Falls

0   Kilometer   0.5

0   Mile   0.5

N

CHATTAHOOCHEE
NATIONAL FOREST

Amicalola Creek

West Ridge
Falls Access Trail

*Amicalola
Falls*

Base of the Falls Trail

16

Pond

Amicalola Falls
State Park Road

Top of the Falls Road

Approach Trail for
the Appalachian Trail

AMICALOLA FALLS
STATE PARK

?

Amicalola

52

*To
Dahlonega*

52

*To
Ellijay*

52

Amicalola Creek

183

*To
Dawsonville*

*Lake
Laurel*

Amicalola Falls, Georgia's pride

steep path. If you do require access, there's an alternate route that begins at the ADA parking area. From here a path leads generally east for about a quarter-mile to the bridge over the upper portion of Amicalola Falls. Although this trail is wheelchair accessible, there is a bit of a grade to it.

You can reach the brink of the falls by driving up Top of the Falls Road to the Upper Amphitheater parking lot. You cannot see the waterfall from the brink, but the creek runs through a lovely picnic area, and the views of the surrounding mountains are spectacular.

This busy state park has a long-term parking area designed to give "thru-hikers" of the Appalachian Trail (AT) a good starting point for their epic journey. The Southern Terminus Approach Trail for the AT takes you up the Amicalola Falls Trail, passes the falls, and then continues to Springer Mountain, where the AT begins (or ends, depending on the direction you hike it).

Miles and Directions

0.0 Walk around the pond and cross a footbridge. Follow the paved path north.

0.3 The pavement ends at a steep stairway leading to the upper deck.

0.35 Reach the upper observation deck for Amicalola Falls (N34°33.999'/W84°14.694'). Backtrack to trailhead.

0.7 Arrive at trailhead.

17 Edge of the World Rapids

Gentle! Also known as EOW, this lovely rapid isn't the tallest, but it covers the full width of Amicalola Creek. The boardwalk leading to it lies within the Dawson Forest WMA, and you must obtain either a Georgia fishing or hunting license or a Lands Pass to hike here. Either can be obtained by visiting www.georgiawildlife.com.

Height: 10 feet
Beauty rating: Good
Distance: 0.84 mile
Difficulty: Easy
Surface: Boardwalk, hard-packed dirt
Hiking time: 20 minutes
Other trail users: None
Blazes: None
County: Dawson

Land status: Dawson Forest Wildlife Management Area–Amicalola Tract
Contacts: (770) 535-5700; www.georgiawildlife.com/dawson-forest-wma
FYI: Lands Pass required—contact (800) 366-2661
Maps: *DeLorme: Georgia Atlas & Gazetteer:* Page 20 A5

Finding the trailhead: *From the junction of GA 53 and GA 183 near Dawsonville*, drive west on GA 53 for 3.6 miles. Turn right into the parking area for Amicalola Creek Access. *From the junction of GA 53 and GA 5 near Tate*, drive east on GA 53 for 15.2 miles. Turn left into the parking area. The trailhead is at the northwest corner of the parking lot. **GPS:** N34°25.577'/W84°12.702'

The Hike

Hike down the steps toward the creek. At the bottom you'll come to a T. Right leads to the wheelchair access trailhead. Go left (west) following the creek downstream and you'll quickly cross under GA 53. Mountain laurel, bear grass, honeysuckle, and a bed of ferns line the walkway, making it particularly enjoyable in spring and summer. Although the hike is easy, there are benches placed occasionally along the path. You may encounter the occasional broken board, but in general the boardwalk is in great shape. Beautiful rapid after rapid greets you before the boardwalk ends at a fork with a blue trail to the left and an informal footpath following the shoreline to the right. Stay right following the shoreline south and you quickly arrive at the base of the splendid Edge of the World Rapids. This rapid spans the full width of Amicalola Creek. Large flat stones rest conveniently at the base, giving you a perfect place to enjoy a picnic, set up a tripod, or dip your feet in the cool clean water. The water is so clear you can see ripples in the sand where the water eddys out at the bank. If you sit long enough, or visit early in the morning, you may spy the grandeur of a great

Edge of the World Rapids covers the full width of Amicalola Creek.

blue heron in flight, coasting effortlessly over the creek. This enjoyable hike offers the steady sound of moving water the entire way, with plentiful birdsong as a wonderful accompaniment. If you want to extend the hike, follow the blue-blazed nature trail, which loops through the surrounding forest.

If you don't want to take the stairs, an ADA path bypasses the steps. To take this route, follow the paved road downhill at the northeast corner of the parking area. At the bottom of the hill there are a few accessible parking places. You can access the boardwalk from there, and it's a mere 0.06 mile from this alternate trailhead to the bottom of the stairs.

Edge of the World Rapids sits not far west of Dawsonville, Georgia. If you're coming from town, you'll pass right by the Atlanta Motorsports Park on your way to the trailhead. This park offers one of the most thrilling opportunities in the South. They have a go-kart track unlike any other, or you can step it up a notch and push the limits on their world-class race course. The location of this park is fitting as Dawsonville is home to the Georgia Racing Hall of Fame.

Miles and Directions

0.0 Hike down the steps.

0.01 Come to a T. Go left (west).

0.05 Bypass the nature trail on the left (east). Stay straight (south).

0.11 Hike underneath GA 53.

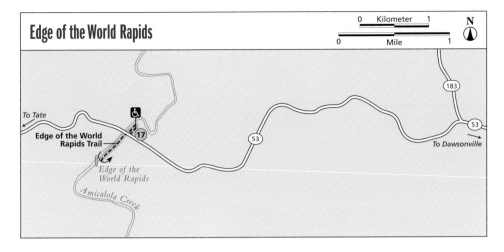

Edge of the World Rapids

0   Kilometer   1

0   Mile   1

N

To Tate

Edge of the World
Rapids Trail

17

Edge of the
World Rapids

Amicalola Creek

183

53

53

To Dawsonville

0.4 The boardwalk ends. Follow
the footpath south along the
shoreline.

0.42 Arrive at Edge of the World
Rapids (N34°25.363'/
W84°13.003'). Backtrack to
trailhead.

0.84 Arrive at trailhead.

*A long wooden boardwalk leads to Edge of the
World Rapids.*

18 Barefoot and Upper Barefoot Falls

Seclusion! The WMA is primarily used for hunting, horses, and mountain biking, so when you visit the falls, you're likely to have it to yourself. The creek is shallow all the way to the base of Barefoot Falls, and a steep narrow path leads quickly upstream to the upper falls.

Height: Barefoot: 25 feet; Upper Barefoot: 30 feet

Beauty rating: Barefoot: good; Upper Barefoot: fair

Distance: 1.75 miles

Difficulty: Moderate

Surface: Wide forest road

Hiking time: 30 minutes

Other trail users: Equestrians, mountain bikers, hunters

Blazes: Green

County: Dawson

Land status: Dawson Forest Wildlife Management Area

Contacts: (770) 535-5700; www.georgiawildlife.com/dawson-forest-wma

FYI: Fee required; trails are closed during firearms deer hunts and before 10 a.m. during archery and turkey seasons. Check with the WMA for specific dates.

Maps: *DeLorme: Georgia Atlas & Gazetteer:* Page 20 B5

Finding the trailhead: *From the junction of GA 9 and GA 369 in Coal Mountain,* drive north on GA 9 for 6.4 miles. Turn left onto Dawson Forest Road. Drive 1.5 miles to a gate at the entrance to the WMA. Continue 0.1 mile. Turn right to pay your fee at the kiosk. Return to the main road and go right. Drive another 2.0 miles on Dawson Forest Road. Turn left onto unmarked Clark Road. Travel 0.8 mile to the dirt road and gate on the right. *From the junction of GA 9 and GA 53 in Dawsonville,* drive south on GA 9 for 5.3 miles. Turn right onto Dawson Forest Road. Follow directions above. The gate is the trailhead. **GPS:** N34°21.103'/W84°10.762'

The Hike

When you stop to pay the day-use fee, you'll notice the envelope only has two options to choose from: horse or bike. That's ok, you can write in "hike," as hiking is allowed within the WMA as well. Parking near the trailhead is sparse, so be sure not to block the roadway or the gate.

From the gate, hike north on the wide, clay forest road (Ram Road) and immediately cross over a narrow orange-blazed footpath running east and west. You'll remain on this forest road nearly the full length of the hike, following green blazes along the way. This "road" is primarily used by equestrians and mountain bikers, although you're likely to have it to yourself. You'll steadily hike downhill almost the entire time, with an elevation loss of about 300 feet from the trailhead to the falls. Birds keep you company as you hike downhill, and it's not until 0.7 mile that you hear any indication of water. At 0.8 mile you'll come to a fork where the green-blazed trail becomes a narrow singletrack leading left (north). Continue straight ahead (east) on the forest

Barefoot Creek: Go on and try it for yourself.

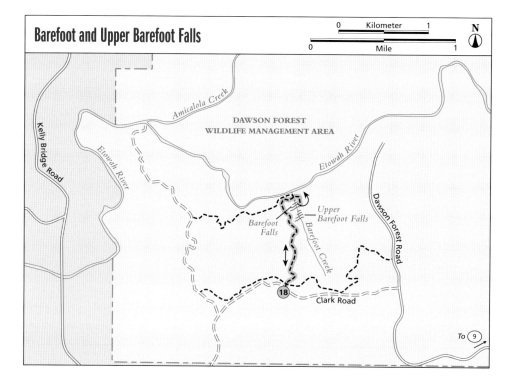

road, toward the sound of a gently moving waterfall. You'll quickly come to a T. Left leads north to a primitive campsite. Go right (southeast) toward the creek, arriving downstream from Barefoot Falls. A plethora of pebbles form the creekbed, and the falls are made by multiple ledges, like a flight of stairs with a landing in the middle. After enjoying the view, cross the shallow creek and follow a footpath upstream and steeply uphill to Upper Barefoot Falls. You'll have to view Upper Barefoot Falls from the side of the falls because the "base" sits near the brink of Barefoot Falls. While the falls are pretty, they're not worth going out of your way for, unless you're seeking isolation. In the warmer months the area can be buggy, including ticks.

Bring a hiking stick to ease the ascent on the way out.

Miles and Directions

0.0 Hike north on the wide trail immediately crossing an orange-blazed footpath.

0.8 Come to a fork. Stay straight (east) on the forest road.

0.82 Come to a T. Go right and reach the base of Barefoot Falls (N34°21.630'/W84°10.694'). Cross the creek and hike upstream.

0.87 Arrive at Upper Barefoot Falls (N34°21.581'/W84°10.664'). Backtrack to the trailhead.

1.75 Arrive at trailhead.

19 Poole's Mill Falls

Wistful! This lovely waterfall is found within a peaceful neighborhood park not far from northern Atlanta. The park is perhaps better known for its history and the covered bridge that crosses over Settingdown Creek near the brink of the falls.

Height: 15 feet
Beauty rating: Good
Distance: 0.3 mile
Difficulty: Easy
Surface: Sidewalk, hard-packed dirt
Hiking time: 10 minutes
Other trail users: None
Blazes: None

County: Forsyth
Land status: Poole's Mill Park
Contacts: www.parks.forsythco.com/
Parks-and-Facilities/Parks/Pooles-Mill-Park
FYI: Nov–Feb 6 a.m.–7 p.m., Mar–Oct
6 a.m.–9:30 p.m.
Maps: *DeLorme: Georgia Atlas & Gazetteer:*
Page 20 C4

Finding the trailhead: *From the junction of GA 369 and GA 372 near Free Home,* drive north on GA 369 for 3.8 miles. Turn right onto Poole's Mill Road. Drive 0.6 mile to the park on the right. **GPS:** N34°17.349'/W84°14.520'

The Hike

A sidewalk leads north into the park where picnic tables, benches, a playground, and a porch swing are present. The path leads past a single picnic shelter and down to the famed Poole's Mill Covered Bridge. The covered bridge was built in 1901, although an uncovered bridge existed well before then. Cross the historic bridge and you can see the brink of the falls to your left. A path leads straight ahead to the base of the falls. During summertime the creek is busier than the playground, and locals splash around near the base of the falls. The waterfall spans the full width of the creek, with a small sliding rock at the far left end of it. If the creek was crystal clear the beauty rating would easily bump up to "very good." But since it has a heavy brown hue, I've given it a "good."

A gristmill once stood near the falls, but the mill was owned by a local Cherokee

Adjacent to a lovely neighborhood park, you'll find Poole's Mill Falls pleasantly waiting.

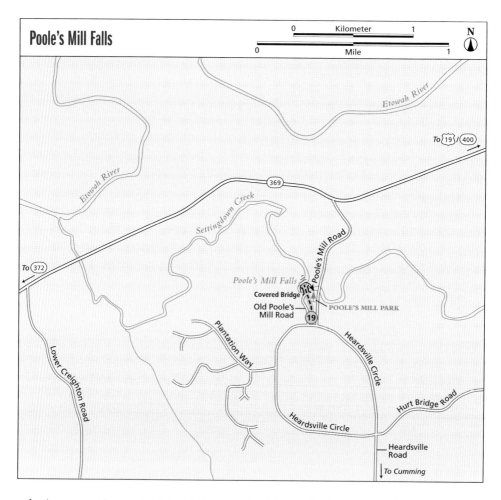

Poole's Mill Falls

businessman, George Welch. Unfortunately, this was in the 1830s when the Indian Removal Act was being enforced across the Southeast, and thousands of Native Americans—including the Seminole, Creek, Choctaw, Chickasaw, and Cherokee tribes—were banished from their homes and land and forced to march west to Oklahoma along the infamous "Trail of Tears." The land was taken from Mr. Welch, but he had signed a treaty sparing him from the horrific Trail of Tears.

Miles and Directions

0.0 Follow the sidewalk northwest into the park.

0.13 Cross the covered bridge.

0.15 Arrive at the base of Poole's Mill Falls (N34°17.485'/W84°14.578'). Backtrack to trailhead.

0.3 Arrive at trailhead.

Northeast Region

Dahlonega, Cleveland, Blairsville Area

20 Falls on Waters Creek

Heavenly! Lively and strong, this one keeps your attention. A popular swimming hole with the locals, it's a great place to cool off from the heat of a sunny day.

Height: 20 feet
Beauty rating: Excellent
Distance: Roadside
Difficulty: Easy
Blazes: None
County: Lumpkin
Land status: Chattahoochee National Forest–Chattooga District

Contacts: (706) 754-6221; www.fs.usda.gov/conf
FYI: Open 7 a.m.–10 p.m.; fee required; restroom, trash cans at parking area
Maps: DeLorme: Georgia Atlas & Gazetteer: Page 15 E7

Finding the trailhead: *From the junction of US 19 and US 129 at Turner's Corner*, drive south on US 19 for 0.5 mile. Turn right onto Dicks Creek Road. Travel 2.8 miles to a right into the parking area. *Note:* Dicks Creek Road becomes FS 34 after 2.2 miles. *From the junction of US 19 and GA 60 north*, drive north on US 19 for 4.7 miles. Turn left onto Dicks Creek Road. Follow directions above. **GPS:** 34°40.741'/W83°56.170'

The immaculate Falls on Waters Creek is stunning every time.

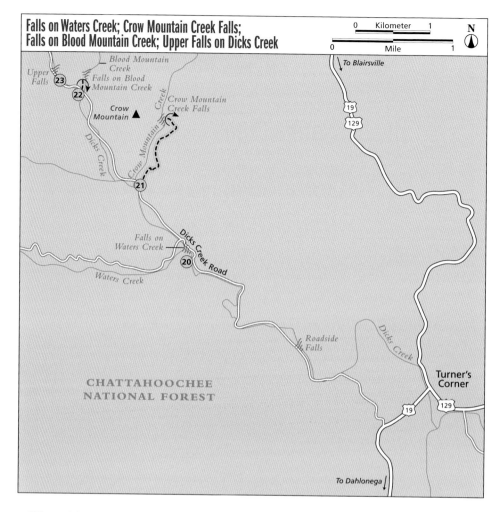

Falls on Waters Creek; Crow Mountain Creek Falls; Falls on Blood Mountain Creek; Upper Falls on Dicks Creek

The Hike

The falls are visible from the roadside, or you can follow a short, rooty path down to the base.

Many activities are enjoyed within the Waters Creek Recreation Area. There are nearly a dozen dispersed primitive campsites along the creek's edge. Several hiking trails are easily accessed, and the creek is considered one of Georgia's trophy trout streams. However, you must follow state fishing regulations before you break out your pole and waders.

21 Crow Mountain Creek Falls

Balanced! From the base of Crow Mountain Creek Falls, the balance of nature comes to mind. Tucked away deep in the forest, the creek makes its way down the mountainside until finally showing itself like a wonderful unexpected gift.

See map on p. 64.
Height: 35 feet
Beauty rating: Good
Distance: 1.54 miles
Difficulty: Moderate to strenuous
Surface: Wide old logging road, narrow hard-packed dirt
Hiking time: 1 hour
Other trail users: Equestrians

Blazes: None
County: Lumpkin
Land status: Chattahoochee National Forest–Chattooga District
Contacts: (706) 754-6221; www.fs.usda.gov/conf
Maps: DeLorme: Georgia Atlas & Gazetteer: Page 15 E7

Finding the trailhead: From the junction of US 19 and US 129 at Turner's Corner, drive south on US 19 for 0.5 mile. Turn right onto Dicks Creek Road. Travel 3.5 miles to a pull-off on the left across from an old logging road blocked by some dirt mounds and just before the fork in the road. **Note:** Dicks Creek Road becomes FS 34 after 2.2 miles. From the junction of US 19 and GA 60 north, drive north on US 19 for 4.7 miles. Turn left onto Dicks Creek Road. Follow directions above. The trailhead is at the foot of the logging road. **GPS:** N34°41.205'/W83°56.597'

The Hike

The trail follows the old roadbed up into the forest, and dirt mounds at the trailhead prevent people from driving four-wheel-drive vehicles up it instead. This is definitely the path less traveled. You'll notice lots of blowdowns where Mother Nature has pushed through the area, leaving a wake of downed trees in her path. Work your way around any natural obstacles, and continue following the rocky roadbed uphill and generally north. At three-quarters of a mile, just before you reach the brink of the falls, follow the side path on a steep scramble downhill to view the falls. This scramble is short, but very steep and not recommended after any rainfall. Bring a hiking stick.

Crow Mountain Creek flows from Crow Mountain and lies within the heart of the Chestatee Wildlife Management Area. Chestatee comes from the Cherokee word *a-tsv-sta-ti-yi*, meaning "firelight place." A popular means of hunting was to set a fire and flush wildlife toward the river where they could be easily killed. The WMA is still popular with hunters, but nowadays they obviously use different means. Many other recreational activities are enjoyed here, including hiking, birding, horseback riding, and fishing in the superb trout waters of Crow Mountain Creek.

Crow Mountain Creek tumbles down to form the falls.

Miles and Directions

0.0 Hike northeast on the old logging road.

0.1 Rock-hop a tributary.

0.25 Cross a tributary.

0.65 Rock-hop another tributary.

0.75 Before reaching the brink of the falls, scramble downhill toward the base of the falls.

0.77 Arrive at Crow Mountain Falls (N34°41.656'/W83°56.393'). Backtrack to trailhead.

1.54 Arrive at trailhead.

22 Falls on Blood Mountain Creek

Enthusiastic! This creek is so alive, and the waterfall is just as impressive as it tumbles down the mountainside. The water juts in and out, around and over the large stones that fill the bed of Blood Mountain Creek.

See map on p. 64.
Height: 120 feet
Beauty rating: Excellent
Distance: 0.1 mile
Difficulty: Moderate
Surface: Hard-packed dirt
Hiking time: 15 minutes
Other trail users: None

Blazes: None
County: Lumpkin
Land status: Chattahoochee National Forest–Blue Ridge District
Contacts: (706) 745-6928, (706) 970-9776; www.fs.usda.gov/conf
Maps: *DeLorme: Georgia Atlas & Gazetteer:* Page 15 E7

Finding the trailhead: *From the junction of US 19 and US 129 at Turner's Corner,* drive south on US 19 for 0.5 mile. Turn right onto Dicks Creek Road. Drive 4.5 miles. Park in a pull-off just after crossing the bridge. *Note:* Dicks Creek Road becomes FS 34 after 2.2 miles. At 3.5 miles stay left at the fork. Drive across the creek. High-clearance vehicles are recommended. *From the junction of US 19 and GA 60 north,* drive north on US 19 for 4.7 miles. Turn left onto Dicks Creek Road. Follow directions above. **GPS:** N34°41.868'/W83°57.135'

The Hike

A narrow dirt path leads steeply up the left bank of the creek to the middle of the falls. This creek is alive with activity, and as you hike upstream you realize how tall it is. When you reach the "viewing area," the water makes a near 90-degree bend before dropping down between two sheer rock walls. On the far side of the creek, a giant cliff looms overhead forming the bank. In contrast to the cliff, brilliant green water beckons you into the crystal-clear pool. The water continues downstream making one lovely drop after another. The falls are approximately 120 feet tall in total, but to me the ideal viewing spot is right here, where the water forms a clean channel between two stone walls making a perfect V at the base of this drop.

Although the hike is short, it's not easy. I don't recommend this hike for children, or dogs. There are several steep dropoffs, root scrambles, and areas where the trail is off camber.

Blood Mountain Creek flows from the upper reaches of Blood Mountain and makes its way south to its confluence with Dicks Creek just downstream from the falls. The mountain and creek are said to have earned their gory name from a brutal battle that was fought between the Cherokee and Creek tribes.

Watch your step.

This portion of Falls on Blood Mountain Creek is tucked away in an amazing little cove.

Folklore has it that the battle was so bloody that the entire mountain turned blood red.

Miles and Directions

0.0 Hike upstream on the left side of the creek.

0.05 Arrive at Falls on Blood Mountain Creek (N34°41.914'/W83°57.121'). Backtrack to the trailhead.

0.1 Arrive at trailhead.

23 Upper Falls on Dicks Creek

Comparable! This is the last among a string of waterfalls that can be reached along this wonderful rural road. Although it sits roadside and isn't the tallest of them all, this waterfall easily matches the others when it comes to beauty.

See map on p. 64.
Height: 20 feet
Beauty rating: Excellent
Distance: Roadside
Difficulty: Easy
County: Lumpkin

Land status: Chattahoochee National Forest–
Blue Ridge District
Contacts: (706) 745-6928, (706) 970-9776;
www.fs.usda.gov/conf
Maps: DeLorme: Georgia Atlas & Gazetteer:
Page 15 E7

Finding the trailhead: *From the junction of US 19 and US 129 at Turner's Corner*, drive south on US 19 for 0.5 mile. Turn right onto Dicks Creek Road. Drive 4.9 miles to a large pull-off on the left. ***Note:*** Dicks Creek Road becomes FS 34 after 2.2 miles. At 3.5 miles stay left at the fork. Drive across the creek. High-clearance vehicles are recommended. *From the junction of US 19 and GA 60 north*, drive north on US 19 for 4.7 miles. Turn left onto Dicks Creek Road. Follow directions above. **GPS:** N34°41.929'/W83°57.323'

Old plows, carts, and farm equipment are often seen along the roadside as you travel through the mountains.

Upper Falls on Dicks Creek is one of many off Dicks Creek Road.

The Hike

This roadside beauty is just as pretty as any other in the area. Standing 20 feet tall, the falls are cradled on the left by big boulders, while the right side makes a clean drop down into the creek. ***Note:*** You must drive across a shallow creek to reach the falls.

This is the fourth and final waterfall found along Dicks Creek Road and FS 34. Although it's roadside and not that tall, it's certainly worth a visit while you're in the area. The recreation area surrounding this lively creek is popular for fishing, camping, hiking, and hunting. If you have time, visit them all!

24 DeSoto Falls

Astonishing! Twice the pleasure here, with both the Lower and Upper DeSoto Falls to visit along the same trail. The Upper Falls is tall and exhilarating as the water drops in tiers down the mountainside. DeSoto's Lower Falls is one-third the size of its upstream sibling, but creates a lot of sound for a smaller waterfall. Like a younger child trying to speak up for itself, this one demands the attention it deserves.

Height: Lower Falls: 30 feet; Upper Falls: 90 feet
Beauty rating: Very good
Distance: 2.2 miles
Difficulty: Moderate
Surface: Hard-packed dirt with a short section of paved road
Hiking time: 1 hour, 15 minutes
Other trail users: None
Blazes: None

County: Lumpkin
Land status: Chattahoochee National Forest–Chattooga District
Contacts: (706) 754-6221; www.fs.usda.gov/conf; USDA Forest Service DeSoto Falls Campground: (706) 745-6928
FYI: Open 7 a.m.–10 p.m.; fee required
Maps: DeLorme: Georgia Atlas & Gazetteer: Page 15 E8

Finding the trailhead: From the junction of US 129 and GA 180 east, drive south on US 129 for 8.9 miles. Turn right into the DeSoto Falls Recreation Area. Take the first left into the large parking area. From the junction of US 129 and US 19 at Turner's Corner, drive north on US 129 for 4.0 miles. Turn left at the sign into the DeSoto Falls Recreation Area. Follow directions above. The trailhead is at the northwest corner of the parking area, near the self-pay station. **GPS:** N34°42.394'/W83°54.914'

The Hike

Follow the wide gravel path through the peaceful picnic area. A bed of ferns surrounds this day-use area, and the only intrusion is the occasional sound of traffic passing by on US 129. The path leads to the campground road where you'll head left hiking into the campground. You'll soon see a small footbridge on your left (west). Cross this footbridge, and a wide gravel path leads right (north) to Upper Falls and left (south) to Lower Falls. The trail to Upper Falls follows the creek upstream, and you can see the campground across the creek. In a quarter-mile you cross another footbridge as you continue hiking north. The trail has a few good climbs to overcome, but nothing too challenging. You'll cross one more footbridge before the path quickly leads to an observation deck at Upper DeSoto Falls. This tall and stoic waterfall drops in several tiers, and the observation deck has you standing right out over the exhilarating creek. The trail to Upper DeSoto Falls is wide, well maintained, and heavily trafficked. Backtrack to the T and now follow the creek downstream, south toward Lower DeSoto Falls. The trek to Lower Falls is narrower and more rugged,

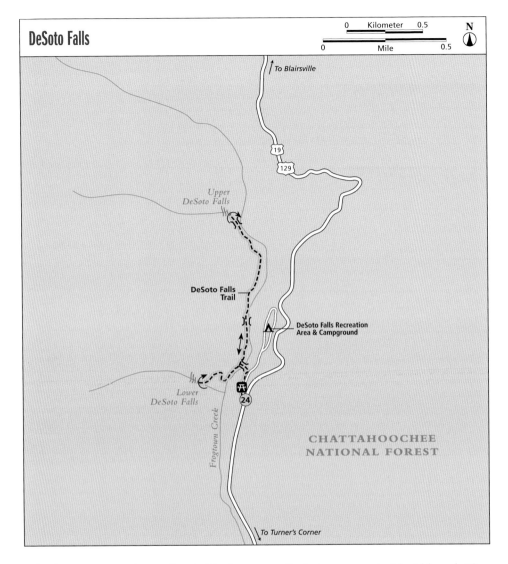

leading you around several switchbacks as you climb the mountainside. Although it's a mere 0.2 mile from the T, the hike to Lower Falls will have you breathing heavy as you ascend. The trail ends at an observation deck at Lower DeSoto Falls. The falls are similar in appearance to the Upper Falls, but the ledges on this one are shallower than its upstream sibling. The water flows over a sheer cliff wall that steps out before dropping again.

DeSoto Falls Scenic Area is named for the Spanish explorer Hernando de Soto. Hernando was the first European to explore the interior of Georgia, which he did in the late 1530s. The falls got their name when some early settlers found a piece of armor near the falls and attributed the relic to de Soto and his men.

An observation deck puts you in the splash zone of Upper DeSoto Falls.

While you're in the area you may want to stop by Neel Gap, aka Walasi-yi Interpretive Center and Mountain Crossings outfitters. Neel Gap is a crossroads along the Appalachian Trail where thru-hikers can restock, buy gear, or stop and spend the night. The stone structure was built in the 1930s around the same time the AT was completed.

Miles and Directions

0.0 Follow the wide gravel path into the picnic area.

0.15 Cross a footbridge and come to a T. Go right (north) toward Upper Falls.

0.4 Cross a footbridge.

0.85 Cross another footbridge. The path leads left toward the falls.

0.9 Arrive at an observation deck at Upper DeSoto Falls (N34°43.017'/W83°54.939'). Backtrack to the T.

1.65 Arrive at the T. Continue straight (south) toward Lower Falls.

1.85 Arrive at Lower DeSoto Falls (N34°42.442'/W83°55.073'). Backtrack to the trailhead.

2.2 Arrive at trailhead.

25 Helton Creek Falls

Gorgeous! Helton Creek is a wonderful place to spend the day. This very short and easy trail takes you to two beautiful waterfalls. The Upper Falls is a popular hangout and swimming hole for the locals. So if it's seclusion you seek, I suggest visiting these falls on a weekday to avoid the heavy traffic of weekend visitors.

Height: Lower Falls: 30 feet; Upper Falls: 50 feet
Beauty rating: Excellent
Distance: 0.3 mile
Difficulty: Easy
Surface: Hard-packed dirt
Hiking time: 20 minutes
Blazes: None

County: Union
Land status: Chattahoochee National Forest-Chattooga District
Contacts: (706) 754-6221; www.fs.usda.gov/conf
Maps: DeLorme: Georgia Atlas & Gazetteer: Page 15 D8

Finding the trailhead: *From the junction of US 129 and GA 180 west,* drive south on US 129 for 1.4 miles. Turn left onto Helton Creek Road. Travel 2.2 miles to a parking area on your right. *From the junction of US 129 and US 19 at Turner's Corner,* drive north on US 129 for 9.2 miles. Turn right onto Helton Creek Road. Follow directions above. The trailhead is at the northwest end of the parking lot. **GPS:** N34°45.201'/W83°53.675'

The Hike

The trail leads down some log steps, and you almost immediately hear the impressive sound of moving water in the distance. The easy-to-follow path leads past the trunks of massive trees that once stood tall in the area. It makes you ponder how many years it took for them to grow so impressively big. In less than 0.1 mile, a set of steps lead to the base of Lower Helton Creek Falls. Large flat rocks give you a place to sit and enjoy the view. When you're ready to move on, continue upstream. The path ends at an observation deck overlooking Upper Helton Creek Falls. The natural beauty here is stunning. A large, pristine swimming hole sits at the base of the falls, and there are plenty of places to take in the scenery, sunbathe after a dip, or

Downed trees add character to the trail.

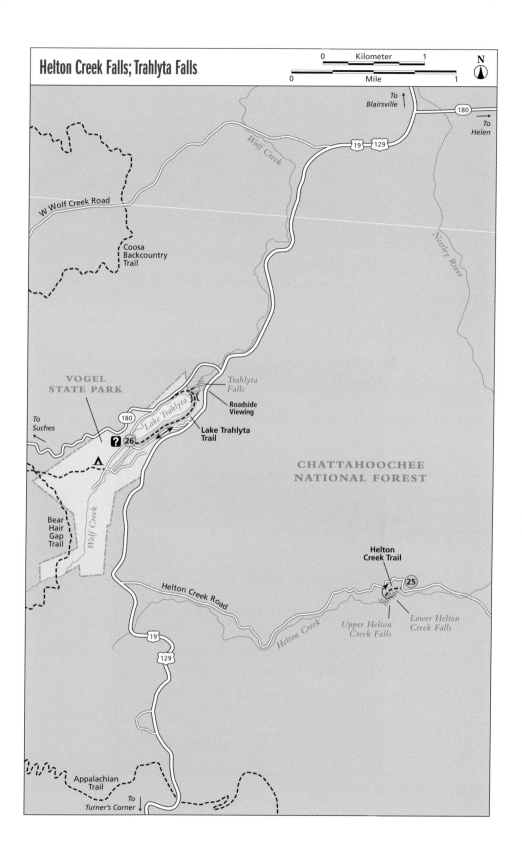

Helton Creek Falls; Trahlyta Falls

0 ——— Kilometer 1

0 ——— Mile 1

N

To
Blairsville

180

19 129

To
Helen

Wolf Creek

W Wolf Creek Road

Coosa
Backcountry
Trail

Nottley River

**VOGEL
STATE PARK**

To
Suches

180

Lake Trahlyta

*Trahlyta
Falls*

Roadside
Viewing

**Lake Trahlyta
Trail**

? 26

⛺

Wolf Creek

Bear
Hair
Gap
Trail

**CHATTAHOOCHEE
NATIONAL FOREST**

**Helton
Creek Trail**

25

Helton Creek Road

Helton Creek

*Upper Helton
Creek Falls*

*Lower Helton
Creek Falls*

19

129

Appalachian
Trail

To
Turner's Corner

lay out a picnic. This is by far one of my favorites. Two fantastic waterfalls along a short, easy hike that the whole family can enjoy. What more could you ask for?

Helton Creek Falls sits in a prime location at the heart of Union County with Vogel State Park just up the road. The area offers hiking trails, mountain biking, and horseback riding for outdoor enthusiasts. If you prefer tamer activities, you could go shopping or tubing in Helen, antiquing in Hiawassee, or try your hand at gem mining in Dahlonega. And of course don't forget the many other waterfalls within easy reach.

Miles and Directions

0.0 Hike west down the steps.

0.07 Cross a tiny tributary.

0.08 Steps on the left lead to Lower Falls.

0.1 Arrive at Lower Helton Creek Falls (N34°45.190'/W83°53.712'). Return to the main trail and hike west upstream.

0.15 Arrive at Upper Helton Creek Falls (N34°45.168'/W83°53.741'). Backtrack to trailhead.

0.3 Arrive at trailhead.

A perfect swim hole waits at Upper Helton Creek Falls.

26 Trahlyta Falls

Lively! This one has spirit and spice and will surely light up your day and bring a smile to your face. Although you can get a great view of Trahlyta Falls from the roadside, an easy lakeside hike allows you to literally reach out and touch the falls as they tumble downstream.

See map on p. 75.
Height: 45 feet
Beauty rating: Excellent
Distance: Roadside or 1.2 miles
Difficulty: Easy
Surface: Wide gravel and mulch, hard-packed dirt
Hiking time: 40 minutes
Other trail users: None

Blazes: None
County: Union
Land status: Vogel State Park
Contacts: (706) 745-2628; www.gastateparks .org/Vogel
FYI: Fee required; 7 a.m.–10 p.m.
Maps: *DeLorme: Georgia Atlas & Gazetteer:* Page 15 D7–D8

Finding the trailhead: *From the junction of US 129 and GA 180 east,* drive south on US 129 for 2.6 miles. Turn right into Vogel State Park. Drive down the hill for 0.4 mile, cross the bridge, and park on the right next to the lake. *From the junction of US 129 and US 19 at Turner's Corner,* drive north on US 129 for 10.3 miles. Turn left into Vogel State Park. Follow directions above. The trailhead is at the southeast end of the parking lot. **GPS:** N34°45.961'/W83°55.394' *Roadside viewing:* The paved pull-off is located 0.1 mile north of the main entrance to Vogel State Park on the west side of US 129.

The Hike

Trahlyta Falls can be viewed from the roadside, or you can hike along the lovely Lake Trahlyta to get a more personal feel for the falls. The trail begins by crossing a foot-bridge over Wolf Creek and then bends left following the shoreline from one end to the other. The lake is surrounded by mountains, and the scenery is exceptional. Occasional benches give you a spot to sit and enjoy the splendid view. Hardy mountain laurel lines the path, with its showy pink blossoms in full form through spring and summer. Trees offer plenty of shade, and birds flutter from one to the next as you hike by. You can hear the occasional car driving by on US 129, but it's not intrusive, and it certainly doesn't overshadow the beautiful setting that surrounds you. Half

Pristine mountains surround Lake Trahlyta.

LEGEND OF PRINCESS TRAHLYTA

Princess Trahlyta was said to have been a true nature lover. She would walk the mountain trails and revel in the splendor of the forest. According to legend, she would sip of the springs, which had a magical power that kept her youthful.

When Princess Trahlyta was kidnapped by the Cherokee warrior Wahsega, he took her far from the safe haven of her mountain home. They say it was her lack of freedom in the forest that killed her, not an act of violence.

According to folklore, passersby who tossed a stone upon her grave would be blessed with good health and good fortune. If you pass her grave today, you'll see that it's plainly marked by a large pile of stones near Stonepile Gap.

a mile into the hike you'll cross a second, much bigger footbridge that passes over a spillway at the east end of the lake. After crossing the footbridge, a narrow path leads downhill to an observation deck at Trahlyta Falls. The deck sits over the top of the creek, giving you an up-close and personal view of the falls. The corner of the deck doubles as a splash zone, where the cool spray of the stream rejuvenates you.

You can practically reach out and touch Trahlyta Falls from the overlook.

This hike is a great place for dogs. There are several spots where they can wade out into the lake. If that isn't enough, this is also an interpretive trail, with signs offering insight about the nature, flora, and fauna found in the area.

Lake Trahlyta was created in the 1930s by the Civilian Conservation Corps, and the lake and falls were named for the Indian princess Trahlyta. In the years before white settlers ever came to live here, there were many great battles between the Creek and Cherokee tribes. Legend has it that the water ran red with blood, and the mountains of Blood and Slaughter were named for the ferocity of these fights. During this wartime, Princess Trahlyta was kidnapped by a suitor she had rejected. She died in captivity and is buried south of the park at Stonepile Gap near the junction of US 19 and GA 60.

Miles and Directions

0.0 Hike south and immediately cross a footbridge. Follow the shoreline of Lake Trahlyta.

0.5 Cross a footbridge and immediately go right (north) on the dirt trail.

0.6 Arrive at Trahlyta Falls (N34°46.199'/W83°54.997'). Backtrack to trailhead.

1.2 Arrive at trailhead.

27 Raven Cliffs Falls

Unique! Raven Cliffs Falls is unlike any other waterfall in the area. A captivating mystery, it's fed by two streams that appear to come right out of the mountain and then plunge perfectly between the cliffs down into the grotto below.

Height: 50 feet
Beauty rating: Excellent
Distance: 5.1 miles
Difficulty: Moderate
Surface: Hard-packed dirt with rooty sections
Hiking time: 2 hours, 35 minutes
Other trail users: None
Blazes: None
County: White

Land status: Chattahoochee National Forest-Chattooga District
Contacts: (706) 754-6221; www.fs.usda.gov/conf
FYI: Fee required; 7 a.m.–10 p.m.; restroom, trash cans near trailhead
Maps: *DeLorme: Georgia Atlas & Gazetteer:* Page 15 E9

Finding the trailhead: *From the junction of GA 75 Alternate and GA 75 (just north of Helen),* drive west on GA 75A for 2.25 miles. Turn right onto GA 348 (Richard B. Russell Scenic Highway). Travel 2.6 miles. Turn left onto FS 244; drive down the hill to the parking area. *From the junction of GA 348 and GA 180,* drive south on GA 348 for 11.2 miles. Turn right onto FS 244. Follow directions above. The trailhead is located next to the bridge. **GPS:** N34°42.591'/W83°47.342'

The Hike

The path immediately crosses a tiny footbridge and leads past a large primitive campsite. You'll quickly cross a second footbridge, and from here the trail follows the creek upstream the entire way. At 0.3 mile you get a clear view of the first of four fabulous, bonus waterfalls en route to Raven Cliffs. The trail continues upstream in a fantasyland of falling water. Another 0.3 mile farther you'll pass the second wonderful bonus waterfall. Shortly after, you'll rock-hop across a wet area, and it seems like you're briefly hiking on a little island. Continue following the creek upstream, and you'll pass the third and perhaps prettiest of the bonus waterfalls. This doubles as a good benchmark, indicating that you're almost at the halfway point. In less than a quarter-mile, you'll hike past the fourth and final bonus waterfall. This one makes two distinct drops, the second of which is an impressive sheer plunge. Along with a wonderful array of waterfalls, this hike also has some intriguing rock formations, not to mention the cliffs and falls that wait at the end of the trail. Shortly after the fourth waterfall, you hike across a second and then third primitive log bridge. Up until now the hike

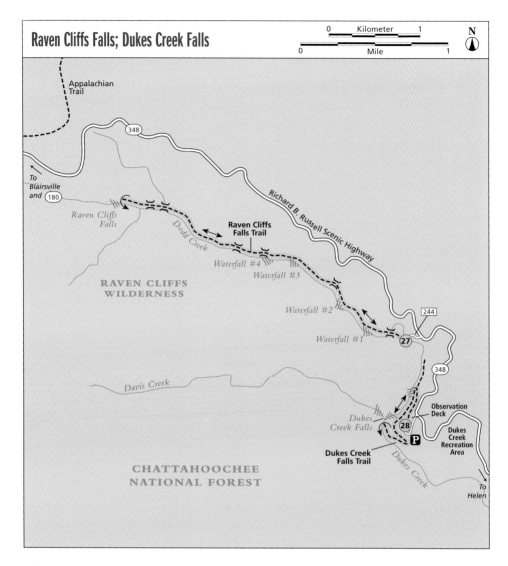

0　　　Kilometer　　1

0　　　Mile　　1

N

Appalachian Trail

348

To Blairsville and 180

Raven Cliffs Falls

Dodd Creek

Raven Cliffs Falls Trail

Richard B. Russell Scenic Highway

Waterfall #4

Waterfall #3

RAVEN CLIFFS WILDERNESS

Waterfall #2

244

Waterfall #1

27

348

Davis Creek

Dukes Creek Falls

Observation Deck

28

P

Dukes Creek Recreation Area

Dukes Creek Falls Trail

Dukes Creek

CHATTAHOOCHEE NATIONAL FOREST

To Helen

has been fairly flat, but beyond this bridge the trail begins to climb. You'll cross two more foot/log bridges before reaching a side path on the left that leads to Lower Raven Cliffs Falls at 2.5 miles. From where you stand, the creek is cradled by boulders and the lower falls sit in a beautiful little cove. This makes a nice little side trip before making the final push uphill to view the grand finale, Raven Cliffs Falls. As you reach the cliffs, you stand in awe of their clean-cut edges and sheer size looming overhead. To see the falls, climb up the steep clay path to the right, following it to the split in the center of the cliffs. Water juts out from between the two giant cliff walls, and you'll surely be delighted when you see it. It's unlike any other waterfall in the state.

Located within the Raven Cliffs Wilderness, this fabulous trail closely follows Dodd Creek, named for Ed Dodd, an environmentalist, national park guide, and

THE AMAZING SALAMANDER

Salamanders are frequently seen at the base of Raven Cliffs Falls. These passive amphibians can be found on every continent except for Antarctica. Some species can grow to be 6 feet long and weigh up to 140 pounds. No need to fear, you won't find these giant salamander species anywhere near the pool at Raven Cliffs. Most species, including those found here, rarely exceed 6 inches.

Salamanders' smooth, slick skin must remain moist at all times or they can die. This explains their presence in the cool mountain water below the falls. Humans are salamanders' worst enemy and the number-one reason for their demise. If you see one along the banks or pools of a mountain stream, please let it be and observe it from afar—perhaps through binoculars, or the lens of a camera, so that it can survive and others can one day see it too.

creator of the *Mark Trail* comic strip. This area was once a popular place for rappelling; however this activity was banned in 1986 to help protect the cliffs from erosion.

Miles and Directions

0.0 Cross the tiny footbridge and hike northwest.

0.13 Cross a footbridge and hike west upstream.

0.3 View the first of four bonus waterfalls (N34°42.662'/W83°47.629').

0.6 Hike past the second bonus waterfall (N34°42.812'/W83°47.815').

0.7 Rock-hop a wet area. Continue upstream (north).

0.77 Cross a log bridge.

1.15 Hike past the third bonus waterfall (N34°43.059'/W83°48.157').

1.35 Hike past the fourth bonus waterfall (N34°43.075'/W83°48.334').

1.38 Cross another log bridge.

1.57 Cross a log bridge.

2.2 Cross a footbridge.

2.35 Cross a log bridge.

2.49 A side path leads left to view Lower Raven Cliffs Falls (N34°43.390'/ W83°49.344)'. Return to the main path and hike west toward the cliffs.

2.55 Arrive at Raven Cliffs Falls (N34°43.402'/W83°49.396'). Backtrack to trailhead.

5.1 Arrive at trailhead.

Colossal cliffs loom over the creek at Raven Cliffs Wilderness Area.

28 Dukes Creek Falls

Fire and ice! Meeting with a fury, two creeks crash together in the most tremendous way! Photos do no justice to the power and might that this masterpiece presents. Sitting side by side, two wonderful waterfalls come together to create Dukes Creek Falls.

See map on p. 80.
Height: 250 feet
Beauty rating: Excellent
Distance: 2.4 miles
Difficulty: Moderate
Surface: Hard-packed dirt, sections of wooden boardwalk; a small portion is wheelchair accessible
Hiking time: 1 hour, 15 minutes
Other trail users: None

Blazes: Green
County: White
Land status: Chattahoochee National Forest-Chattooga District
Contacts: (706) 754-6221; www.fs.usda.gov/conf
FYI: Fee required; 7 a.m.–10 p.m.; restroom, trash cans near trailhead
Maps: *DeLorme: Georgia Atlas & Gazetteer:* Page 15 E9

Finding the trailhead: *From the junction of GA 75 Alternate and GA 75 (north of Helen),* drive west on GA 75A for 2.25 miles. Turn right onto GA 348 (Richard B. Russell Scenic Highway). Travel 1.6 miles to a left into Dukes Creek Recreation Area. *From the junction of GA 348 and GA 180,* drive south on GA 348 for 12.1 miles. Turn right into the Dukes Creek Recreation Area. The trailhead is at the south side of the parking area. **GPS:** N34°42.107'/W83°47.366'

The Hike

From the parking area walk down the steps and head right (west). You can hear the falls from the trailhead although they are far by foot. As the crow flies the creek is near, but for us bipedal people we have to take the long way. At 0.1 mile you'll get a glimpse of the falls in the distance, but on a foggy day you'll have to wait. Beyond this "observation deck" the trail continues to a T near the creek. As you follow the creek downstream, the wide gravel path gives you an aerial view of the beautiful cascades below. You'll even pass a bonus waterfall at the half-mile mark. Less than half a mile from this waterfall the trail makes a hard switchback to the right and transforms from a wide gravel trail to a narrow dirt footpath. This path descends steadily until you reach a wooden observation deck at the base of Dukes Creek Falls. Two waterfalls are collectively known as Dukes Creek Falls. The left is tall, with a commanding presence. The falls on the right are much shorter, but full of character. This creek crashes down over large boulders before it collides and converges with the other.

Dukes Creek is credited as the starting place for the great Georgia gold rush. In 1828 a prospector named Fred Logan made the first find along this powerful waterway. His discovery stirred the first significant gold rush in US history.

Two creeks converge to form the dazzling Dukes Creek Falls.

Miles and Directions

0.0 Follow the paved path west.

0.1 An observation spot offers views of the falls in the distance. Continue hiking northeast.

0.32 Come to a T at the creek. Go left (southwest).

0.5 Hike past a bonus waterfall in the creek below.

0.9 Make a switchback to the right (west).

1.2 Arrive at Dukes Creek Falls (N34°42.152'/W83°47.497'). Backtrack to trailhead.

2.4 Arrive at trailhead.

29 Horse Trough Falls

Wondrous! Horse Trough Falls truly makes you wonder how such a tiny creek at the top could feed such a massive waterfall and then in an instant returns to a simple little forest stream. Nature certainly is amazing. This one is recommended for hikers of all ages and abilities.

Height: 70 feet
Beauty rating: Very good
Distance: 0.2 mile
Difficulty: Easy
Surface: Wide gravel trail
Hiking time: 10 minutes
Other trail users: None
Blazes: Green

County: Union
Land status: Chattahoochee National Forest-Chattooga District
Contacts: (706) 754-6221; www.fs.usda.gov/conf
FYI: 7 a.m.–10 p.m.
Maps: *DeLorme: Georgia Atlas & Gazetteer:* Page 15 D9

Finding the trailhead: *From the junction of GA 75 and GA 356,* drive north on GA 75 for 8.0 miles. Turn left onto FS 44. Travel 4.5 miles. Turn right into the Upper Chattahoochee River Campground, pass the bathhouse, and park at the day-use parking. **Note:** You must drive across a shallow creek on the way to the trailhead. *From the junction of GA 75 and GA 180,* drive south on GA 75 for 2.5 miles. Turn right onto FS 44. Follow directions above. The trailhead is at the north-northwest end of the parking area. **GPS:** 34°47.521'/W83°47.119'

The Hike

A wide gravel trail leads into the woods and over a footbridge. Interpretive signs offer information about the nature around you, giving you a self-guided tour of the forest. The short, easy-to-follow path soon leads to an observation deck at the base of Horse Trough Falls.

Named for and flowing from Horsetrough Mountain, the falls and mountain are located within the Mark Trail Wilderness. Oddly enough, Mark Trail is a fictional character from a comic strip that was first penned in the mid-1900s. The character was a photojournalist and magazine writer who quelled the evils of those doing ecological and environmental misdeeds. Well before his time, he would have fit right into today's eco-friendly society.

A ring around the stem of any wild mushroom may be an indication that it is poisonous.

Horse Trough Falls

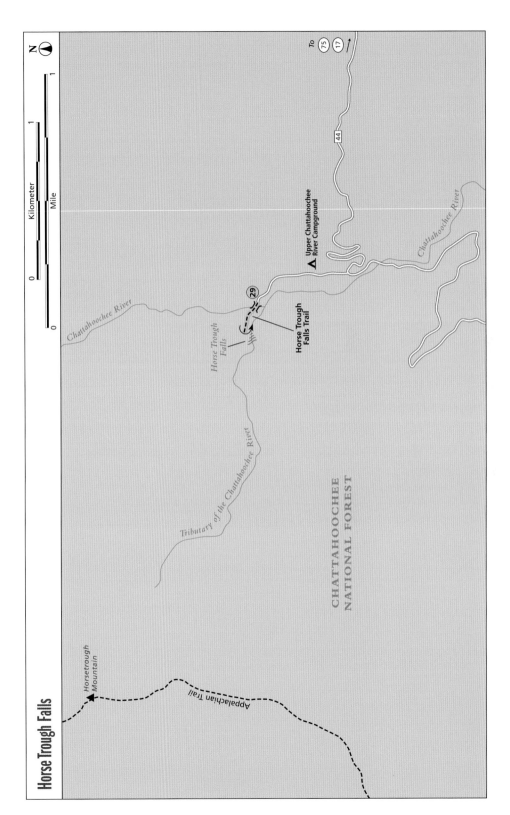

Horse Trough Falls is far prettier in person.

Miles and Directions

0.0   Follow the path north toward the falls.

0.1   Arrive at the base of Horse Trough Falls (N34°47.555/W83°47.200). Backtrack to trailhead.

0.2   Arrive at trailhead.

30 High Shoals Falls

Twice the treat! This terrific trail offers two incredible waterfalls. The first is Blue Hole Falls. In a word . . . inviting! The waters of the Blue Hole open their arms and inspire you to spend the afternoon picnicking and basking in their delight. Next you'll reach High Shoals Lower Falls. Like the talons of an eagle catching its prey, the water clings to the rock as it swoops down the mountainside.

Height: Blue Hole: 25 feet; High Shoals Lower Falls: 100 feet
Beauty rating: Excellent
Distance: 2.04 miles
Difficulty: Moderate to strenuous
Surface: Hard-packed dirt
Hiking time: 1 hour, 10 minutes
Other trail users: None

Blazes: Green (sparsely placed)
County: Towns
Land status: Chattahoochee National Forest-Blue Ridge District
Contacts: (706) 745-6928, (706) 970-9776; www.fs.usda.gov/conf
Maps: *DeLorme: Georgia Atlas & Gazetteer:* Page 15 C9

Finding the trailhead: *From the junction of GA 75 and GA 356,* drive north on GA 75 for 10.1 miles. Turn right onto Indian Grave Gap Road (FS 283). Travel 1.3 miles to the small parking area on the left. *From the junction of GA 75 and GA 180,* drive south on GA 75 for 0.5 mile. Turn left onto Indian Grave Gap Road (FS 283). Follow directions above.

The trailhead for High Shoals Trail (#19) is at the north end of the parking area. (**Note:** Indian Grave Gap Road fords a small creek. On days when water levels are high, you may need a high-clearance vehicle to ford the creek.) **GPS:** N34°48.980'/W83°43.618'

The Hike

This wide and heavily trodden trail makes a steady descent. By half a mile you'll reach the creek. As you hike past a primitive campsite, you'll see the remains where a footbridge once stood. Follow the creek downstream less than a tenth of a mile and cross the creek on a makeshift "bridge." Some creative hikers used planks from the old bridge, a downed tree, and their ingenuity to create this crafty passageway. After crossing the creek, head left (north) following the creek downstream. You'll cross a pair of footbridges before a side path on the left that leads down to Blue Hole Falls. This side path is just past some boulders that are inset in the middle of the trail. An observation deck gives you a perfect view of the falls and the spectacular swim hole that accompanies it. A deep blue-green pool forms at the base from the steady stream of rushing water. Each time I visit I'm always astounded. This is definitely one of my favorites!

Backtrack to the main trail and continue north descending deeper into the forest. Within a tenth of a mile you'll come to a T. Go left following the sound of the falls. The path leads around a few switchbacks before you arrive at High Shoals Falls. You

High Shoals Falls; Gurley Creek Falls; Joel Creek Falls

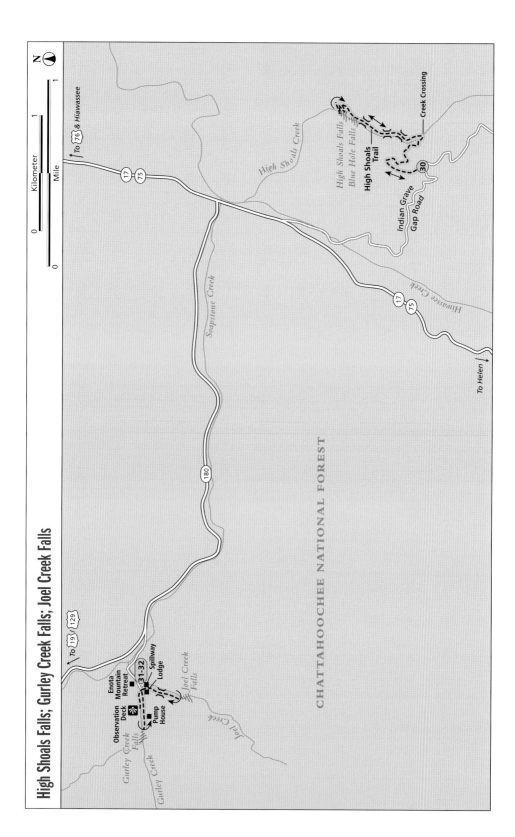

Blue Hole Falls creates a pristine pool at the base.

don't quite realize how much of a descent you made, until you're hiking back out. Bring a stick to ease the ascent.

These waterfalls make their home within the High Shoals Scenic Area. The area covers 170 acres, and there are actually five waterfalls in succession along High Shoals Creek. In an effort to protect the area, only two have a designated and well-maintained trail.

Indian Grave Gap Road was named for Indian Grave Gap, which sits at 3,120 feet. Given the history of this area, there's a good chance it was aptly named.

Miles and Directions

0.0 Follow the wide path north.

0.45 Cross the creek and head left (north).

0.5 Cross a footbridge.

0.55 Cross a footbridge.

0.72 Cross a footbridge.

0.77 Follow the side path leading left (southwest) to Blue Hole Falls (N34°49.288'/ W83°43.346').

0.82 Arrive at Blue Hole Falls. Backtrack to the main trail. Continue hiking northeast.

0.92 Come to a T, go left (west).

1.07 Arrive at High Shoals Lower Falls (N34°49.352'/W83°43.318'). Backtrack to trailhead.

2.04 Arrive at trailhead.

31 Gurley Creek Falls

Verve! As you follow the creek uphill and upstream, you can't help but enjoy the sights and sounds it has to offer. Gurley Creek flows enthusiastically downstream, and you're treated from one spirited cascade to the next. When you reach the main drop, it does not disappoint. This one is full of life, vim, and vigor!

See map on p. 88.
Height: 200 feet
Beauty rating: Very good
Distance: 0.5 mile
Difficulty: Moderate
Surface: Hard-packed dirt
Hiking time: 20 minutes
Other trail users: None

Blazes: None
County: Towns
Land status: Privately owned Enota Mountain Retreat; open to public
Contacts: (706) 896-9966; www.enota.com
FYI: Fee required; 8 a.m.–6 p.m.
Maps: *DeLorme: Georgia Atlas & Gazetteer:* Page 15 C9

Finding the trailhead: *From the junction of GA 180 and GA 75 near Hiawassee,* drive west on GA 180 for 2.6 miles. Turn left into Enota Mountain Retreat. Follow signs to Lodge/Office. *From the junction of GA 180 and US 129 in Choestoe,* drive east on GA 180 for 10.0 miles. Turn right into Enota Mountain Retreat. Follow directions above. The trailhead is on the north side of the lodge on the first gravel road leading left (west). **GPS:** N34°50.276'/W83°46.551'

The Hike

Prior to hiking here you must check in at the lodge, where you can get a trail map and further guidance to the trailhead if needed. Once you've paid the day-use fee, head to the right (north) side of the lodge. From here you'll see two gravel roads that lead left. Follow the first one west toward the Apache and Cherokee cabins, where you'll see signs toward the waterfall. Beyond the cabins a narrow dirt path leads upstream alongside Gurley Creek. The trail makes a fairly steep climb nearly due west and after two-tenths of a mile you'll pass the remnants of an old pump house. You can see the main drop of the falls from here, or scramble down a dirt path to the base of this main drop. The falls are 200 feet in total, but it drops in sections. To me, this is the preferred way to see the falls, since you can get up close and personal. Plus the trail follows the creek, so that's always a bonus, even if you have to climb steeply uphill.

Another option lets you see the waterfall in its entirety, but this view is from afar. To get this alternate viewpoint, return to the lodge and hike west on that second gravel road mentioned earlier. You'll hike past a long, slender building and follow the creek upstream. The path ends at a small observation deck. From here you can view the falls from afar through the foliage. These two views are very different from one another. If you're able to make the uphill climb, I highly recommend the first option.

Left: This friendly fellow roams freely with some other furry friends at Enota Mountain Retreat. Right: Gurley Creek Falls, a terrific treat accessed at Enota Mountain Retreat

Cabins, camping, a trout pond, and a small farm with goats, pigs, chickens, and rabbits all grace this lovely piece of property. Not to mention they have miniature horses that roam freely around the property. The horses are extremely friendly, and you may be lucky enough to encounter one. The Enota Mountain Retreat is run by a nonprofit organization, and whether you come for the day, or plan to stay, you'll surely enjoy your time here. Visit Joel Creek Falls while you're here (Hike 32). That trailhead is on the south side of the lodge.

Miles and Directions

0.0 Hike past the lodge toward the cabins.

0.1 Follow the narrow dirt path west.

0.2 Hike past the old pump house.

0.25 Arrive at Gurley Falls (N34°50.276'/W83°46.777'). Backtrack to trailhead.

0.5 Arrive at trailhead.

32 Joel Creek Falls

Legit! At 400 feet tall, this one is the real deal. It's difficult to see the falls in its entirety, but the portion that you do spy is quite unique. The waterfall makes a big bend in the middle, which looks like it's flowing sideways rather than downward.

See map on p. 88.
Height: 400 feet
Beauty rating: Good
Distance: 0.4 mile
Difficulty: Moderate
Surface: Hard-packed dirt
Hiking time: 15 minutes
Other trail users: None

Blazes: None
County: Towns
Land status: Privately owned Enota Mountain Retreat; open to the public
Contacts: (706) 896-9966; www.enota.com
FYI: Fee required; 8 a.m.–6 p.m.
Maps: *DeLorme: Georgia Atlas & Gazetteer:* Page 15 C9

Finding the trailhead: *From the junction of GA 180 and GA 75 near Hiawassee,* drive west on GA 180 for 2.6 miles. Turn left into Enota Mountain Retreat. Follow signs to Lodge/Office. *From the junction of GA 180 and US 129 in Choestoe,* drive east on GA 180 for 10.0 miles. Turn right into Enota Mountain Retreat. Follow directions above. Trailhead is located to the right of the spillway, which is behind the lodge to the left (south). **GPS:** N34°50.276'/W83°46.551'

The Hike

Prior to hiking here you must check in at the lodge, where you can get a trail map and further guidance to the trailhead if needed. After paying your day-use fee, head to the left (south) of the lodge. You'll pass an old fire engine and a few rental cabins hiking toward the small spillway. To the right of the spillway walk up the steps and follow the path alongside the small pond that feeds it. The trail quickly leads across a pair of footbridges as you head into the forest. The closer you get to the falls, the more the trail climbs, leading you to an open area where you can view the falls in the distance. This one is unique. It makes a bend in the middle of the falls, as if the water is stretching itself out flowing sideways down the mountainside.

You'll hike past this old engine on the way to Joel Creek Falls.

Joel Falls makes a surprisingly hard bend in the middle of the falls.

Enota Mountain Retreat is a nonprofit organization that boasts a small farm, camping, cabins, a trout pond, organic garden, and more. Whether you stay here or not, you're likely to enjoy your visit. A highlight is the miniature horses that roam freely around the property. These hospitable horses are so sweet and friendly, they'll come right up and nudge you begging for a gentle pet. Visit Gurley Creek Falls while you're here (Hike 31). That trailhead is on the north side of the lodge.

Miles and Directions

0.0 From the lodge, hike toward the spillway.

0.05 Hike up the steps, and south past the pond.

0.08 Cross a footbridge.

0.09 Cross another footbridge.

0.2 Arrive at an opening in the trail to view Joel Falls (N34°50.110'/W83°46.615'). Backtrack to trailhead.

0.4 Arrive at trailhead.

33 Cupid Falls

Unsuspecting! This certainly is an unexpected find. Unlike the typical waterfalls found deep within the forest, this one sits behind the campus of Young Harris College. It's one of those hidden gems that you would never even know existed if you weren't told they were here. Enjoy this blessing in disguise.

Height: 20 feet
Beauty rating: Very good
Distance: Roadside
Difficulty: Easy
County: Towns

Land status: Jeff Davis Memorial Park
FYI: Dawn to dusk
Maps: *DeLorme: Georgia Atlas & Gazetteer:* Page 15 B8

Finding the trailhead: *From the junction of US 76 and GA 66 in Young Harris,* drive east on US 76 for 0.1 mile. Turn right onto Maple Street. Drive 0.1 mile to a stop sign. Continue straight through the college campus for 0.4 mile to a pull-off on the left. (*Note:* Along the way Maple Street becomes Thomas Town Road.) *From the junction of US 76 and GA 515 near Young Harris,* drive west on US 76 for 3.2 miles. Turn left onto Maple Street. Follow directions above. **GPS:** N34°56.107'/W83°50.459'

The Hike

You're likely to find a spot in the small roadside parking area next to the fence line, but if you find this area is full, a larger parking lot sits 0.1 mile past the falls. The only thing indicating the name of this quaint neighborhood park is a plaque mounted on a single stone. A handful of picnic tables rest amid the grassy area next to the creek, and a single porch-style loveseat swing sits upstream from the falls. You can see the falls from the grassy area next to where you parked, or follow a short scramble path down to the creek at

Tucked away behind Young Harris College you'll find the glorious Cupid Falls.

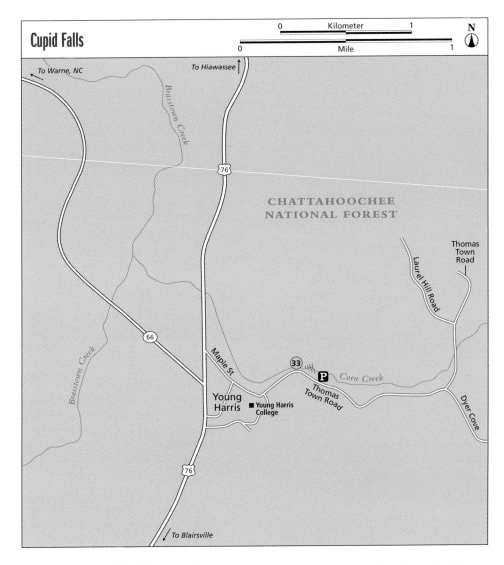

Cupid Falls

CHATTAHOOCHEE
NATIONAL FOREST

the base of the falls. The crystal-clear water beckons you to spend a few refreshing moments wading in the creek. While this park doesn't offer much as far as amenities, there's a peaceful feel about it, and the falls are as pretty as any other in the north Georgia mountains.

Young Harris has a small-town feel, but it's just minutes from Hiawassee, which has everything you need from music to wineries, and galleries to gardens. The town of Young Harris sits just west of Lake Chatuge, arguably one of the prettiest lakes in the region. It is surrounded by tall mountains—the tallest of these being Brasstown Bald, which sits just to the south of Young Harris—and the many fingers of this lovely lake create captivating coves of crystal-clear green water. Every which way you turn there are amazing views, and splendid adventures ready for you to explore.

34 Anna Ruby Falls

Showy! Located adjacent to Unicoi State Park, Anna Ruby Falls is one of the most popular waterfalls in the area. Although overcrowded, the falls are quite beautiful and worth a visit. Don't expect seclusion here, and you won't be disappointed.

Height: 153 feet, 50 feet
Beauty rating: Excellent
Distance: 0.8 mile
Difficulty: Moderate
Surface: Paved path; considered wheelchair accessible
Hiking time: 30 minutes
Other trail users: None
Blazes: None
County: White

Land status: Chattahoochee National Forest-Chattooga District
Contacts: Anna Ruby Falls Visitor Center; (706) 878-3574; www.fs.usda.gov/conf
FYI: Open 9 a.m.–7 p.m. from Memorial Day to Labor Day; 9 a.m.–5 p.m. after Labor Day; fee required; gift shop, restrooms, vending machines, trash cans at the trailhead
Maps: DeLorme: Georgia Atlas & Gazetteer: Page 15 E9

Finding the trailhead: *From the junction of GA 356 and GA 75,* drive north on GA 356 for 1.25 miles. Turn left onto Anna Ruby Falls Road. Travel 2.4 miles to the gate/fee booth. Pay the fee and continue another 0.9 mile to where the road dead-ends at the parking area. *From the junction of GA 356 and GA 197,* drive south on GA 356 for 9.35 miles. Turn right onto Anna Ruby Falls Road. Follow directions above. **GPS:** N34°45.469'/W83°42.605'

The Hike

A paved path makes a steady incline, following the creek upstream until you arrive at a footbridge. Cross the bridge and continue on the now steeper ascent until you arrive at the observation decks at the base of Anna Ruby Falls. Although this is considered wheelchair accessible, be aware, the path makes a very steep uphill climb. Interpretive signs along the way describe many of the natural features, and benches are provided for those needing a break from the incline.

The two waterfalls that make up Anna Ruby Falls sit side by side and unite to form Smith Creek, which flows directly into Unicoi Lake.

Shortly after the Civil War, the falls and the many acres surrounding them belonged to Col. John H. Nichols. Sadly, Colonel Nichols was a widower who had lost not just his wife but also his two infant sons. All that was left for this decorated war veteran was his daughter, Anna Ruby. She lives on infinitely through the splendor of Smith and York Creeks as they create the natural wonder known as Anna Ruby Falls.

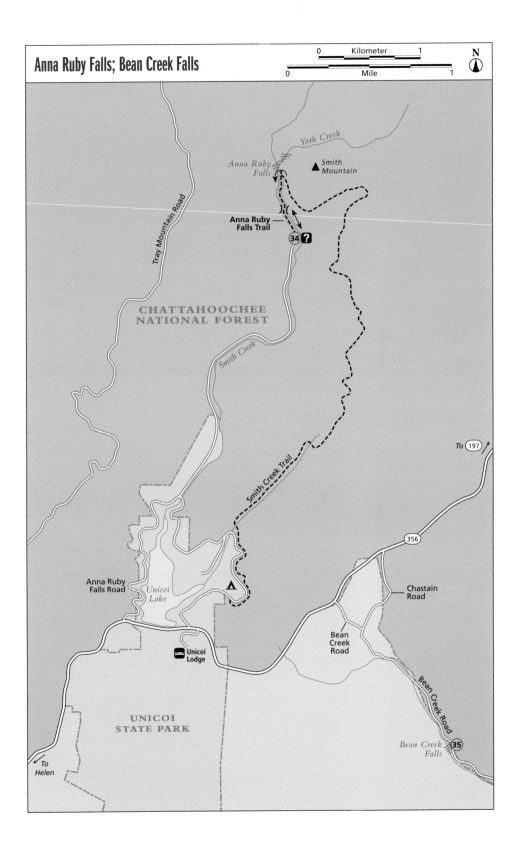

York Creek drops over a sheer cliff to create the second half of Anna Ruby Falls.

Miles and Directions

0.0 Hike north on the paved path.

0.2 Cross a footbridge.

0.4 Arrive at Anna Ruby Falls (N34°45.813/W83°42.731). Backtrack to trailhead.

0.8 Arrive at trailhead.

35 Bean Creek Falls

Beefy! A thick wall of dark stone forms the face of this roadside waterfall as it makes a double drop into the shallow creek below. Bean Creek Falls has an ideal location, not far from downtown Helen, and across the way from the unbeatable Unicoi State Park. While you're in the area this makes a nice pit stop if you want to get a quick waterfall fix.

See map on p. 97.
Height: 20 feet
Beauty rating: Very good
Distance: Roadside
Difficulty: Easy

County: White
Land status: Private property
Maps: *DeLorme: Georgia Atlas & Gazetteer:* Page 15 E10

Finding the trailhead: *From the junction of GA 356 and GA 197,* drive west on GA 356 for 7.9 miles. Turn left onto Bean Creek Road. Travel 0.2 mile to a stop sign. Go right following Bean Creek Road for 0.9 mile to the falls on the right. *From the junction of GA 356 and GA 75 near Helen,* drive east on GA 356 for 2.7 miles. Turn right onto Bean Creek Road. Follow directions above.
GPS: N34°42.822'/W83°41.665'

The Hike

Wild roses line the steep bank of creek standing between you and the beautiful Bean Creek Falls. The falls make an abrupt drop right along the roadway, and the edge of the road seems to drop off just as steeply, so use caution while you're taking a peek and a picture. Remember this is on private property, so no matter how pretty the falls are and how tempting it is to get a closer look, resist the temptation, or you will be trespassing.

While you're in the area, the nearby Unicoi State Park is well worth a visit. The park has camping, cabins, and a fabulous lodge. Hiking, mountain biking, paddling, and even a zipline are among the many adventures this park has to offer. If you prefer a tamer trip, the alpine town of Helen is a wonderful place to visit, and it's just down the road. On your way to town don't forget to stop in for some hot boiled peanuts at Fred's Famous Peanuts near the junction of GA 356 and GA 75.

Bean Creek Falls, an impressive roadside treat

36 Soque River Falls

Historic! Although this isn't the tallest waterfall in the area, it's steeped in history, and the roadside location offers easy access to those who may not be able to delve deep into the forest. The neighboring pottery shop, Mark of the Potter, whose parking lot you're using to see the falls, is a fantastic place to visit while you're here. The pottery is wonderfully made, and there's even a mini waterfall that flows in the basement of this iconic landmark.

Height: 15 feet
Beauty rating: Very good
Distance: Roadside
Difficulty: Easy
County: Habersham

Land status: Private property
Contacts: (706) 947-3440; www.markofthe potter.com
Maps: DeLorme: Georgia Atlas & Gazetteer: Page 16 E1

Finding the trailhead: *From the junction of GA 197 and GA 255 in Batesville,* drive south on GA 197 for 2.0 miles to the parking area on the left just south of Mark of the Potter. *From the junction of GA 197 and GA 385 in Clarkesville,* drive north on GA 197 for 10.1 miles to the parking area on the right just south of Mark of the Potter. **GPS:** N34°43.744'/W83°35.307'

The Hike

From the parking area all you need to do is look upstream and you'll see the splendid Soque River Falls dropping down over boulders adjacent to the Mark of the Potter pottery shop. The falls are not very tall, but they are multifaceted and wonderful to watch. Once you've enjoyed the show from here, stop in the pottery shop and the thrills will continue. The shop has a team of first-class artisans who keep the shelves stocked with plenty of pottery to choose from. As you explore the shop, step out onto the back deck where you get a closer view of the falls and have the opportunity to feed the shop's prodigious pet trout. Feeding the trout here has been a tradition for decades, dating back to when this structure was a working mill. The river powered a gristmill for many years, and you can

Mark of the Potter gives you a great view of Soque River Falls.

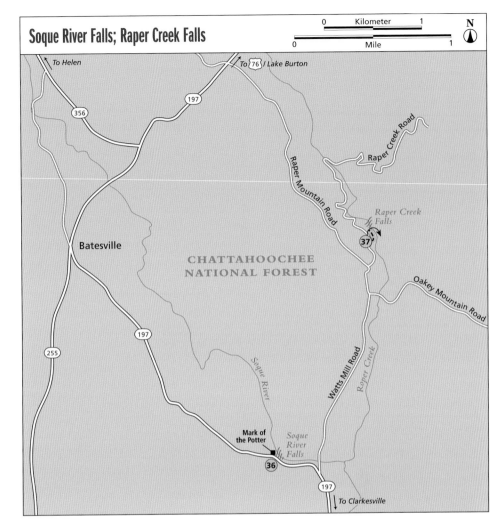

still see the remnants of the mill works near the foundation of the structure. If you venture down to the basement, you'll see another very small "waterfall" where the water rolls down over a small stone wall. As you leave the structure you should do so with pride, knowing that you just stood inside a historical landmark that has graced northeast Georgia for centuries.

Take time to stop and smell the flowers.

37 Raper Creek Falls

Flexible! The trail ends at an area where you can overlook the falls from above. This is an ideal vantage point to see this wacky waterfall. It drops in two tiers sitting nearly side by side.

See map on p. 101.
Height: 40 feet
Beauty rating: Very good
Distance: 0.2 mile
Difficulty: Moderate
Surface: Hard-packed dirt
Hiking time: 10 minutes
Other trail users: None

Blazes: None
County: Habersham
Land status: Chattahoochee National Forest–Chattooga District
Contacts: (706) 754-6221; www.fs.usda.gov/conf
Maps: *DeLorme: Georgia Atlas & Gazetteer:* Page 16 D1

Finding the trailhead: *From the junction of GA 197 and GA 356 near Batesville,* drive north on GA 197 for 0.8 mile. Turn right onto Raper Mountain Road. Drive 1.7 miles. Turn left onto Raper Creek Road. Travel 0.25 mile to a small pull-off on the right. *From the junction of GA 197 and US 76 north of Lake Burton,* drive south on GA 197 for 10.6 miles. Turn left onto Raper Mountain Road. Follow directions above. The trailhead is in the pull-off. **GPS:** N34°44.950'/W83°34.666'

The Hike

The trailhead is in the pull-off and you can clearly see where the path makes a scramble north and downhill to the falls. Although you can see the falls from the road, the view is much better if you make the short hike down to it. Plus, you get to hike past an impressive rock overhang with a giant tree growing out of it. Near the falls you'll see a rudimentary homemade sign that reads "Cindy Falls," although I've never seen this listed anywhere as an official name for the falls. The waterfall is unique. Upstream of the falls the creek is just chugging along, doing its thing, and suddenly it comes to a dead stop as it's halted by a large stone in the middle of the creek. This boulder brings the water to a stop at the brink of the falls and then diverts it down to the right where it makes a freefall plunge down to the creek below. The water falls in two tiers, but they are offset from one another. Although it's short, the terrain has some steep aspects to it. I've rated it as "moderate" for a difficulty level. Nonetheless, this distinctive waterfall is certainly worth a quick scramble to see.

The creek and falls could certainly have a better name, but so be it. Raper Creek has its headwaters near the unbeatable shores of Lake Burton and makes its confluence to the south into the serene Soque River. Although the name is unpleasant, the creek is surrounded by gorgeous mountains, and outdoor opportunities abound.

A stone set in the middle of the creek redirects the flow of Raper Creek Falls.

Miles and Directions

0.0   Scramble down the path toward the falls.

0.1   Arrive at Raper Creek Falls (N34°44.970'/W83°34.674'). Backtrack to trailhead.

0.2   Arrive at trailhead.

38 Sliding Rock on Wildcat Creek

Thrilling! A popular waterslide and swimming hole with the local kids, the cool refreshing waters of Wildcat Creek make for a fun and exciting time. I've occasionally slid down this one myself.

Height: 20 feet
Beauty rating: Excellent
Distance: Roadside
Difficulty: Easy
Blazes: None
County: Rabun

Land status: Chattahoochee National Forest-Chattooga District
Contacts: (706) 754-6221; www.fs.usda.gov/conf
Maps: DeLorme: Georgia Atlas & Gazetteer: Page 16 C1

Finding the trailhead: *From the junction of GA 197 and US 76*, drive south on GA 197 for 4.85 miles. Turn right onto West Wildcat Road (FS 26). Travel 1.5 miles to the rockslide on the left. *From the junction of GA 197 and GA 356*, drive north on GA 197 for 6.3 miles. Turn left onto West Wildcat Road (FS 26). Follow directions above. **GPS:** N34°50.071'/W83°36.381'

The Hike

A short climb down the bank from the roadside takes you to the base of the Sliding Rock on Wildcat Creek. Special thanks go out to Brian at Burton Woods Cabins for sharing this fun and special place with us all!

Caution: There may be logs, rocks, etc. underneath the water at the base of this and all "sliding rocks." Please use caution and always swim the area prior to making your initial slide.

Near Lake Burton, Wildcat Creek is located within the Lake Burton Wildlife Management Area. Besides housing this great local swimming hole, the 12,600-acre WMA is well known for activities such as hunting, fishing, and

Exceptional beauty awaits along Wildcat Creek.

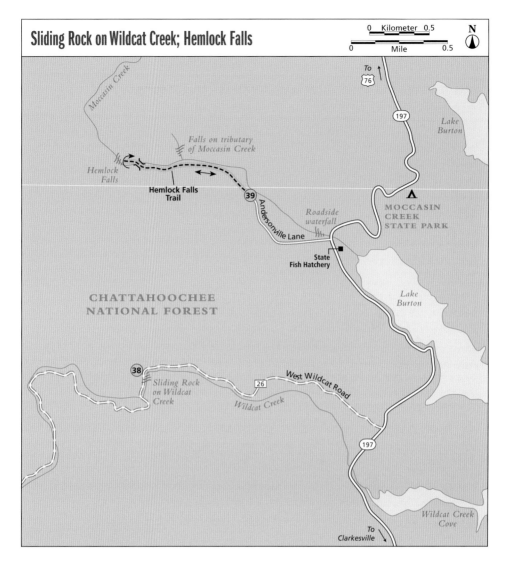

Sliding Rock on Wildcat Creek; Hemlock Falls

0 Kilometer 0.5

0 Mile 0.5

N

To US 76

197

Lake Burton

Moccasin Creek

Falls on tributary of Moccasin Creek

Hemlock Falls

Hemlock Falls Trail

39

Andersonville Lane

Roadside waterfall

MOCCASIN CREEK STATE PARK

State Fish Hatchery

CHATTAHOOCHEE NATIONAL FOREST

Lake Burton

38

Sliding Rock on Wildcat Creek

Wildcat Creek

26

West Wildcat Road

197

Wildcat Creek Cove

To Clarkesville

hiking. Birders and those simply out for an afternoon picnic will enjoy the area as well.

39 Hemlock Falls

Light and lively! Hemlock Falls is among my favorites. Not only is the waterfall a beauty, but the hike offers incredible views as it follows Moccasin Creek upstream over the full length of the hike. This creek is easily one of the finest in the region.

See map on p. 105.
Height: 15 feet
Beauty rating: Excellent
Distance: 1.9 miles
Difficulty: Easy
Surface: Hard-packed dirt
Hiking time: 50 minutes
Other trail users: None

Blazes: Green
County: Rabun
Land status: Chattahoochee National Forest–Chattooga District
Contacts: (706) 754-6221; www.fs.usda.gov/conf
Maps: DeLorme: Georgia Atlas & Gazetteer: Page 16 C1

Finding the trailhead: *From the junction of GA 197 and US 76*, drive south on GA 197 for 3.6 miles. Turn right onto Andersonville Lane (immediately after passing Moccasin Creek State Park). Travel 0.4 mile to a three-way intersection. Go straight ahead at the intersection and continue another 0.1 mile to where the road dead-ends at the trailhead. *From the junction of GA 197 and GA 356*, drive north on GA 197 for 7.0 miles. Turn left onto Andersonville Lane. Follow directions above. **Note:** A beautiful spillway sits on the right along Andersonville Lane. The marked trailhead is at the northeast end of the parking lot. **GPS:** N34°50.880'/W83°35.817'

The Hike

This wide path makes its way northwest into the woods and leads past an amazing forest of ferns. Bypass any side paths leading to the creek, and follow the main trail in a nearly straight line upstream. The cool air that commonly accompanies a creekside hike is ever present here. Even on the hottest summer day, the refreshing air and shade of rhododendron tunnels offers a reprieve. As you follow Moccasin Creek it seems to be one long rapid, a swiftly moving masterpiece. If this wasn't exhilarating enough, at 0.4 mile a bonus waterfall flows in from the opposite (north) bank. A bench made of trees gives you a perfect place to sit and enjoy the view. As you continue hiking you'll find this creek is alive with activity! Each cascade outshines the last as the water barrels down the mountain. You'll follow an easy uphill grade, and a quarter-mile past the first falls you'll cross a footbridge over another small but beautiful waterfall. Continue hiking upstream and the trail ends near an open sandy area at the base of Hemlock Falls. An inviting swim hole greets you, enticing you to submerge into the crisp clean water.

Moccasin Creek is one of the most beautiful in the region. It passes through a hardwood forest mixed with plentiful rhododendron and mountain laurel. Pine, oak, birch, and hemlock trees all prevail. The mouth of the creek meets the astounding

WATER MOCCASINS

Commonly known as "cottonmouths," water moccasins are a venomous species of snake. They are widespread throughout the South and known for their aggressive nature. These pit vipers can be identified by their large diamond-shaped head, which has a pit on each side of it, located between the nostril and the eye. These pits are where the venom is stored. The snake's hollow fangs act like hypodermic needles, injecting venom into its prey. If you get bit by any snake, venomous or not, stay calm and immediately seek medical attention.

Lake Burton adjacent to the aptly named Moccasin Creek Campground. If you're looking for a place to camp while in the area, this one is just minutes from the trailhead. Aside from hiking and boating, trout fishing is also a popular activity here. How could it not be, with the Burton Trout Hatchery as its neighbor.

Miles and Directions

0.0 Hike northwest.

0.4 View a waterfall flowing in from the opposite bank.

0.65 Cross a footbridge over another small waterfall (N34°51.027'/ W83°36.190').

0.95 Arrive at Hemlock Falls (N34°51.153'/W83°36.666'). Backtrack to trailhead.

1.9 Arrive at trailhead.

Pull up a stone and take in the beauty at Hemlock Falls.

40 Denton Branch Falls

Splendid! Denton Branch Falls is one you'll probably have to yourself—and a splendid experience it should be.

Height: 40 feet
Beauty rating: Very good
Distance: 0.6 mile
Difficulty: Easy
Surface: Hard-packed dirt
Hiking time: 20 minutes
Other trail users: None
Blazes: None

County: Rabun
Land status: Chattahoochee National Forest-Chattooga District
Contacts: (706) 754-6221; www.fs.usda.gov/conf
Maps: *DeLorme: Georgia Atlas & Gazetteer:* Page 16 A1

Finding the trailhead: *From the junction of US 76 west and US 441,* drive west on US 76 for 7.9 miles. Turn right onto Persimmon Road. Travel 4.0 miles. Turn left onto Tallulah River Road (FS 70). Drive 6.5 miles. Turn right onto the unmarked dirt Denton Branch Road (first right after Chapple Lane). Follow Denton Branch Road for 0.2 mile to the end at the creek. *From the junction of US 76 and GA 197,* go east on US 76 for 3.0 miles. Turn left onto Persimmon Road. Follow directions above. The trailhead is at the end of Denton Branch Road where the dirt road meets the creek. **GPS:** N34°59.038'/W83°33.173'

The Hike

This hike has you immediately rock-hopping across the creek. Once you're on the other side, the trail follows an old logging road northeast into the forest. In less than 0.1 mile the trail narrows to a traditional footpath. Because it's off the beaten path, it doesn't see a lot of traffic. The upside: You're likely to have it to yourself. The downside: It can be a little overgrown in the warmer months. At the time of my last visit, there were several downed trees across the narrow footpath, but these thigh-high obstacles were easy enough to get over. The path follows the creek upstream, and you'll pass giant boulders up on the hillside standing guard over the waterway. Ignore any small side paths that lead off the main trail and continue hiking generally east and upstream. At two-tenths of a mile you'll pass Lower Denton Branch Falls. The lower falls drops in two distinct sections as the water swoops down the mountainside. A tenth of a mile upstream you'll rock-hop the creek, which lands you on a little island at the base of Denton Branch Falls. There's no mistaking Denton Branch Falls; this bold and beautiful waterfall makes a free-falling plunge over a large rock

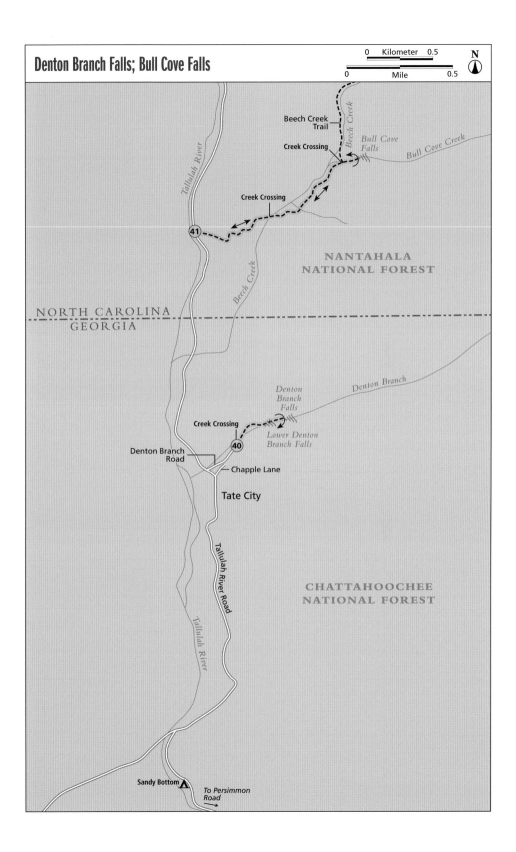

Denton Branch Falls; Bull Cove Falls

0   Kilometer   0.5

0   Mile   0.5

N

Tallulah River

Beech Creek Trail

Beech Creek

Creek Crossing

Bull Cove Falls

Bull Cove Creek

Creek Crossing

41

NANTAHALA
NATIONAL FOREST

Beech Creek

NORTH CAROLINA
GEORGIA

Denton Branch

Denton Branch Falls

Creek Crossing

Lower Denton Branch Falls

40

Denton Branch Road

Chapple Lane

Tate City

CHATTAHOOCHEE
NATIONAL FOREST

Tallulah River Road

Tallulah River

Sandy Bottom

To Persimmon Road

overhang. Ferns and flowers in spring-time, wild berries in summer, fall foli-age in autumn, and icicles dangling in winter make this a trail for all seasons.

Located within the Southern Nan-tahala Wilderness, Denton Branch, along with many other creeks, is part of the Tallulah River Basin. What that means is that they all flow into and feed the mighty Tallulah River. As you make your way to the trailhead, be sure to take a moment to appreciate this spectacular river as you pass it by. With its plentiful cascades, this river is always a pleasure. If you wanted to extend your stay, and don't mind a rugged off-grid experience, there are three fantastic primitive campgrounds along Tallulah River Road: Tallulah River, Tate Branch, and Sandy Bottom. Each of these is waterfront, resting comfort-ably along the banks of the rowdy Tal-lulah River.

A short hike leads to Denton Branch Falls.

Miles and Directions

0.0 Cross the creek and follow the logging road north.

0.2 Hike past Lower Denton Branch Falls (N34°59.126'/W83°33.012').

0.29 Rock-hop the creek.

0.3 Arrive at Denton Branch Falls (N34°59.137'/W83°32.940'). Backtrack to trailhead.

0.6 Arrive at trailhead.

41 Bull Cove Falls (North Carolina)

Solitary! Along with solitude you may also find snails, snakes, salamanders, and wet feet. Resting in a remote area of the Nantahala National Forest, Bull Cove Falls is almost aloof, standing out in a stately manner above the many playful smaller cascades that fill the creek. Although Bull Cove Falls is located in North Carolina, I've included it here due to its proximity to Denton Branch Falls, which is definitely worth a visit while you're in the area.

See map on p. 109.
Height: 40 feet
Beauty rating: Good
Distance: 2.0 miles
Difficulty: Strenuous
Surface: Hard-packed dirt
Hiking time: 1 hour, 30 minutes
Other trail users: None

Blazes: Blue
County: Clay
Land status: Nantahala National Forest-Tusquitee District
Contacts: (828) 837-5152; www.fs.usda.gov/main/nfsnc
Maps: *DeLorme: Georgia Atlas & Gazetteer:* Page 16 A1

Finding the trailhead: *From the junction of US 76 west and US 441,* drive west on US 76 for 7.9 miles. Turn right onto Persimmon Road. Travel 4.0 miles. Turn left onto Tallulah River Road (FS 70). Drive 7.7 miles (entering North Carolina) to a parking area on the left. *Note:* You'll have to drive across a shallow creek along FS 70. *From the junction of US 76 and GA 197,* drive east on US 76 for 3.0 miles. Turn left onto Persimmon Road. Follow directions above. The trailhead for Bull Cove Falls is located on the opposite (east) side of the road from where you parked and approximately 50 feet to the south. **GPS:** N34°59.891'/W83°33.393'

The Hike

The marked trailhead for "Trail #378" sits on the opposite side of the forest road from where you parked. The first 0.15 mile follows a narrow path steeply uphill. When you reach the top of the ridge, the trail bends left and descends down to Beech Creek. Depending on water levels, this may or may not be a dry foot crossing. Once you're across follow the trail that heads left and upstream. This section of the hike isn't heavily trodden, so it can be a bit overgrown. Regardless, it's still easy enough to follow. During the warmer months this overgrown foliage can make it a bit buggy, so have some repellent at the ready. Just shy of a mile you'll make your third water crossing. Immediately after crossing, you'll come to a fork. Left (north) is the main path you were following. Go right (east) on an obscure footpath that follows the creek upstream. To reach the falls you'll

▶ The southern yellow jacket is commonly mistaken for a bee when in fact it's a wasp. These sinister stingers often live in underground nests, and a single colony can contain as many as 100,000 yellow jackets.

Left: A lush green forest greets you at Bull Cove. Right: The bushwhack to Bull Cove Falls is worth the work.

have to do a bit of bushwhacking and some creative rock scrambling, but it's worth the effort. Choose your best route, and you soon arrive at the base of Bull Cove Falls.

This hike sits in the shadow of Big Scaly Mountain, which grandly stands over 5,000 feet tall. It has a variety of wildflowers, berries, ferns, and reishi mushrooms among many other forms of flora that keep you entertained over the length of the hike. Please beware! While hiking the final creekside portion of this trail, my dog Mikey and I were *viciously* attacked by yellow jackets from an underground nest. I highly recommend carrying Benadryl with you or, if you have known allergies, an EpiPen, just in case.

You can't help but notice Tate City as you pass through on your way to the trailhead. What really stands out is the barn with "See Tate City" in bold letters and the official road sign that reads "Tate City—Population 32 +/-." This sleepy little town is said to be one of the oldest settled areas in these mountains. It was once a thriving community known for its corundum mines. When the mines dried up, the town became a lumber camp. After the lumber boom ended, Tate City eventually evolved into what you see today.

Miles and Directions

0.0 Follow the trail steeply uphill east.

0.4 Cross Beech Creek and head left (east).

0.57 Rock-hop a tributary.

0.9 Cross the creek and immediately head right (east) on a narrow footpath.

1.0 Arrive at Bull Cove Falls (N35°00.186'/W83°32.567'). Backtrack to trailhead.

2.0 Arrive at trailhead.

42 Kilby Mill Falls

Seasonal! Although this one has potential, in spring and summer an abundance of brush blocks your view. Visit in the colder months when the foliage thins out and you'll appreciate the best that this waterfall has to offer.

Height: 50 feet
Beauty rating: Fair
Distance: 0.4 mile
Difficulty: Easy
Surface: Hard-packed dirt
Hiking time: 15 minutes
Other trail users: None
Blazes: None

County: Rabun
Land status: Chattahoochee National Forest–Chattooga District
Contacts: (706) 754-6221; www.fs.usda.gov/conf
Maps: *DeLorme: Georgia Atlas & Gazetteer:* Page 16 B2

Finding the trailhead: *From the junction of US 76 west and US 441,* drive west on US 76 for 7.9 miles. Turn right onto Persimmon Road. Drive 7.4 miles to a pull-off on the right before crossing a bridge near the entrance to Ramah Darom. **Note:** Along the way Persimmon Road becomes Patterson Gap Road. *From the junction of US 76 and GA 197,* drive east on US 76 for 3.0 miles. Turn left onto Persimmon Road. Follow directions above. The trailhead is next to the pull-off on the southeast side of the bridge. **GPS:** N34°56.859'/W83°29.661'

The Hike

The trailhead is at the pull-off. Follow the footpath northeast into the forest. Halfway to the falls you'll rock-hop across a tributary. Continue northeast, and at 0.2 mile you'll come to an open area where you can view Kilby Mill Falls just upstream diagonally. Although this waterfall has potential, I gave it a beauty rating of "fair" because there's so much brush between you and the falls. If you really wanted to get a better view, you could always wade out into the creek, or visit in winter when the foliage has thinned out.

The falls are found on Persimmon Creek, named for the persimmon tree. There are a variety of persimmon trees, which produce a very sweet fruit with a plum to pear consistency. If you find a chalky, dry taste in your mouth, don't be turned away. You simply ate one that wasn't quite ripe yet. Give it another try with a ripe one; you won't be disappointed.

To get a good view of Kilby Mill Falls, you'll have to wade out into the creek.

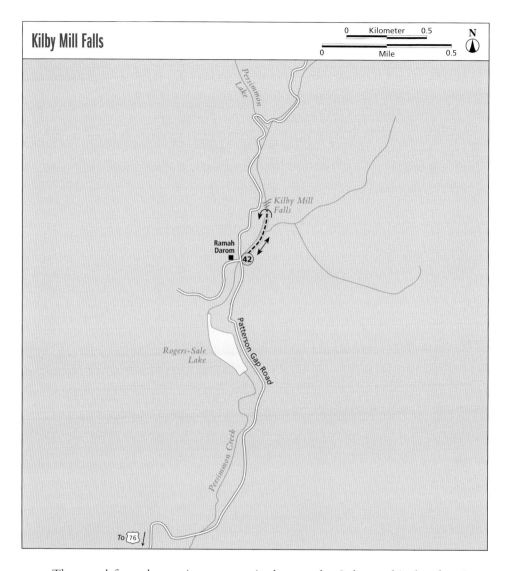

The wood from the persimmon tree is also popular. It has multicolored grain, often with dark hues in the center. This durable species is used to make a number of things, including golf club heads.

Miles and Directions

0.0 Hike northeast into the forest.

0.1 Rock-hop a tributary.

0.2 Arrive at Kilby Mill Falls (N34°57.021'/W83°29.556'). Backtrack to trailhead.

0.4 Arrive at trailhead.

43 Bad Branch Falls

Chiseled! Tall cliffs surround the area where Bad Branch Falls flows over a clean face of stone. The water washes down to form Bad Branch Creek, which is one of many in the area that feed into the lovely Seed Lake. You'll enjoy splendid views of the lake as you drive along the shoreline en route to the trailhead.

Height: 40 feet
Beauty rating: Good
Distance: 0.4 mile
Difficulty: Easy
Surface: Hard-packed dirt, short wet rocky section
Hiking time: 15 minutes
Other trail users: None

Blazes: None
County: Rabun
Land status: Chattahoochee National Forest-Chattooga District
Contacts: (706) 754-6221; www.fs.usda.gov/conf
Maps: *DeLorme: Georgia Atlas & Gazetteer:* Page 16 D1

Finding the trailhead: *From the junction of US 441 and US 76 east,* drive south on US 441 for 8.9 miles. Turn right onto Old 441 south. Travel 2.5 miles. Turn left onto Lake Rabun Road. Continue 6.2 miles. Turn left onto Low Gap Road (where Lake Rabun Road becomes Seed Lake Road). Immediately turn left. Drive over the bridge across Seed Lake. Travel 0.4 mile. Turn right onto Crow Creek Road. Drive 2.9 miles to a pull-off on the right before you reach Lake Seed Campground. *Note:* As you're driving to the falls, at one point it seems as though you're entering someone's driveway. Be respectful. Drive slowly. *From the junction of US 441 and the north end of the Riley C. Thurmond Bridge,* drive north on US 441 for 1.7 miles. Turn left onto Old 441 south. Follow directions above. *From the junction of GA 197 and SR 356,* drive north on GA 197 for 3.0 miles. Turn right onto Burton Dam Road. Travel 7.2 miles. Turn right onto Low Gap Road (along the way, Burton Dam Road becomes Seed Lake Road). Follow directions above. *From the junction of GA 197 and US 76,* drive south on GA 197 for 8.2 miles. Turn left onto Burton Dam Road. Follow directions above. The trailhead is directly across from the pull-off. **GPS:** N34°46.030'/W83°31.113'

The Hike

The trail to Bad Branch Falls follows an old logging road generally south nearly the entire way. When the path putters out near the creek, you can't help but notice the giant cliffs directly in front of you. The cliffs easily stand over 100 feet tall and will have you standing in awe as you look into the face of nature. A damp, rocky path briefly follows the narrow creek upstream to the base of the falls. It's as though Mother Nature took a chisel to the stone and cleanly carved out a perfectly flat face where the water flows down. You can see some circular holes in the rock walls as well,

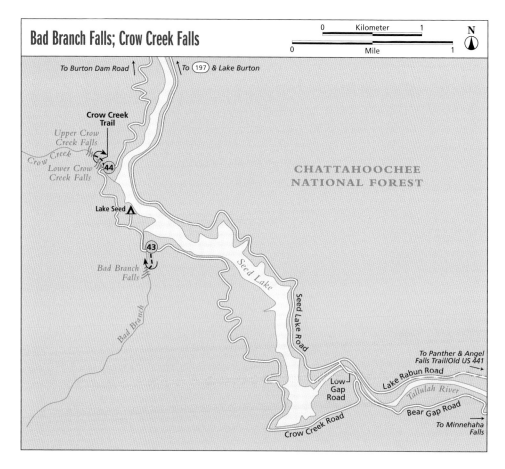

Bad Branch Falls; Crow Creek Falls

perhaps where some blasting was done many years ago when this area was used as a quarry. While you're in the area I highly recommend that you couple this hike with a few neighboring others. Crow Creek, Minnehaha, and Haven Falls are all nearby. All of these are short, fairly easy hikes, and the waterfalls are fantastic!

Miles and Directions

0.0 Hike southwest on the logging road.

0.15 Reach the creek. Go left (south) upstream on the rocky path.

0.2 Arrive at Bad Branch Falls (N34°45.922'/W83°31.160'). Backtrack to trailhead.

0.4 Arrive at trailhead.

44 Lower and Upper Crow Creek Falls

Crisp! Although this isn't a very tall waterfall, there's something about it that just draws you in. Crisp, clean ledges form the face of the falls, and the water keeps a perfect tempo as it falls from one ledge to the next.

See map on p. 116.
Height: Lower Crow Creek: 6 feet; Upper Crow Creek: 12 feet
Beauty rating: Very good
Distance: 0.25 mile
Difficulty: Easy
Surface: Hard-packed dirt
Hiking time: 10 minutes
Other trail users: None
Blazes: None
County: Rabun
Land status: Chattahoochee National Forest-Chattooga District
Contacts: (706) 754-6221; www.fs.usda.gov/conf
Maps: DeLorme: Georgia Atlas & Gazetteer. Page 16 D1

Finding the trailhead: *From the junction of US 441 and US 76 east,* drive south on US 441 for 8.9 miles. Turn right onto Old 441 south. Travel 2.5 miles to a left onto Lake Rabun Road. Continue 6.2 miles. Turn left onto Low Gap Road (where Lake Rabun Road becomes Seed Lake Road). Immediately turn left. Drive over the bridge across Seed Lake. Travel 0.4 mile. Turn right onto Crow Creek Road. Drive 3.8 miles to a pull-off on the right just past a gated forest road. *From the junction of US 441 and the north end of the Riley C. Thurmond Bridge,* drive north on US 441 for 1.7 miles. Turn left onto Old 441 south. Follow directions above. *From the junction of GA 197 and SR 356,* drive north on GA 197 for 3.0 miles. Turn right onto Burton Dam Road. Travel 7.2 miles. Turn right onto Low Gap Road (along the way, Burton Dam Road becomes Seed Lake Road). Follow directions above. *From the junction of GA 197 and US 76,* drive south on GA 197 for 8.2 miles. Turn left onto Burton Dam Road. Follow directions above. The gated forest road is the trailhead—trail #24. **GPS:** N34°46.457'/W83°31.438'

The Hike

As you look upstream from the trailhead, you can immediately see the Lower Falls on Crow Creek. Although it's small, it's a pretty little cascade, and a nice treat on your way to the upper falls. The trail follows the creek upstream and you quickly come to the base of Upper Crow Creek Falls. This is a beautiful little cascade. And although it stands a mere 12 feet tall, the beauty of this bold creek, and the way the water drops from one perfectly cut ledge to the next, is exceptional. As a matter of fact, this is among my favorite waterfalls, despite its size. I also suggest hiking to Bad Branch, Minnehaha, and Haven Falls while you're in the area. They are all nearby, and all splendid and unique waterfalls. On top of that, they are all short and fairly easy hikes.

Crow Creek isn't to be confused with Crow Mountain Creek Falls, which is west of here near Turner's Corner, Georgia. If you were not aware, crows are among the

Crow Creek Falls drop perfectly from one ledge to the next.

most intelligent species of animals in the world. They have the largest brain-to-body ratio of all avians that fly, and have exceptional communication skills using a complex language unique to the species.

Miles and Directions

0.0 Walk over the dirt mound on the path to the right of the creek.

0.03 Hike past Lower Crow Creek Falls (N34°46.525'/W83°31.522').

0.12 Arrive at Upper Crow Creek Falls (N34°46.478'/W83°31.458'). Backtrack to trailhead.

0.25 Arrive at trailhead.

45 Minnehaha Falls

Terrrific! Since the first edition of this book, the trail to Minnehaha Falls has exploded with people. If you want it to yourself, aim for a weekday and keep your fingers crossed. The falls are bold, boisterous, and teeming with character. If you're in the area, it's definitely worth a visit, even if you have to share the "laughing waters" of Minnehaha.

Height: 55 feet
Beauty rating: Excellent
Distance: 0.4 mile
Difficulty: Easy to moderate
Surface: Hard-packed dirt
Hiking time: 15 minutes
Other trail users: None
Blazes: None

County: Rabun
Land status: Chattahoochee National Forest–Chattooga District
Contacts: (706) 754-6221; www.fs.usda.gov/conf
Maps: *DeLorme: Georgia Atlas & Gazetteer: Page 16 D2*

Finding the trailhead: *From the junction of US 441 and US 76 east,* drive south on US 441 for 8.9 miles. Turn right onto Old 441 south. Travel 2.5 miles to a left onto Lake Rabun Road. Continue 6.2 miles. Turn left onto Low Gap Road (where Lake Rabun Road becomes Seed Lake Road). Immediately turn left again, driving over the bridge across Seed Lake. After approximately 0.1 mile, Low Gap Road makes a sharp bend to the right and a dirt road continues straight ahead. This dirt road is Bear Gap Road. Follow it for 1.5 miles to a small pull-off on the left. *From the junction of US 441 and the north end of the Riley C. Thurmond Bridge,* drive north on US 441 for 1.7 miles. Turn left onto Old 441 south. Follow directions above. *From the junction of GA 197 and SR 356,* drive north on GA 197 for 3.0 miles. Turn right onto Burton Dam Road. Travel 7.2 miles. Turn right onto Low Gap Road (along the way, Burton Dam Road becomes Seed Lake Road). Follow directions above. *From the junction of GA 197 and US 76,* drive south on GA 197 for 8.2 miles. Turn left onto Burton Dam Road. Follow directions above. **GPS:** N34°44.973'/W83°28.749'

The Hike

The hike to Minnehaha follows the Falls Branch Trail (#147). It begins by leading up some steps and then continues to follow a heavily trodden dirt path uphill. The trail is easy to follow whether you have it to yourself or have to share it with the masses. Within 0.2 mile you're standing at the base of this big, boisterous, and beautiful waterfall. Regardless of weather patterns, this one always has a bold flow to it. The water drops from one ledge to the next, each a bit deeper than the one before, and the fresh cool breeze generated at the base is truly exhilarating! The falls rests near the beautiful shores of Lake Rabun, and you're likely to enjoy the drive along the lakeshore as much as the hike. Pop in to see the neighboring Bad Branch, Crow Creek, and Haven Falls while you're in the area.

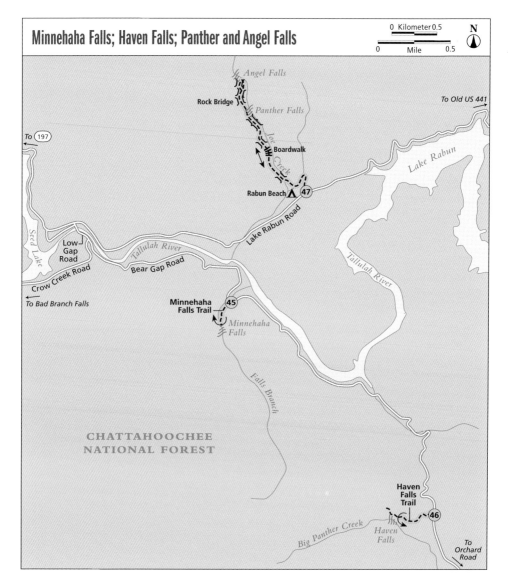

Minnehaha Falls; Haven Falls; Panther and Angel Falls

Minnehaha is a fictional Native American woman who was the lover of the main character in Henry Wadsworth Longfellow's poem "The Song of Hiawatha." Hiawatha, founder of the Iroquois confederacy, and the fictional Minnehaha have lent their names to several places. The name of the waterfall is often incorrectly translated as "laughing water," when in fact the true meaning of Minnehaha is "curling water" or "waterfall."

The trail to Minnehaha Falls is one of the most popular hikes in the area.

Miles and Directions

0.0 Hike up the steps.

0.2 Arrive at Minnehaha Falls (N34°44.848'/W83°28.819'). Backtrack to trailhead.

0.4 Arrive at trailhead.

46 Haven Falls

Magical! The beauty of Haven Falls is astounding! Its two-tiered nature and crisp freefall give this one a unique footprint. Although it's very different from Panther Creek Falls, they share Big Panther Creek, and both land squarely on the Author's Favorites list.

See map on p. 120.
Height: 50 feet
Beauty rating: Excellent
Distance: 0.8 mile
Difficulty: Easy
Surface: Hard-packed dirt
Hiking time: 20 minutes
Blazes: None

Other trail users: None
County: Habersham
Land status: Chattahoochee National Forest-Chattooga District
Contacts: (706) 754-6221; www.fs.usda.gov/conf
Maps: *DeLorme: Georgia Atlas & Gazetteer.* Page 16 E2

Finding the trailhead: *From the junction of Glen Hardman Road and US 441 in Turnerville,* follow Glen Hardman Road for 0.1 mile. Turn right onto Old US 441. Drive 0.3 mile. Turn left onto Orchard Road. Travel 1.0 mile. Turn right onto Bear Gap Road. Travel 2.3 miles to a logging road with jeep-blocking mounds on the left (just past Glen Ellen Springs). Park in front of the mounds, or in the pull-off on the right. *From the junction of GA 197 and SR 356,* drive north on GA 197 for 3.0 miles. Turn right onto Burton Dam Road. Travel 7.2 miles. Turn right onto Low Gap Road (along the way, Burton Dam Road becomes Seed Lake Road). Immediately turn left. Drive over the bridge across Seed Lake. After approximately 0.1 mile, Low Gap Road makes a sharp bend to the right and a dirt road continues straight ahead. This dirt road is Bear Gap Road. Follow it for 2.7 miles to a fork. Go left. Drive another 1.5 miles to the forest road with jeep-blocking mounds. This is the trailhead. **GPS:** N34°43.729'/W83°27.269'

The Hike

Follow the old logging road northwest into the forest. The logging road briefly winds around for 0.3 mile and leads you to a fork. The main trail continues straight (northwest), but you can see and hear the falls to the left. Follow the side trail on the left 0.1 mile directly southwest to the falls. Your attention is immediately captured. There are two distinct and unique portions of the falls. The upper area has a large "rock house" that creates a cavern where you can go behind the falls. The water makes a clean, free-falling plunge over the leading ledge of this "rock house." It then lands on a flat area rolling down over a staircase made of stone, which forms the lower portion of the falls. It's like the "rock house" has a stoop leading right to its pearly gates. The beauty here is truly exceptional! And better yet, unlike its very popular neighbor Minnehaha Falls, you're likely to have this one to yourself. Although there are no blazes, the route is easy to follow.

Left: You'll pass this lovely water mill en route to Haven Falls. Right: You can go behind Haven Falls.

Miles and Directions

0.0 Follow the logging road northwest.

0.3 Follow the side path southwest toward the falls.

0.4 Arrive at Haven Falls (N34°43.713'/W83°27.557'). Backtrack to trailhead.

0.8 Arrive at trailhead.

47 Panther and Angel Falls

Sumptuous! The trail to Panther and Angel Falls gives the hiker two waterfalls for the price of one. Fairly similar in appearance, each resembles a staircase carved out by Mother Nature. You can't help but wonder how long it took to create such a phenomenon.

See map on p. 120.
Height: Panther: 50 feet; Angel: 65 feet
Beauty rating: Good
Distance: Panther: 1.8 miles; Angel: 2.4 miles
Difficulty: Panther: easy to moderate; Angel: moderate to strenuous
Surface: Hard-packed dirt
Hiking time: Panther: 55 minutes; Angel: 1 hour, 20 minutes

Other trail users: None
Blazes: Green
County: Rabun
Land status: Chattahoochee National Forest–Chattooga District
Contacts: (706) 754-6221; www.fs.usda.gov/conf
Maps: *DeLorme: Georgia Atlas & Gazetteer:* Page 16 D2

Finding the trailhead: *From the junction of US 441 and US 76 east,* drive south on US 441 for 8.9 miles. Turn right onto Old 441 south. Drive 2.5 miles. Turn left onto Lake Rabun Road. Drive 4.5 miles to a parking area on the right. *From the junction of US 441 and the north end of the Riley C. Thurmond Bridge,* drive north on US 441 for 1.7 miles. Turn left onto Old 441 south. Follow directions above. *From the junction of GA 197 and GA 356,* drive north on GA 197 for 3.0 miles. Turn right onto Burton Dam Road. Travel 9.6 miles to a parking area on the left. *From the junction of GA 197 and US 76,* drive south on GA 197 for 8.2 miles. Turn left onto Burton Dam Road. Follow directions above. The marked trailhead leads north from the parking area. **GPS:** N34°45.622'/W83°28.216'

The Hike

Those of you that have hiked here before are in for a surprise. The Forest Service has rerouted the trail, and you no longer begin from inside the Rabun Beach Campground, that is, unless you're camping there. The trailhead is now located outside the gated campground, which allows for better access to the public. Hike north on the newly cut trail and within a tenth of a mile you follow a narrow creek upstream through a tunnel of mountain laurel. After rock-hopping the creek you'll follow it back downstream on the other side. The creek is super peaceful. It's small and passive but has a very pleasant flow. That coupled with a nice variety of birds singing makes this reroute thoroughly enjoyable. You'll cross your first footbridge near the old trailhead with a small waterfall just upstream. From the footbridge the path follows Joe Creek upstream making a steady but fairly gentle climb until you reach Panther Falls. Stone ledges are stacked one above the next to form the falls; it literally looks like a staircase that you could walk right up to the top. Resist the temptation: The rocks are

BIG CATS

Oddly enough, the genus *Panthera* does not classify what is typically referred to as a panther. The big cats with the *Panthera* classification are jaguars, lions, tigers, and leopards. These colorful cats are the only ones that can roar. The mountain lion (*Felis concolor*), which is commonly referred to as cougar, puma, and regionally as panther, belongs to the genus *Felis*. Identified by their solid-colored coats, many of these big cats are threatened or endangered. These feral felines were said to be extinct in the Southern Appalachians, although several sightings have been reported throughout the region in recent years.

covered with very slick algae. Instead, wade out into the creek. The water is shallow and the flow is passive enough that you can walk right up to the last drop of the falls and dip your head in the cool, crisp creek water.

From the base of Panther Falls the path leads steeply uphill around a switchback and past the brink of Panther Falls. Stay on the marked path; the brink of any waterfall is dangerous! The rooty path leads past some very pretty cascades that keep you entertained as you climb. You'll crisscross back and forth over Joe Creek before coming to a fork. Either way quickly leads to Angel Falls, as this section of the trail forms a small loop. An observation deck crosses in front of Angel Falls before leading back to the

Bed-size tree trunks adorn the trail.

Left: Stone stair steps form the face of Panther Falls. Right: Angel Falls rolls right below the observation deck.

fork. Angel Falls is similar in appearance to Panther Falls, but this one is narrower and taller. If you visit in the warmer months, Angel Falls may be a bit overgrown, making it hard to enjoy the full view of the falls.

With 25 miles of shoreline, charming Lake Rabun has been a popular recreation area for over a century. Since the days of the Depression when the first home sites were built, people have enjoyed the area for all its natural beauty. Outdoor opportunities include hiking, fishing, boating, swimming, picnicking, and camping.

Miles and Directions

0.0 Hike north into the forest.

0.12 Rock-hop the creek.

0.35 Cross a footbridge.

0.6 Cross a boardwalk.

0.65 Cross a footbridge over a tributary.

0.7 Rock-hop a tiny tributary.

0.8 Cross a footbridge.

0.85 Cross a footbridge.

0.9 Arrive at Panther Falls (N34°46.077'/W83°28.633'). Continue climbing on the trail.

1.1 Cross a rock bridge.

1.12 Cross a footbridge.

1.15 Come to a fork, either way leads 0.05 mile to the falls.

1.2 Arrive at Angel Falls (N34°46.267'/W83°28.689'). Return to the trailhead.

2.4 Arrive at trailhead.

48 Panther Creek Falls

Grandeur! Like a Phoenix in flight, this waterfall is absolutely amazing. Ablaze with beauty, this is a wonderful place for a picnic or to take a quick dip. Easily making the Author's Favorites list, Panther Creek Falls is one of the most beautiful waterfalls in the area. As a result, it gets quite a few hikers, especially on the weekends. If you're lucky enough to have it to yourself, savor the moment. It's not likely to last.

Height: 75 feet
Beauty rating: Excellent
Distance: 7.0 miles
Difficulty: Moderate to strenuous
Surface: Hard-packed dirt
Hiking time: 3 hours, 15 minutes
Other trail users: None
Blazes: Green

County: Habersham
Land status: Chattahoochee National Forest–Chattooga District
Contacts: (706) 754-6221; www.fs.usda.gov/conf
FYI: Fee required; 7 a.m.–10 p.m.
Maps: *DeLorme: Georgia Atlas & Gazetteer:* Page 16 E2

Finding the trailhead: *From the junction of US 441 and US 76 east,* drive south on US 441 for 13.1 miles. Turn right onto Old Historic 441. Travel 1.5 miles to the parking area on the right. *From the junction of US 441 and GA 17 Alternate,* drive north on US 441 for 3.0 miles. Turn left onto Glenn Hardman Road just south of mile marker 18. Travel 0.1 mile to a stop sign. Go right and drive 1.0 mile to the parking area on the left. *From the junction of GA 197 and US 76,* drive south on GA 197 for 7.1 miles. Turn left onto Raper Mountain Road. Travel 1.8 miles to a stop sign. Go left onto Oakey Mountain Road (which becomes New Liberty Road) and drive 7.3 miles. Turn left onto Orchard Road. Drive 5.1 miles. Go left onto Old Historic Highway 441. Travel 0.6 mile to the parking area on the left. *From the junction of GA 197 and GA 356,* drive north on GA 197 for 0.8 mile. Turn right onto Raper Mountain Road. Follow directions above. The marked trailhead is across the street (southeast) from the parking area on the east side of Old Historic Highway 441. **GPS:** N34°41.930'/W83°25.166'

The Hike

The narrow trail almost immediately crosses underneath US 441 and remains fairly flat as you follow Big Panther Creek downstream. A half-mile into the hike you'll cross under some power lines, the last sign of civilization that you'll see as you head into the sweet solitude of the forest. The expected presence of rhododendron and mountain laurel grace the trail, as does a wide variety of wildflowers, especially in springtime. Despite its length, this trail is heavily trodden and easy to follow. In less than a mile, you'll hike below a very cool rocky outcropping. I mention this particular feature not only because it's unique, but also because years ago you had to climb up the rocks near here to continue on the trail. At 1.4 miles you'll cross a footbridge over Big Panther Creek, which is easily one of the prettiest creeks in the region. The

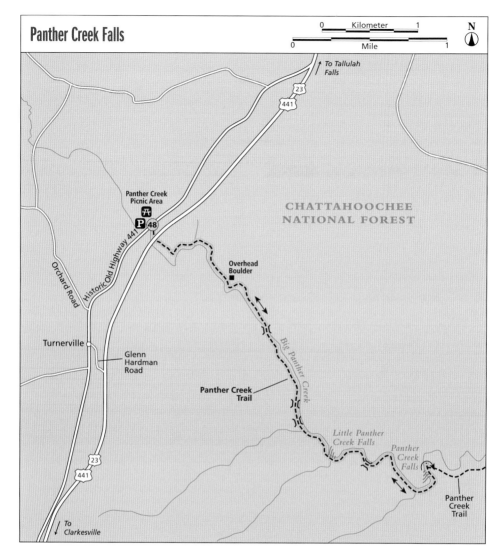

Panther Creek Falls

0   Kilometer   1

0   Mile   1

N

To Tallulah Falls

23

441

Panther Creek Picnic Area

48

CHATTAHOOCHEE NATIONAL FOREST

Overhead Boulder

Orchard Road

Historic Old Highway 441

Turnerville

Glenn Hardman Road

Panther Creek Trail

Big Panther Creek

Little Panther Creek Falls

Panther Creek Falls

Panther Creek Trail

23

441

To Clarkesville

rocks are placed in just the right spots to create a flow that is unmatched. Even if you don't hike the full distance to the falls, you're sure to enjoy this glorious trail: birds singing, cascades splashing about in the creek, and a variety of wildflowers popping up here and there. The fresh sweet smell of honeysuckle, rock formations, burls: This trail really has it all. As you stroll downstream through the forest, you'll cross a few footbridges over tributaries. Nearly two-thirds of the way into the hike, you'll reach an open area next to the creek at the base of Little Panther Creek Falls. Although this is a nice treat, it's nothing compared to the grand finale. Continue hiking downstream, and after crossing your fourth and final footbridge, the path climbs up and along some steep cliff ledges that form the bank of Big Panther Creek. Guy wires help keep you safe, but if you're afraid of heights, you'll probably find this section of

Panther Creek Falls is by far a favorite.

the hike a bit challenging. Carefully hike up and over, and the trail soon returns to flat level ground. After rock-hopping a tributary, the path rises again over a second precarious creekside cliff rise. When you return to flat ground, bypass any trails to the right, staying downstream along Big Panther Creek. After passing one final guy wire cliff crossing, the trail swings around some large boulders near the brink of the falls. Continue hiking downstream and you'll be rewarded with the most perfect, pristine sandy beach at the base of Panther Creek Falls. A large, inviting swim hole is one of the finest in the state. You could literally just pitch a hammock and a tent and spend your life here. This is one of my absolute favorite waterfalls.

Not only is the trail to the falls spectacular, but the area downstream is equally as exceptional. So much so that the US Forest Service has designated nearly 600 acres as the Panther Creek Botanical Area. This area is protected due to the richness and diversity of plant life—flora that is typically uncommon in northern Georgia. The creek here lies directly over the Brevard Fault, giving the soil below an excessive amount of limestone content. It's this high concentration of limestone that allows the area to support such rare vegetation.

Miles and Directions

0.0 Hike south and cross under US 441.

0.45 Rock-hop a tributary.

0.5 Hike under some power lines.

Left: People often turn bowls and other decorative pieces out of burls like this. Right: The Georgia mountains are full of friendly faces.

0.85 Come to a rocky outcropping hanging over the trail. Go south-southeast hiking under and around the boulders.

1.4 Cross a footbridge over Big Panther Creek.

1.9 Cross a footbridge.

2.1 Cross a footbridge.

2.38 Arrive at Little Panther Creek Falls (N34°40.676'/W83°23.927').

2.4 Log-hop across a wet-weather tributary.

2.75 Cross a footbridge.

3.2 Rock-hop a tributary.

3.5 Arrive at Panther Creek Falls (N34°40.636'/W83°23.290'). Backtrack to trailhead.

7.0 Arrive at trailhead.

49 Henderson Falls

Pacifying! Although it's small with not much flow, there's a peaceful calm about this lovely little waterfall. You'll find it nestled away in a neighborhood park in the town of Toccoa, often overshadowed by the much taller and tragic Toccoa Falls.

Height: 10 feet
Beauty rating: Good
Distance: 0.2 mile
Difficulty: Easy
Surface: Sidewalk
Hiking time: 5 minutes
Other trail users: None
Blazes: None

County: Stephens
Land status: Henderson Falls Park
Contacts: (706) 886-1334; www.cityoftoccoa
.com/henderson-falls-park.cfm
FYI: 7 a.m.–9 p.m.
Maps: *DeLorme: Georgia Atlas & Gazetteer:*
Page 16 G3

Finding the trailhead: *From US 123 in Toccoa,* drive north on Broad Street for 0.4 mile. Turn left onto GA 17A (Falls Road). Drive 0.2 mile. Turn right onto Henderson Falls Road. Travel 0.4 mile to the park on the left. *From the junction of US 23 and GA 17 Alternate in Hollywood,* drive south on GA 17A for 9.4 miles. Turn left onto Henderson Falls Road. Follow directions above. The trailhead is the footbridge on the east side of the parking lot. **GPS:** N34°35.471'/W83°19.972'

The Hike

Tennis courts, a playground, an amphitheater, a picnic shelter, and a nature trail all grace the peaceful neighborhood park that houses Henderson Falls. A pair of footbridges lead from the parking lot over the tiny creek and into the main body of the park. You can cross either one of them and then follow the creek downstream along the sidewalk. Just past the restrooms you'll see the steps on the left that lead to the base of the falls. There are no blazes, and no need for them. A small platform sits near the base where a perfect little swimming hole awaits. Visitors can view the falls from the platform, or better yet, jump from it and fully feel the fresh clear creek water firsthand. The falls make a freefall over a

Pinxter flowers are part of the rhododendron family.

Henderson Falls; Toccoa Falls

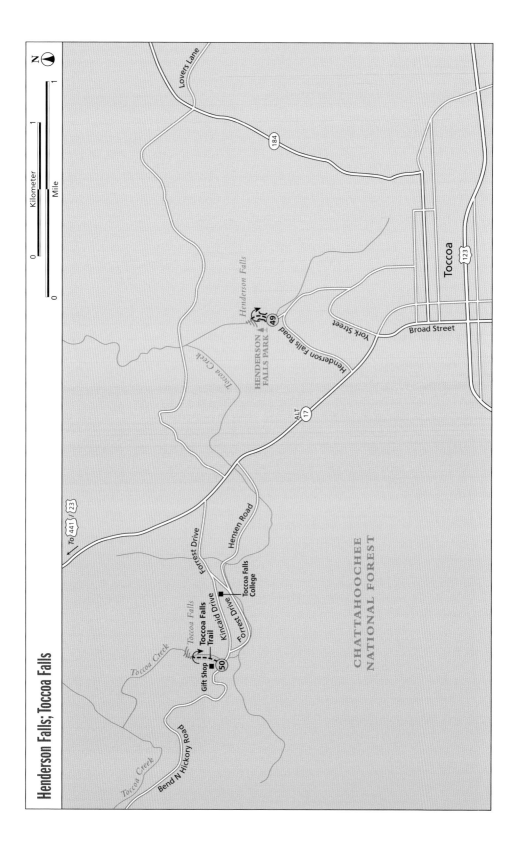

Clear green water gathers at the base of Henderson Falls.

rock ledge much like its neighbor the majestic Toccoa Falls. Although this one is on a much smaller scale than Toccoa Falls, they are both worth a visit while you're in the area.

If you plan your visit during the month of May, perhaps you can coincide with the Taste of Toccoa. This fabulous food and wine festival is held annually in the historic downtown district of Toccoa.

Miles and Directions

0.0 Cross the footbridge and hike north on the sidewalk.

0.1 Hike down the steps on your left and arrive at Henderson Falls (N34°35.531'/ W83°19.971'). Backtrack to trailhead.

0.2 Arrive at trailhead.

50 Toccoa Falls

Toccoa Falls is absolutely delightful. One of the few waterfalls that make a true free-fall, its beauty is indescribable. Despite the lack of privacy here, this highly recommended waterfall makes the Author's Favorites list.

See map on p. 132.
Height: 186 feet
Beauty rating: Excellent
Distance: 0.2 mile
Difficulty: Easy
Surface: Wide gravel trail
Hiking time: 15 minutes
Other trail users: None

Blazes: None
County: Stephens
Land status: Toccoa Falls College
Contacts: (706) 886-7299, ext. 5257; www
.tfc.edu
FYI: Fee required; 9 a.m.–sundown
Maps: *DeLorme: Georgia Atlas & Gazetteer:*
Page 16 F3–G3

Finding the trailhead: *From the junction of US 441 and US 76 east,* drive south on US 441 for 18.4 miles. Turn left onto Alternate GA 17 (GA 17A). Drive south for 8.3 miles to the entrance to Toccoa Falls College on the right. Go through the gate and come to a stop sign. Go straight, following the signs for Toccoa Falls and Gift Shop. At 0.8 mile from GA 17A, arrive at the parking area for the falls. *From the junction of US 441 and GA 17,* drive north on US 441 for 3.6 miles. Turn right onto GA 17A. Follow directions above. **GPS:** N34°35.645'/W83°21.643'

The Hike

Located on the campus of Toccoa Falls College, the falls are accessed through the gift shop. Toccoa Falls is suitable for all ages; both young and old will enjoy this one. If the gift shop is closed, the gate next to it should be open. A wide gravel trail follows the creek upstream leading to the base of Toccoa Falls.

Toccoah means "beautiful" in Cherokee, which makes this waterfall aptly named indeed. However beautiful it may be, this was once the site of a horrible tragedy. In 1977 a dam above the falls broke, causing a flood so ferocious that it killed thirty-nine unsuspecting people, injured more than sixty others, and caused millions of dollars in damage. With the help of local, state, and federal agencies, the college was able to rebuild and remain open. The loss of life that day will never be forgotten. A memorial stands near the base of the falls to honor those who did not survive the devastation.

Miles and Directions

0.0 From the gift shop or gate, hike north following the creek upstream.
0.1 Arrive at Toccoa Falls (N34°35.772'/W83°21.617'). Backtrack to trailhead.
0.2 Arrive at trailhead.

51 Waterfalls of Tallulah Gorge

Tallulah Gorge offers some of the most incredible views in the area. Seven breathtaking waterfalls can be seen here, five of which are easily visible from the rim of the gorge. The North and South Rim Trails essentially lead you around the circumference of the gorge offering views of Oceana and L'Eau d'Or Falls, Tallulah Gorge Dam, Tempesta and Hurricane Falls, and Caledonia Cascade. These waterfalls are visible from various numbered overlooks. Two additional trails dip deep into the gorge, one leading to Hurricane Falls and the other taking you to the funnest spot in the gorge . . . Bridal Veil Falls (aka Sliding Rock).

Height: 46 to 96 feet
Beauty rating: Excellent
Distance: North and South Rim Trails 2.5 miles, modified loop; Gorge Floor Trail distance varies depending on which return route you take to the trailhead.
Difficulty: North and South Rim Trails: easy to moderate; gorge access and Gorge Floor Trail: strenuous
Surface: Rubber mulch path, man-made steps; bouldering down to Bridal Veil Falls

Hiking time: 2 hours to hike the rim trails; up to an entire day exploring the gorge floor
Other trail users: None
Blazes: White
County: Rabun and Habersham
Land status: Tallulah Gorge State Park
Contacts: (706) 754-7970; www.gastateparks .org
FYI: Fee required; Gorge Floor Trail requires a permit
Maps: DeLorme: Georgia Atlas & Gazetteer: Page 16 E3

Finding the trailhead: *From the junction of US 441 and US 76 east,* drive south on US 441 for 10.6 miles. Turn left onto Jane Hurt Yarn Road. Travel 0.4 mile to a fork in the road with stone pillars to the right. Go right here. Stop at the guard gate and pay the fee. Continue downhill to the parking lot and Interpretive Center (IC). *From the junction of US 441 and GA 17 Alternate in Hollywood,* drive north on US 441 for 8.1 miles. Turn right onto Jane Hurt Yarn Road. Follow directions above. The trail begins behind the IC. **GPS:** N34°44.394'/W83°23.434'

The Hike

A web of trails offers endless options as you explore this spectacular state park. The trail system begins behind the IC where a path quickly leads to a T. To the left you will find Overlook #2, #1, and Inspiration Point sequentially. Near Overlook #2 you will also find a steep set of steps that leads down into the gorge. Be advised, you must register at the IC and have a permit in hand before you hike into the gorge. The park issues one hundred permits per day, and they are free of charge. To the right

L'Eau d'Or Falls is best viewed from Overlook 2 and 3 along the north rim of Tallulah Gorge.

at the T, the North Rim Trail follows the north rim of the gorge from Overlook #3 to #5. Each overlook offers unique views of the many waterfalls within and the gorge itself. You will see detailed information for each below in the Miles and Directions for this hike. Beyond Overlook #5 the path climbs a few steps and leads you south across the bridge on US 441. Once you reach the south end of the bridge, a sidewalk-style trail cuts back east where the South Rim Trail begins. This trail leads you from Overlook #6 to #10. Again, each offers a unique view of the waterfalls and gorge as described below. Before you reach Overlook #8 you will see a second set of steps leading steeply down into the gorge. A suspension bridge crosses the river and ties this set of stairs to the set mentioned earlier near Overlook #2. These steps also bring you down to the base of Hurricane Falls. The falls are thunderous, and an immaculate green pool sits at the base. Despite how inviting this pool appears, there is NO SWIMMING ALLOWED. The Tallulah River is fierce, and it is not safe to swim here, period. There is however, another place in the gorge where you are welcome to swim—Bridal Veil Falls. This exhilarating waterfall is also known as Sliding Rock, and for a good reason. The river flows over a long, smooth stone slope that you can literally slide right down, landing in a perfect plunge pool at the base. After sliding once, you'll find yourself quickly climbing up the banks to do it again.

To reach Bridal Veil Falls you will have to go right at the fork along the South Rim Trail. This fork is located between the stairs that go into the gorge, and Overlook #8. By going right at this fork you will begin hiking on the Sliding Rock Trail. The path leads generally southeast and quickly takes you under some power lines. Within a tenth of a mile you will hike past the south Wallenda tower (the north Wallenda tower is across the gorge near Overlook #1). This tower once stood tall above the gorge and was used in 1970 by Karl Wallenda, who successfully walked a tightrope (without a net!) across the windy Tallulah Gorge from Overlook #1 on the north rim to this very tower on the south rim. Sixteen years later, Professor Leon performed the same feat traveling in the opposite direction. Beyond the tower you will begin a rugged, rocky downhill trek to Bridal Veil Falls. Although the descent is only 0.3 mile, it is challenging and there is no specific trail per se to follow. When you reach the gorge floor, you're in for a treat! Bridal Veil Falls forms a 90-foot rockslide, so bring a towel and your suit and have some fun with it.

So many options are available within this sensational state park. Choose a route that works for you and enjoy the explorations.

At nearly 1,000 feet deep and 2 miles long, Tallulah Gorge creates a picturesque setting unlike any other. The dam, built in 1913, changed the river's flow forever. Several times a year, however, the Georgia Power Company (which owns the dam) performs "aesthetic" water releases and whitewater releases for kayakers. They open the dam and allow you to get a peek at what the river once was in all its splendor. These water releases are performed annually on the first two weekends in April and the first three weekends in November.

Miles and Directions

North and South Rim Trails

- **0.0** Hike west on the paved path.
- **0.05** Arrive at a T. Go right (west) toward Overlook #3. (**Option:** Go left (east) toward Overlook #1 and Inspiration Point.)
- **0.1** Arrive at Overlook #3 (N34°44.395'/W83°23.547'). View L'Eau d'Or Falls, then go right (west) toward Overlook #4.
- **0.13** Cross a footbridge.
- **0.3** Arrive at Overlook #4 (N34°44.433'/W83°23.673'). View Tallulah Gorge Dam. Continue hiking west.
- **0.35** Arrive at Overlook #5 (N34°44.426'/W83°23.729'). Enjoy gorge views from the west end. Continue hiking west.
- **0.37** Cross a footbridge.
- **0.39** Cross a footbridge.
- **0.45** Hike up the steps on the right and follow the sidewalk south over the US 441 bridge.
- **0.58** Arrive at the south end of the bridge. Follow the sidewalk east toward Overlook #6.

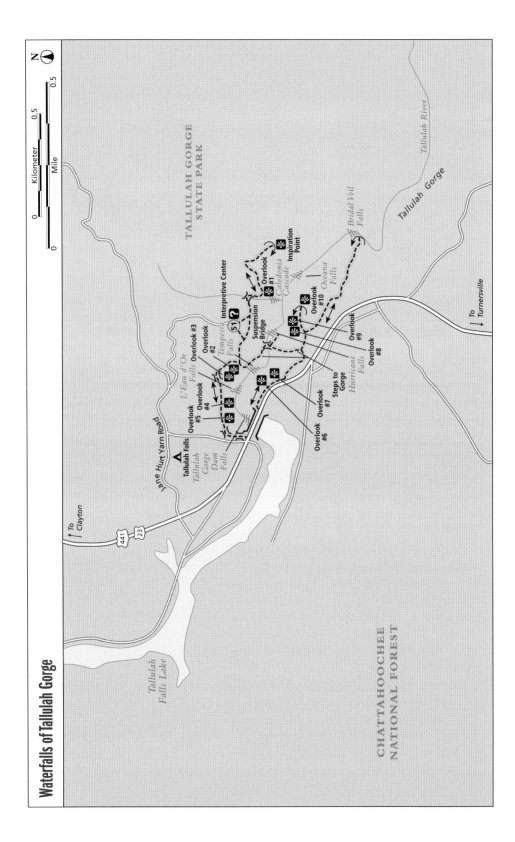

Waterfalls of Tallulah Gorge

Ninety feet of sheer fun awaits at Bridal Veil Falls.

0.7 Arrive at Overlook #6 (N34°44.310'/W83°23.601'), which offers views of Hawthorne Pool at the base of L'Eau d'Or Falls. Continue hiking south.

0.73 Arrive at Overlook #7 (N34°44.267'/W83°23.570'). Tempesta Falls can be seen from here. Continue hiking south.

0.88 Bypass the steps leading into the gorge. We'll return here later.

0.91 Come to a fork. Right (southeast) is the route to the gorge floor. Go left (east) toward Overlook #8.

0.95 Arrive at Overlook #8 (N34°44.224'/W83°23.417'). This is the best place to view Hurricane Falls from the rim. Continue hiking east.

1.00 Arrive at Overlook #9 (N34°44.229'/W83°23.366'). Here you'll get slight views of Hurricane Falls upstream and a decent view of Oceana Falls downstream. Continue hiking southeast.

1.03 Arrive at Overlook #10 (N34°44.218'/W83°23.352'). No waterfall views here, but it offers fantastic views of the gorge itself. Backtrack to the steps mentioned above at 0.88 mile.

1.18 Arrive at the steps. Hike down into the gorge (permit required).

1.32 Reach a fork at the suspension bridge. Go right (southeast) toward Hurricane Falls.

1.37 Arrive at the base of Hurricane Falls (N34°44.293'/W83°23.436'). Backtrack to the suspension bridge.

1.42 Cross the bridge and climb the steps on the north side of the gorge.

1.52 Arrive at Overlook #2 (N34°44.368'/W83°23.552'). In my opinion, this is the best place on the north rim to view L'Eau d'Or Falls. Hike north toward Overlook #3.

1.55 Arrive near Overlook #3. Go right (east) back toward the trailhead.

1.6 Arrive at the first T mentioned above at 0.05 mile. Go right (east-southeast) toward Overlook #1.

1.7 Bypass a trail on the left that also leads to the IC/trailhead.

1.77 Cross a footbridge and hike past the north Wallenda tower.

1.82 Arrive at Overlook #1 (N34°44.322'/W83°23.318'). Oceana Falls can be viewed downstream on the gorge floor. Continue east to Inspiration Point.

2.07 Arrive at Inspiration Point (N34°44.284'/W83°23.170'). From here you view Oceana Falls and L'Eau d'Or Falls and get spectacular views of the gorge itself. Backtrack to the trail leading to the IC/trailhead mentioned at 1.7 miles.

2.44 Go right (north) toward the IC/trailhead.

2.5 Arrive at the IC/trailhead.

Sliding Rock Trail

From the fork mentioned at 0.91 mile above, hike southeast and pass under the power lines.

0.1 Hike past the south Wallenda tower. Make your way steeply downhill over rocks and boulders.

0.4 Arrive at Bridal Veil Falls (N34°44.091'/W83°23.086'). Backtrack to the South Rim Trail.

0.8 Arrive back on the South Rim Trail. Backtrack to the trailhead on whichever route you choose.

Note: Distance to trailhead varies depending on which route you take:

2.62 Via the South and North Rim Trail

2.13 Via the South Rim Trail and suspension bridge (bypassing Hurricane Falls and returning directly to the trailhead).

Options: For an easy hike, hike the North Rim Trail only, but skip the section from Overlook #1 to Inspiration Point. Easy to moderate: Hike the complete North Rim Trail or hike the complete North and South Rim Trails. Moderate to strenuous: Hike down into the gorge to the platform at the base of Hurricane Falls. Strenuous: Hike both the North and South Rim Trails and also the Sliding Rock Trail.

52 Mill Shoals on Stekoa Creek

Serene! The creek makes an abrupt drop creating the picture-perfect painting here. There's a calming peace that washes over you as you stand downstream from this mystical waterfall. The trail is fairly easy to follow, and the closer you get to the falls the steeper the terrain becomes. When you reach the creek, a brief bushwhack leads upstream to the falls. I assure you, whatever challenges this hike presents, it's worth the work.

Height: 35 feet
Beauty rating: Very good
Distance: 2.5 miles
Difficulty: Moderate to strenuous
Surface: Hard-packed dirt
Hiking time: 1 hour, 15 minutes
Other trail users: None
Blazes: None

County: Rabun
Land status: Chattahoochee National Forest–Chattooga District
Contacts: (706) 754-6221; www.fs.usda.gov/conf
Maps: DeLorme: Georgia Atlas & Gazetteer: Page 16 D3

Finding the trailhead: *From the junction of US 441 and US 76 east in Clayton*, drive south on US 441 for 6.8 miles. Turn left onto East Wolf Creek Road. Drive 3.7 miles. Turn right onto Wolf Creek Church Road. Drive for 0.2 mile to a fork. Go right on FS 515. Continue driving until you've gone 1.5 miles from US 441. Turn left onto an unmarked dirt road. Travel 0.1 mile to the end. *From the junction of US 441 and GA 17 Alternate in Hollywood*, drive north on US 441 for 11.9 miles. Turn right onto East Wolf Creek Road. Follow directions above. The trailhead is the guardrail "gate" at the northeast end of the parking area. **GPS:** N34°48.036'/W83°20.890'

The Hike

A single piece of guardrail acts as a gate at the trailhead. Go around the "gate" and hike east on the wide roadbed. The trail leads steadily downhill to a fork. Stay right (east) as you continue to follow the wide forest road. The farther into the forest you go, the more overgrown the logging road becomes. A half-mile from the fork, you'll hike through a clearing. At the far end of the clearing, stay left and the forest road becomes evident again. Beyond the clearing, pine needles carpet the trail and it's

You'll pass the historic Wolf Creek Church Cemetery on the way to the Mill Shoals trailhead.

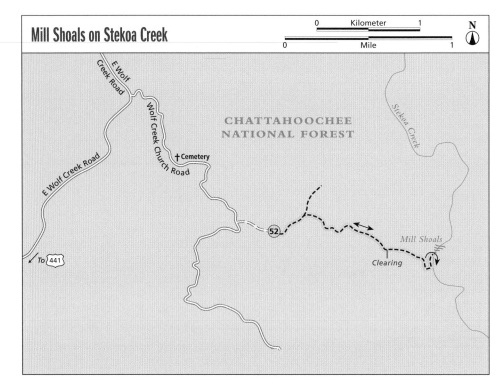

not until the 1.0-mile mark when you begin to hear heavy moving water. From here the trail narrows and the descent becomes steeper than before.

When you reach the creek the trail seems to abruptly end. Go left here following Stekoa Creek north upstream. This is a near bushwhack as you follow the overgrown narrow path toward the sound of the falls. I assure you the falls are worth a few nicks and scratches. After rock-hopping a tributary, the path leads out to the creek, downstream from Mill Shoals on Stekoa Creek.

The falls sit in a private and peaceful portion of Stekoa Creek, where sand and stone give you a perfect place to sit and enjoy the water as it passes by. This is a great place for a picnic. You may even see footprints in the sand from deer, raccoon, bobcat, or bear. The creek has a pleasant greenish hue, but the water flows

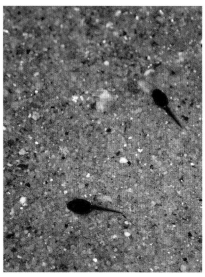

Tadpoles are born with gills so they can breathe underwater.

Mill Shoals brings beauty to Stekoa Creek.

downstream from Clayton and acts as a drainage for the community. Regardless of how inviting it may appear, I recommend that you skip a dip and stay ashore for this one.

Be sure to stop at the Wolf Creek Church Cemetery on the way to the trailhead. This historic graveyard has been around for nearly two centuries. The church was established in 1851, and as you stroll between grave sites you'll see headstones dating back to the Civil War era.

Miles and Directions

0.0 Hike east on the logging road.

0.2 Come to a fork, go right (east).

0.7 Hike through a clearing and the trail bends left (east).

1.1 The forest road ends at the creek. Go left (north), hiking upstream.

1.2 Rock-hop a tributary and follow the path out toward the creek.

1.25 Arrive downstream from Mill Shoals (N34°47.924'/W83°19.907'). Backtrack to trailhead.

2.5 Arrive at trailhead.

53 Stonewall Falls

Reflection! Stonewall Falls is loaded with perfect ledges for sitting and reflecting on the natural beauty that surrounds you. The softly spilling water encourages thoughts of peace, harmony, and wonder.

Height: 25 feet
Beauty rating: Very good
Distance: Roadside
Difficulty: Easy
Other trail users: Mountain bikers
Blazes: None
County: Rabun

Land status: Chattahoochee National Forest–Chattooga District
Contacts: (706) 754-6221; www.fs.usda.gov/conf
Maps: *DeLorme: Georgia Atlas & Gazetteer:* Page 16 C2

Finding the trailhead: *From the junction of US 76 west and US 441,* drive west on US 76 for 0.2 mile. Turn left onto Main Street. Travel 3.2 miles to a four-way stop sign. Continue straight through the stop sign and drive another 2.25 miles. Turn right onto FS 20. (Along the way, Main Street becomes Old Highway 441.) Drive 1.7 miles to the falls at the end of the road. (**Note:** At 1.2 miles on FS 20 you'll pass a designated parking area with a small day-use fee. FS 20 is a rough, bumpy ride. If you don't have a high-clearance vehicle, park here and walk the extra 0.5 mile down FS 20 to see the falls.) *From the junction of US 76 and GA 197,* drive east on US 76 for 10.7 miles. Turn right onto Main Street. Follow directions above. **GPS:** N34°49.234'/W83°27.003'

The Hike

Stonewall Falls sits northwest from where you parked and is visible from the creek's edge.

You might think this waterfall is named for the stone wall that makes up a portion of the falls—a ledge so perfect you can even sit upon it. It's more likely, however, that it was named for Gen. Thomas Jonathan "Stonewall" Jackson. Jackson was a Confederate general during the Civil War and was arguably one of the best tactical commanders in US history. Ironically, in 1863 he was accidentally shot by one of his own men. He survived the shooting with the amputation of one arm but then caught pneumonia, which led to his death 8 days later.

You can drive right up to see Stonewall Falls.

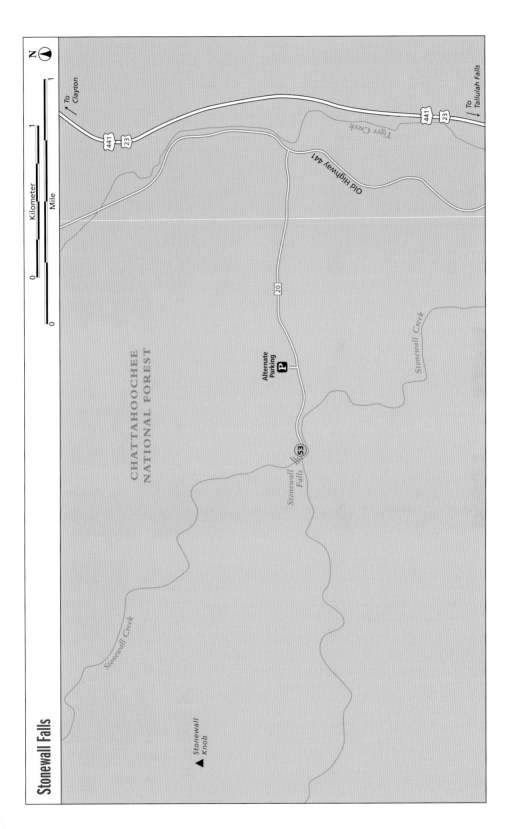

Stonewall Falls

54 Becky Branch Falls

Ticklish! Becky Branch tap dances down the rocks, with each droplet of water tickling the moss on its way to the base. This hike briefly has you hiking on the famed Bartram Trail. William Bartram was a nature enthusiast, explorer, botanist, and pioneer who traveled throughout the South in the late 1700s. He also was quite an impressive artist, drawing all of the natural resources he discovered along the way.

Height: 20 feet
Beauty rating: Very good
Distance: 0.3 mile
Difficulty: Moderate
Surface: Hard-packed dirt
Hiking time: 20 minutes
Other trail users: None
Blazes: Yellow

County: Rabun
Land status: Chattahoochee National Forest-Chattooga District
Contacts: (706) 754-6221; www.fs.usda.gov/conf
Maps: *DeLorme: Georgia Atlas & Gazetteer:* Page 16 C3

Finding the trailhead: *From the junction of US 441 and US 76 east,* drive north on US 441 for 0.2 mile. Turn right onto Rickman Drive. Travel 0.5 mile to a stop sign. Turn right onto Warwoman Road. Drive 2.3 miles. Turn right onto Warwoman Dell Lane. Drive down the hill 0.1 mile and park. *From the junction of US 441 and GA 246,* drive south on US 441 for 7.4 miles. Turn left onto Warwoman Road. Follow directions above. *From the junction of Warwoman Road and GA 28,* go west on Warwoman Road for 11.0 miles. Turn left onto Warwoman Dell Lane. Follow directions above. The trailhead is on the west side of the parking area at the area information sign. **GPS:** N34°35.531'/W83°19.971'

The Hike

There are two trailheads for Becky Branch Falls located within the Warwoman Dell picnic area. This enables you to make a loop out of this hike. The eastern trailhead sits near a few dried-up trout ponds. This is where the hike will end as described in this text. Not far from here you'll see the western trailhead with a large information signpost. Begin here, and follow the yellow-blazed path upstream. You'll go around a few short switchbacks before reaching Warwoman Road. *Carefully* cross the busy road, and continue upstream until you reach a footbridge crossing in front of Becky Branch Falls. The falls are beautiful, and easy to reach. Sweet berries, wildflowers, and the sound of moving water all overshadow the sound of cars whizzing by on the busy road.

A footbridge crosses over Becky Branch Falls.

After enjoying the falls, cross the footbridge, and the path now leads back downstream on the opposite bank of the creek. When you reach the road, again *carefully* cross it and follow the path downstream. You'll hike past the old trout ponds before ending at that eastern trailhead.

Warwoman Dell has a nice picnic area and is named for Nancy Ward, a Cherokee woman who lived in the area. According to Cherokee legend, Nancy was touted as the "last warwoman in the East." In 1755 she fought side by side with her husband in the war against the Creek. When he was killed in battle, she took up his rifle and led the Cherokee to victory. Following this battle, Ward was given the moniker *tsi-ge-yu,*

Becky Branch Falls; Martin Creek Falls

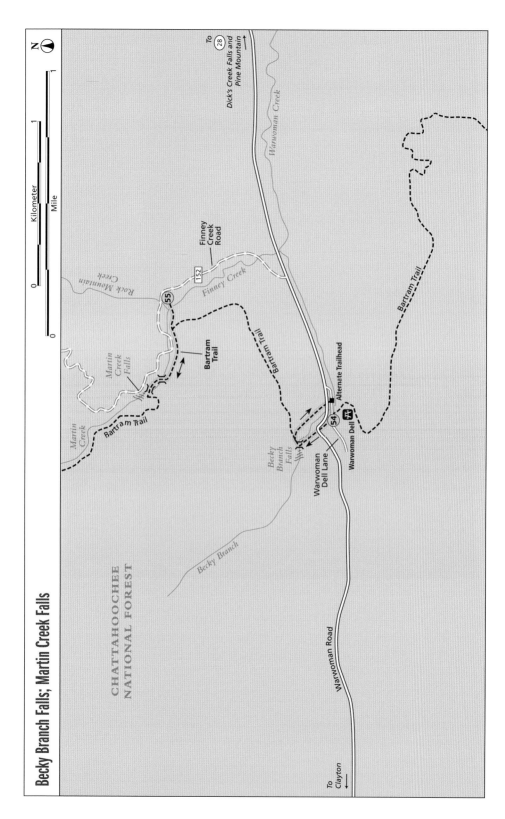

THE FIRST AMERICAN NATURALIST

William Bartram was perhaps the very first American-born naturalist and illustrator of nature. Bartram spent years traveling on foot, exploring the southeastern regions of the United States during the late 1700s. His travels began and ended in Philadelphia, Pennsylvania, where he was born, and he passed through eight states along the way.

As he made his way through the countryside, Bartram gathered and illustrated all the flora and fauna he could. He was one of the first people to draw and describe hundreds of plant, bird, and animal species. Bartram isn't only famous for his collection of nature; he is also credited for documenting the Native American tribes he encountered.

A trail named in his honor closely follows the paths taken by William Bartram himself more than 200 years ago. A well-marked, 37-mile portion of the Bartram Trail runs throughout the mountains of north Georgia. For a wealth of information regarding the man, his travels, and the trail that bears his name, visit www.bartramtrail.org.

Cherokee for "warwoman." She was so beloved and respected by her people that she was allowed to sit in on council meetings and assist in making decisions for the tribe.

Miles and Directions

0.0 Hike northwest toward Warwoman Road.

0.05 Carefully cross Warwoman Road and pick the trail up directly across the street. Hike northwest.

0.15 Arrive at Becky Branch Falls (N34°53.034'/W83°21.143'). Cross the footbridge over the falls and hike southeast downstream.

0.25 Carefully cross Warwoman Road. Continue hiking downstream.

0.3 Arrive at the alternate trailhead.

Old trout ponds add intrigue to the Becky Branch hike.

55 Martin Creek Falls

Playful! Martin Creek Falls is a perfect place to frolic and splash about in the water as it spills over stones in the creek. This fabulous two-tiered waterfall is among my favorites.

See map on p. 148.
Height: 40 feet
Beauty rating: Excellent
Distance: 0.94 mile
Difficulty: Easy to moderate
Surface: Hard-packed dirt
Hiking time: 35 minutes
Other trail users: None

Blazes: Yellow
County: Rabun
Land status: Chattahoochee National Forest–Chattooga District
Contacts: (706) 754-6221; www.fs.usda.gov/conf
Maps: *DeLorme: Georgia Atlas & Gazetteer:* Page 16 B3

Finding the trailhead: *From the junction of US 441 and US 76 east,* drive north on US 441 for 0.2 mile. Turn right onto Rickman Drive. Travel 0.5 mile to a stop sign. Turn right onto Warwoman Road. Drive 2.8 miles. Turn left onto Finney Creek Road (FS 152). Drive 0.4 mile just past the small creek to where the road makes a sharp left and heads uphill. Just before this left, look to your left and see a small pull-in to a primitive campsite. Pull in and park here. *From the junction of US 441 and GA 246,* drive south on US 441 for 7.4 miles. Turn left onto Warwoman Road. Follow directions above. *From the junction of Warwoman Road and GA 28,* go west on Warwoman Road for 10.5 miles. Turn right onto Finney Creek Road (FS 152). Follow directions above. The trailhead is at the southwest corner of the parking area. **GPS:** N34°53.513'/W83°20.569'

The Hike

The narrow overgrown trail begins at the back of the primitive campsite and leads south into the forest. You quickly come to an obscure fork. Go right and rock-hop the creek. After crossing the creek, head right and follow the footpath west as it climbs. You soon reach a T at the more defined Bartram Trail. Go right on the wide yellow-blazed trail following the swiftly moving creek upstream. You'll pass some beautiful cascades before the creek transforms into a shallow, passive, slow-moving stream. Nature truly is amazing; it's as though this is two different waterways. There are some fantastic primitive campsites on the opposite bank where backpackers enjoy creekside camping at its best. You'll rock-hop over back-to-back tiny wet-weather tributaries before crossing a footbridge over Martin Creek. The trail continues upstream with yellow blazes leading your way. A second footbridge crosses the creek one last time near the base of Martin Creek Falls. Immediately after the footbridge you'll come to a T. Left (east) follows the Bartram Trail deeper into the forest. Go right, and the trail abruptly ends at an observation deck overlooking the falls.

Solitude is likely to be yours on the Martin Creek Falls trail.

The Bartram Trail was named for William Bartram, a young nature enthusiast who chronicled his travels across the South in the late 1700s. In Bartram's day, this was known as Falling Branch Falls. It later came to be known as Martin Creek Falls for Gen. Joseph Martin, who served in the Georgia, North Carolina, and Virginia legislatures. Martin had forged close ties with the Cherokee tribe, and his diplomatic efforts are said to have played an integral part in our success in the Revolutionary War.

Close ties indeed. One of his five wives was the Cherokee princess Elizabeth "Betsy" Ward, daughter of the famous "warwoman" Nancy Ward.

Miles and Directions

0.0 Hike south into the forest.

0.03 Come to a fork. Go right (west).

0.05 Rock-hop the creek and head right, hiking west and uphill.

Martin Creek Falls is formed by two terrific tiers.

0.15 Come to a T at the Bartram Trail. Go right (west).

0.35 Cross a footbridge.

0.45 Cross a footbridge and immediately come to a T. Go right (west).

0.47 Arrive at Martin Creek Falls (N34°53.562'/W83°20.959'). Backtrack to trailhead.

0.94 Arrive at trailhead.

56 Dick's Creek Falls

Amazing! Dick's Creek is unique in that it flows directly into the Wild and Scenic Chattooga River. At the base of the falls, the creek pushes out into Section III of the Chattooga near a splendid natural feature known as Dick's Creek Ledge. The ledge is formed by a series of stones that span the full width of the river, creating a Class III+ rapid. You'll be entranced by the beauty and strength of the waterfall, river, and rapid here.

Height: 60 feet
Beauty rating: Excellent
Distance: 1.0 mile
Difficulty: Easy
Surface: Hard-packed dirt
Hiking time: 30 minutes
Other trail users: None
Blazes: None

County: Rabun
Land status: Chattahoochee National Forest-Chattooga District
Contacts: (706) 754-6221; www.fs.usda.gov/conf
Maps: *DeLorme: Georgia Atlas & Gazetteer: Page 16 C4*

Finding the trailhead: *From the junction of US 441 and US 76 east,* drive north on US 441 for 0.2 mile. Turn right onto Rickman Drive. Travel 0.5 mile to a stop sign. Turn right onto Warwoman Road. Drive 5.2 miles. Turn right onto Sandy Ford Road. Drive 0.6 mile to an intersection with John Houck Road. Stay left, crossing the bridge and continuing on Sandy Ford Road until you've driven a total of 4.2 miles from Warwoman Road. The small parking area is on the left just after fording the creek. *From the junction of US 441 and GA 246,* drive south on US 441 for 7.4 miles. Turn left onto Warwoman Road. Follow directions above. *From the junction of Warwoman Road and GA 28,* drive west on Warwoman Road for 8.1 miles. Turn left onto Sandy Ford Road. Follow directions above. To reach the trailhead walk south along the road for about 100 feet to the Bartram Trail on the left. **GPS:** N34°52.005'/W83°15.131'

The Hike

Disregard the trail that leads out from the middle of the parking area. Instead, hike 100 feet farther down the road and you'll see where the Bartram Trail crosses the road. Go left following the famous yellow-blazed Bartram Trail north into the forest. You can't help but notice the impressively large trees, and it's quite possible that some of the bigger specimens were in their infantile stages when William Bartram walked this very route nearly 250 years ago. Just beyond the halfway point, you'll cross a footbridge over the passive-moving Dick's Creek. Not far past this footbridge, you'll reach an intersection where the Bartram Trail continues straight (north) and the Dick's Creek Falls Trail #60 heads off to the right (east). Go right here, and immediately cross a footbridge. The path quickly brings you alongside the brink of the falls. Continue hiking downstream and within 0.05 mile you'll see some scramble

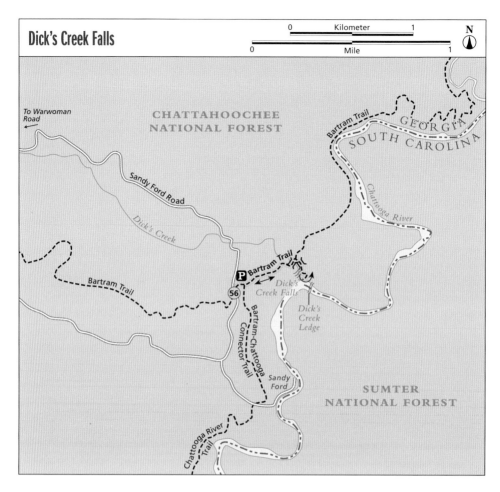

paths leading out to the river to the base of Dick's Creek Falls. The falls spill out into the Chattooga River just downstream from Dick's Creek Ledge, a river-wide rapid that drops a shelf of smooth stone. This river never disappoints! It has earned the designation of Wild and Scenic River, and you can clearly see why when you visit Dick's Creek Falls. The falls flow over a beautiful rock face before plunging down into the river. And with the rapid resting near the base, this one gives you a two for one when it comes to exceptional natural features.

While you're here, if you continue driving past the trailhead on Sandy Ford Road, in less than a mile the road ends at "Sandy Ford." Sandy Ford is a beautiful sandy beach along the river's edge and a popular local hangout. The area is heavily used nearly year-round, so don't expect to have it to yourself.

The famed Chattooga River forms the state line between Georgia and South Carolina, although prior to 1816, the state line sat farther east in South Carolina. The boundary was extended through a treaty with the Cherokee, moving the state line to its current location with the river running right through it.

Dick's Creek Ledge runs the full width of the Chattooga River.

Miles and Directions

0.0 Hike northeast on the Bartram Trail.

0.05 Bypass Trail #54 on the right (southwest). Continue hiking east.

0.28 Cross a footbridge over Dick's Creek.

0.3 Come to an intersection with Trail #60 on the right (east). Go right and immediately cross a footbridge.

0.4 Reach the brink of Dick's Creek Falls. Continue downstream.

0.45 Follow a side path scramble down to the river.

0.5 Arrive at the base of Dick's Creek Falls (N34°52.063'/W83°14.766'). Backtrack to trailhead.

1.0 Arrive at trailhead.

57 Sarahs Creek Falls

Spirited! This is one of the smallest waterfalls in this book, but it's full of life and certainly worth a visit. Crystal-clear water flows over a creek-wide bed of rugged rock, and a picture-perfect pool gathers at the base, enticing you to wade out into the waterway.

Height: 10 feet
Beauty rating: Excellent
Distance: 0.1 mile
Difficulty: Easy
Surface: Hard-packed dirt
Hiking time: 5 minutes
Other trail users: Anglers
Blazes: None

County: Rabun
Land status: Chattahoochee National Forest–Chattooga District
Contacts: (706) 754-6221; www.fs.usda.gov/conf
Maps: *DeLorme: Georgia Atlas & Gazetteer:* Page 16 B4

Finding the trailhead: *From the junction of US 441 and US 76 east,* drive north on US 441 for 0.2 mile. Turn right onto Rickman Drive. Travel 0.5 mile to a stop sign. Turn right onto Warwoman Road. Drive 8.5 miles. Turn left onto Sarahs Creek Road (FS 156). Drive 1.9 miles to the campground on the left. Enter the campground and follow the road to a pull-off near campsite #1. **Note:** Along Sarahs Creek Road the pavement ends at 0.6 mile. *From the junction of US 441 and GA 246 in Dillard,* drive south on US 441 for 7.4 miles. Turn left onto Warwoman Road. Follow directions above. *From the junction of Warwoman Road and GA 28,* go west on Warwoman Road for 4.8 miles. Turn right onto Sarahs Creek Road (FS 156). Follow directions above. The trailhead is to the left (east) of campsite #1. **GPS:** N34°55.528'/W83°15.761'

The Hike

A narrow footpath leads from campsite #1 back into the forest and follows the creek downstream. In less than a tenth of a mile, you're standing at the base of Sarahs Creek Falls. The campground is small but wonderful. It's one of those little-known gems that the locals frequent for weekend getaways. There are only five campsites here, and occupancy is first come, first served. Arrive early if you want to snag a site here. The waterfall is also slight in size, but equally as splendid as the campground that houses it. A series of small rocks are perfectly placed to form a pristine pool at the base of the falls. Although it's only 10 feet tall, it's exceptionally pretty, and very easy to reach. The whole family can enjoy this one. The kids can fish in the creek or wade out into the pool formed at the base. Whether you pop in for a peek, or make a weekend trip of it, this one is certainly worth the drive up the winding forest road to visit.

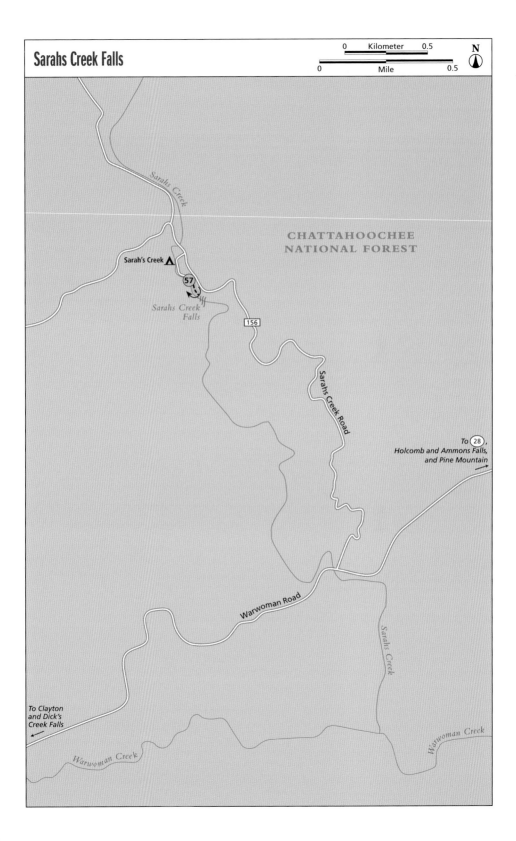

Sarahs Creek Falls

0 Kilometer 0.5

0 Mile 0.5

N

Sarahs Creek

CHATTAHOOCHEE
NATIONAL FOREST

Sarah's Creek

57

Sarahs Creek
Falls

156

Sarahs Creek Road

To 28,
Holcomb and Ammons Falls,
and Pine Mountain

Warwoman Road

Sarahs Creek

To Clayton
and Dick's
Creek Falls

Warwoman Creek

Warwoman Creek

Sarahs Creek Falls lie a mere tenth of a mile from Sarah's Creek Campground.

Miles and Directions

0.0 Follow the creek downstream.

0.05 Arrive at Sarahs Creek Falls (N34°55.486'/W83°15.723'). Backtrack to trailhead.

0.1 Arrive at trailhead.

58 Holcomb and Ammons Falls

Twice the pleasure! First you're greeted with massive and mighty Holcomb Falls, towering overhead and flowing strength and force. This mighty power is soon followed by the calming waters of Ammons Falls.

Height: Holcomb: 120 feet; Ammons: 40 feet
Beauty rating: Very good
Distance: Holcomb: 0.6 mile; Ammons: 1.1 miles
Difficulty: Strenuous
Surface: Hard-packed dirt
Hiking time: 45 minutes
Other trail users: None
Blazes: None
County: Rabun
Land status: Chattahoochee National Forest-Chattooga District
Contacts: (706) 754-6221; www.fs.usda.gov/conf
Maps: *DeLorme: Georgia Atlas & Gazetteer: Page 16 A4*

Finding the trailhead: *From the junction of US 441 and US 76 east,* drive north on US 441 for 0.25 mile. Turn right onto Warwoman Road. Travel 9.8 miles. Turn left onto Hale Ridge Road. Drive 6.7 miles to the end at Overflow Creek Road. Park where you can near the intersection. *From the junction of US 441 and GA 246,* drive south on US 441 for 7.4 miles. Turn left onto Warwoman Road. Follow directions above. *From the junction of Warwoman Road and GA 28,* drive west on Warwoman Road for 3.9 miles. Turn right onto Hale Ridge Road. Follow directions above. The marked trailhead is on the north side of Overflow Creek Road at the intersection with Hale Ridge Road. **GPS:** N34°58.719'/W83°15.979'

The Hike

Resting at the trailhead lies a large stone marker with the trail name etched into it. The trailhead is at the intersection of Hale Ridge Road and Overflow Creek Road on the north side of Overflow Creek Road. The narrow trail leads north making a rapid descent into the forest. Just past a tenth of a mile you'll cross a tiny footbridge, and you begin to hear the sound of the falls in the distance. About two-tenths farther and you're crossing a footbridge over Holcomb Falls. This is one impressive waterfall. Standing tall at 120 feet, this beauty tumbles down the mountainside and then passes right below the footbridge that you're standing upon to view it. It's multifaceted with a number of drops, splashes, and swirls that capture your gaze. Beyond Holcomb Falls the trail begins to climb as steeply as you came in with the steady sound of Ammons Creek urging you on. At 0.5 mile bypass the trail on your left (south) and continue hiking northwest and uphill on the main trail. That

▶ You can tell the age of a tree by counting the "annual rings" on the trunk. Each ring is the approximate equivalent of 1 year of age. Hence the name annual rings.

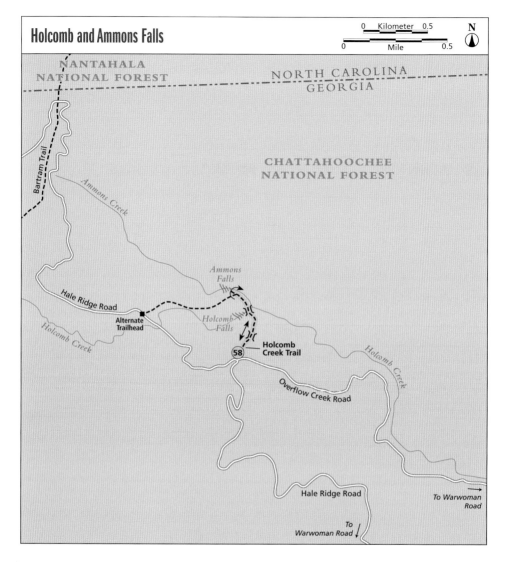

Holcomb and Ammons Falls

NANTAHALA
NATIONAL FOREST

NORTH CAROLINA
GEORGIA

CHATTAHOOCHEE
NATIONAL FOREST

Bartram Trail

Ammons Creek

Ammons
Falls

Hale Ridge Road

Alternate
Trailhead

Holcomb
Falls

Holcomb Creek

58

Holcomb
Creek Trail

Holcomb Creek

Overflow Creek Road

Hale Ridge Road

To Warwoman
Road

To
Warwoman Road

side trail leads to Hale Ridge Road about 0.6 mile northwest of the trailhead where you began this hike. Not far from that fork the trail ends at an observation deck over the middle of Ammons Falls. A white wash of water flows steadily down the mountain to form Ammons Falls. In the middle of the falls, a large boulder juts out toward you, splitting the stream into two.

Juvenile maple, oak, and poplar accompanied by rhododendron and ferns line the narrow footpath, but you'll also hike past some massive trees along this trail. Thankfully they escaped the terror of the timber age. Make sure you take your time and appreciate these spectacular specimens.

Although they are located along the same trail, these two waterfalls are actually on separate creeks: Holcomb and Ammons.

Left: A footbridge crosses over the base of Holcomb Falls. Right: A large boulder juts out in the middle of Ammons Falls, splitting the stream in two.

Miles and Directions

0.0 Hike north into the forest.

0.13 Cross a footbridge.

0.3 Cross a footbridge over Holcomb Creek Falls (N34°58.906'/W83°15.933')

0.5 Bypass a trail on the left (south).

0.55 Arrive at Ammons Falls (N34°59.014'/W83°16.007'). Backtrack to trailhead.

1.1 Arrive at trailhead.

59 Ada-Hi Falls

Aspiring! Like a weeping wall, Ada-Hi Falls is more of a trickle than a waterfall and the water seems to seep from the rock face. The spring that feeds this simple flow is a mere 300 feet above the waterfall, so it doesn't have much time to collect the momentum and volume that most other falls have. Although the waterfall itself isn't much to see, the trail and road to the trailhead are excellent for viewing a variety of wildflowers.

Height: 35 feet
Beauty rating: Good
Distance: 0.4 mile
Difficulty: Moderate
Surface: Man-made steps, rooty dirt path
Hiking time: 20 minutes
Other trail users: None
Blazes: Green

County: Rabun
Land status: Black Rock Mountain State Park
Contacts: (706) 746-2141; www.gastateparks .org
FYI: 7 a.m.–10 p.m.
Maps: *DeLorme: Georgia Atlas & Gazetteer:* Page 16 B3

Finding the trailhead: *From the junction of US 441 and US 76 east,* drive north on US 441 for 3.0 miles. Turn left onto Black Rock Mountain Parkway and drive up the mountain. At approximately 1.0 mile you'll see a large sign for Black Rock Mountain State Park on the left. Don't turn left here. Continue straight ahead until you reach the entrance gate to the park. Enter the park and continue up the mountain until you come to a fork. Go left at the fork to the campground entrance. Park on the right just before the campground office. *From the junction of US 441 and GA 246,* drive south on US 441 for 4.6 miles. Turn right onto Black Rock Mountain Parkway. Follow directions above. The trailhead is on the east side of the road opposite the parking area. **GPS:** N34°54.380'/W83°24.464'

The Hike

The hike begins by leading down a few flights of steps and into the forest. Beyond the stairs, the green-blazed trail transforms into a rooty dirt path making a rapid descent toward the falls. You'll see benches along the path giving you a resting place for the way back uphill, and an abundance of wildflowers along the path makes it worth every step.

As you near the falls you'll cross a footbridge and hike down several more flights of man-made steps. The trail ends at an observation deck alongside Ada-Hi Falls. A wall of stone forms the face of the falls, and moss and plant life bring the stone to life. This one is highly dependent on recent rainfall. Water levels vary from barely a trickle to a decent steady flow.

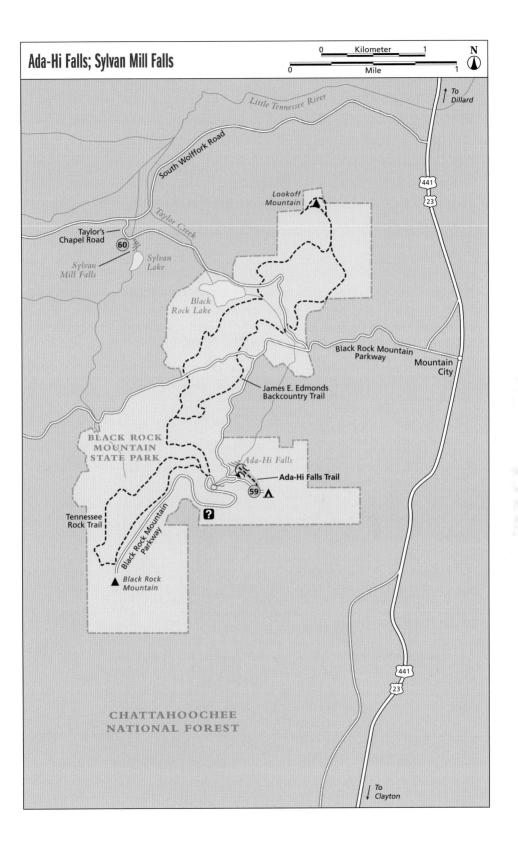

Ada-Hi Falls; Sylvan Mill Falls

0 Kilometer 1

0 Mile 1

N

To Dillard

Little Tennessee River

South Wolffork Road

441
23

Taylor Creek

Lookoff Mountain

Taylor's Chapel Road

60

Sylvan Mill Falls

Sylvan Lake

Black Rock Lake

Black Rock Mountain Parkway

Mountain City

James E. Edmonds Backcountry Trail

BLACK ROCK MOUNTAIN STATE PARK

Ada-Hi Falls

Ada-Hi Falls Trail

59

?

Tennessee Rock Trail

Black Rock Mountain Parkway

Black Rock Mountain

441
23

CHATTAHOOCHEE NATIONAL FOREST

To Clayton

WHERE THE WATER SPLITS

The Eastern Continental Divide (ECD) is an imaginary line where the water "splits" and flows in either one direction or the other. The ECD primarily follows the ridgeline and high peaks of the Appalachian Mountain Range.

Simply put, all the streams, creeks, and rivers east of the divide eventually flow from one to the next until they make their way out to the Atlantic Ocean. All the water flowing on the west side of the ECD either flows directly into the Gulf of Mexico or to the Mississippi River, which then carries it out to the Gulf.

Named for the Cherokee word for "forest," Ada-Hi sits at the highest elevation of any waterfall in Georgia. This makes sense because it's found within Black Rock Mountain State Park. At 3,640 feet this is Georgia's highest-elevation state park. The park is named for the sheer cliffs of dark-colored biotite gneiss, which seem far more impressive than Ada-Hi Falls. On a clear day you can see four states (Georgia, North Carolina, South Carolina, and Tennessee) from atop Black Rock Mountain.

An overlook leads right up to Ada-Hi Falls.

Groundhogs are similar to beavers, but they prefer dry land.

Miles and Directions

0.0 Hike down the steps.

0.14 Cross a footbridge.

0.2 Arrive at Ada-Hi Falls (N34°54.479'/W83°24.568'). Backtrack to trailhead.

0.4 Arrive at trailhead.

60 Sylvan Mill Falls

Pristine! A picturesque scene is perfectly painted around Sylvan Mill Falls. This one is a wonderful treat for a roadside waterfall. A water wheel and colorful gardens surround the falls, making this one look as if it came right out of a fairy tale.

See map on p. 163.
Height: 50 feet
Beauty rating: Excellent
Distance: Roadside
Difficulty: Easy
Blazes: None
County: Rabun

Land status: Private property—Sylvan Falls Mill Bed and Breakfast
Contacts: (706) 746-7138; www.sylvanfalls mill.com
Maps: DeLorme: Georgia Atlas & Gazetteer: Page 16 B2

Finding the trailhead: From the junction of US 441 and US 76 east, drive north on US 441 for 4.25 miles. Turn left onto South Wolffork Road. Travel 2.2 miles. Turn left onto Taylor's Chapel Road. Drive 0.2 mile to the falls on the right. From the junction of US 441 and GA 246, drive south on US 441 for 3.3 miles. Turn right onto South Wolffork Road. (Be sure to bypass North Wolffork Road.) After turning onto South Wolffork Road, follow directions above. **GPS:** N34° 55.655' W83° 25.224'

The Hike

Sylvan Mill Falls can be viewed from the roadside. The bed-and-breakfast that gives this waterfall a home has lovely gardens that sit at the base of the falls and a wonderful water wheel to the right. At 27 feet, this is one of the largest water wheels in the United States and has been in operation for 178 years. This glorious gristmill still grinds flour today for use in the B&B, or you can buy a bag and take it home with you.

THE 100-MILE RULE

More and more people in today's green eco-friendly society are becoming aware of their "carbon footprint." One way to reduce your footprint is to try to live by the "100-Mile Rule," which encourages people to try to "eat local." The idea is to purchase only products that are grown, raised, or made within 100 miles of your home.

Local produce is fresher, animals are range fed, and it supports the local economy. You're not only helping the environment but are making an investment in your health as well. While it can be difficult to eat 100 percent local, every little bit helps. Keep this in mind the next time you step into the grocery store.

A large water wheel is run by the hydro power of Sylvan Mill Falls.

A quick visit to this neighborhood waterfall is worth the trip. Or perhaps you'll opt to stay at the eco-friendly Sylvan Falls Mill Bed and Breakfast, which proudly uses "local, regional, organic and sustainable" products.

61 Darnell Creek Falls

Boisterous! This slender waterfall puts on a spectacular show as it squeezes between the rocks. With easy access and boisterous beauty, it's easy to see why this is a popular local hangout. It happens to be one of my favorite falls as well.

Height: 30 feet
Beauty rating: Excellent
Distance: 0.2 mile
Difficulty: Easy
Surface: Gravel forest road
Hiking time: 10 minutes
Other trail users: 4-wheel-drive vehicles
Blazes: None

County: Rabun
Land status: Chattahoochee National Forest-Chattooga District
Contacts: (706) 754-6221; www.fs.usda.gov/conf
Maps: DeLorme: Georgia Atlas & Gazetteer: Page 16 B3

Finding the trailhead: *From the junction of GA 246 and US 441 in Dillard*, drive south on US 441 for 1.9 miles. Turn left onto Kellys Creek Road. Drive 0.9 mile. Turn right onto Darnell Creek Road. Travel 0.4 mile to a fork. Go left onto FS 150. Travel 0.4 mile to a pull-off at an unmarked forest road on the right. This forest road is the "trail." *From the junction of US 441 east and US 76 east in Clayton*, drive north on US 411 for 5.7 miles. Turn right onto Kellys Creek Road. Follow directions above. **GPS:** N34°57.601'/W83°21.493'

The Hike

The "trail" leads in a near straight line as you hike down the muddy, bumpy forest road FS 150. If you have a high-clearance vehicle, you can drive down if you prefer. The road ends at a primitive campsite near the base of the falls. This is a very popular hangout and local swimming hole, and when you see it you'll see why. Large rocks at the base give visitors a perfect place to sun themselves after taking a dip in the cool, mountain stream. The splash zone that this one creates is really something! It churns and bounces, swirling the creek in every direction. It's just spectacular, which is surprising for such a small waterfall.

Darnell Creek is one of many that flow into and form the Little Tennessee River.

Fleabane daisies have many thin petals around a center yellow disc.

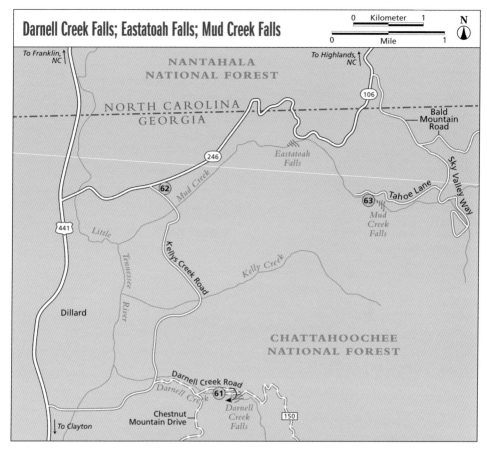

Darnell Creek Falls; Eastatoah Falls; Mud Creek Falls

0 Kilometer 1

0 Mile 1

N

To Franklin, NC

To Highlands, NC

NANTAHALA NATIONAL FOREST

NORTH CAROLINA
GEORGIA

Bald Mountain Road

106

Eastatoah Falls

246

Mud Creek

62

63

Tahoe Lane

Mud Creek Falls

Sky Valley Way

441

Little

Tennessee River

Kellys Creek Road

Kelly Creek

Dillard

CHATTAHOOCHEE NATIONAL FOREST

Darnell Creek Road

Darnell Creek

61

Darnell Creek Falls

150

Chestnut Mountain Drive

To Clayton

Mountains abound in the northeast region of Georgia.

Darnell Creek Falls is small but stunning.

The river begins near this confluence and flows north through Georgia, North Carolina, and Tennessee where it ends at the Tennessee River not far from Knoxville.

If you enjoy wine and local flavor, stop by for a tasting at 12 Spies Vineyard. The vineyard sits just minutes from the trailhead in Rabun Gap. The atmosphere is pleasant and views of the vineyards and mountains are thoroughly enjoyable.

Miles and Directions

0.0 Hike southeast down the forest road.

0.1 Arrive at Darnell Creek Falls (N34°57.551'/W83°21.384'). Backtrack to trailhead.

0.2 Arrive at trailhead.

62 Eastatoah Falls

Panache! This roadside beauty stands tall on the mountainside but oftentimes goes unnoticed. The stretch of highway that Eastatoah Falls keeps watch over isn't very viewer friendly, so use caution, and keep your roadside visit brief.

See map on p. 169.
Height: 200 feet
Beauty rating: Good
Distance: Roadside
Difficulty: Easy

County: Rabun
Land status: Private property
Maps: *DeLorme: Georgia Atlas & Gazetteer:* Page 16 A3

Finding the trailhead: *From the junction of US 441 and US 76 east,* drive north on US 441 for 7.7 miles. Turn right onto GA 246. Drive approximately 1.0 mile to a pull-off on the right just past Kellys Creek Road. *From the Georgia–North Carolina state line,* drive south on US 441 for 0.7 mile. Turn left onto GA 246. Follow directions above. **GPS:** N34 59.459'/W83 21.543'

The long yellow legs and reddish chest and shoulders are telltale signs of the red-shouldered hawk.

The Hike

Eastatoah Falls can be viewed from the roadside. From the pull-off, look east to get a glimpse of the falls flowing down the mountainside in the distance. I recommend bringing binoculars or a good zoom lens if you really want to appreciate it. Also known as Falls on Ford Mountain and Falls on Mud Creek, this one is located on private property, so the best you can do is view it from afar. If you want an up-close and personal experience, visit its upstream sibling Mud Creek Falls (Hike 63).

One reasonable theory for the name of the falls is that it comes from the Cherokee village of Eastertoy. Hundreds of years ago Eastertoy was located in the town of Sky Valley, near present-day Dillard, Georgia. Through the years, *Eastertoy* evolved into *Eastatoah*.

Magnolia trees are a Southern staple.

63 Mud Creek Falls

Healthy! Sitting tall at 3,320 feet, Sky Valley boasts the highest city in the state. It lures people from all over for its famous Fall Festival. But whether you visit in autumn or any time of the year, Mud Creek Falls is sure to impress. Unlike its downstream sibling Eastatoah Falls, which is viewed from afar, you can sit right at the base of this one, and trust me, you will feel the power and might as the water thunders down the mountain. The roar and breeze generated by the sheer force of nature is mesmerizing.

See map on p. 169.
Height: 85 feet
Beauty rating: Excellent
Distance: Roadside
Difficulty: Easy

County: Rabun
Land status: Town of Sky Valley
Maps: *DeLorme: Georgia Atlas & Gazetteer:* Page 16 A3

Finding the trailhead: *From the junction of GA 246 and US 441 in Dillard,* drive east on GA 246 for 4.0 miles to the GA/NC state line. Continue driving north into North Carolina on NC 106 for 0.3 mile. Turn right onto Old Mud Creek Road. Drive 0.3 mile and the road becomes Bald Mountain Road as you reenter Georgia. Continue driving 0.6 mile. Turn right onto Sky Valley Way. Drive 0.5 mile. Turn right onto Tahoe Lane. Travel 0.7 mile to the falls at the end of the road. Park alongside the road, *not* in the accessible parking area. **GPS:** N34°59.022'/W83°20.023'

The Hike

You've hit the jackpot! Mud Creek Falls is just phenomenal, and easy to reach so the whole family can enjoy it. You can view the falls from the roadside or walk a mere 200 feet down the wide path to stand at the base. The creek thunders down over smooth stone as it forms the falls. This 85-foot beauty drops in two tiers, before passing by the big boulders resting near the base. These boulders give visitors a perfect place to sit as the creek mesmerizes you with its power and might. If you prefer traditional seating, there's a picnic table near the base. Every sense is exhilarated as you take in the scenery. The roar of water, the cool clean overspray, and the wind generated by this outstanding specimen rejuvenates your very soul.

If you're up for a hike, the half-mile Trees Trail follows the creek

This Sky Valley overlook is located off GA 246.

Mud Creek thunders downstream, forming Mud Creek Falls.

downstream. This path identifies nearly twenty different species of trees, from hemlock to hickory and beech to birch. The Trees Trail ends at a footbridge, but the path continues creekside for another 0.5 mile to GA 246. It's definitely worth the drive up into North Carolina, which swings back into Georgia, when you have this one waiting for you. It's certainly one of my favorites and may be yours too. Sky Valley has big beautiful homes, a golf course, tennis, and townhouses. If you plan to stay awhile, many rental options are available.

South Carolina Waterfalls

The Upcountry

Westminster to Clayton, GA

64 Bull Sluice

Hi-fidelity! This Class V rapid falls and flows perfectly over the rocky-bottomed river floor along Section III of the Wild and Scenic Chattooga River. With strength and serenity, it heightens all of your senses and holds your gaze.

Height: 10 feet
Beauty rating: Very good
Distance: 0.4 mile
Difficulty: Easy
Surface: Paved path, gravel trail
Hiking time: 20 minutes
Other trail users: Whitewater rafters
Blazes: None
County: Rabun, Georgia; Oconee, South Carolina

Land status: Chattahoochee National Forest-Chattooga District/Sumter National Forest-Andrew Pickens District
Contacts: (706) 754-6221 / (864) 638-9568; www.fs.usda.gov
Maps: *DeLorme: South Carolina Atlas & Gazetteer:* Page 16 B1; *DeLorme: Georgia Atlas & Gazetteer:* Page 16 C4

Finding the trailhead: *From the junction of US 76 east and US 441 in Clayton, Georgia,* drive east on US 76 for 8.2 miles. The parking lot is on the left just after crossing the Chattooga River Bridge. *From the junction of US 76 and US 123,* drive west on US 76 for 17.7 miles. Just before crossing the Chattooga River Bridge, pull into a parking area on the right. The trailhead is at the northeast end of the parking lot next to the pavilion. **GPS:** N34°48.902'/W83°18.307'

The Hike

Follow the wide paved path downhill toward the river. This path is an access point for whitewater rafters and kayakers to head out on Section IV of the river, so the path is wide enough for groups of people to carry their rafts. In less than 0.1 mile you'll see a gravel path leading off to the right (north) as the main trail makes a U-turn to the left and continues downhill. If you stay on the pavement, it leads to a lovely sandy beach alongside the Chattooga. Save that for later, and go right on the gravel path. This path also ends at the river at a small overlook near the base of Bull Sluice. You'll enjoy splendid views of the river from this vantage point, and the rapid crashes down with all the enthusiasm you would expect from this impressive waterway.

Bull Sluice is located along a stretch of the Chattooga that has been protected since the spring of 1974. The river proudly has national forest on both sides, giving it

Bull Sluice

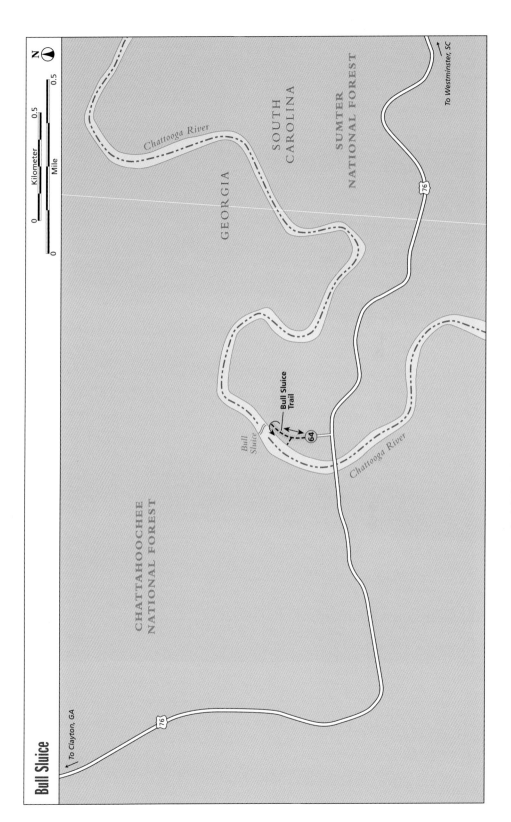

Bull Sluice Trail

Bull Sluice

Chattooga River

Chattooga River

GEORGIA

SOUTH CAROLINA

CHATTAHOOCHEE NATIONAL FOREST

SUMTER NATIONAL FOREST

To Clayton, GA

To Westminster, SC

N

Kilometer

Mile

64

76

76

Bull Sluice, a raging rapid flowing free on the Chattooga River

a wonderful buffer zone on which no commercial roads or development is allowed. It's said that the rocks forming the riverbed were carved out over a span of 600 to 750 million years.

Each rapid is classified on a standardized scale according to difficulty. The International Scale of River Difficulty ranges from the tamest Class I rapid to the most

Survey markers often mark the Forest Service property lines.

difficult, often "unrunnable," Class VI. Bull Sluice sits toward the tougher end of that scale as a Class IV+ rapid.

Miles and Directions

0.0 Hike northeast down the paved path.

0.06 Go right (north) on the gravel side trail.

0.2 Arrive at Bull Sluice (N34°49.020'/W83°18.275'). Backtrack to trailhead.

0.4 Arrive at trailhead.

65 Fall Creek Falls

Inspiring! Like the wings of a dove flapping in the wind, Fall Creek Falls brings a similar offering of peace. This short but steep scramble rewards you with a refreshing flow and an inviting shallow pool at the base.

Height: 60 feet
Beauty rating: Very good
Distance: 0.2 mile
Difficulty: Moderate
Surface: Hard-packed dirt
Hiking time: 20 minutes
Other trail users: None
Blazes: None

County: Oconee
Land status: Sumter National Forest–Andrew Pickens District
Contacts: (864) 638-9568; www.fs.usda.gov/scnfs
Maps: *DeLorme: South Carolina Atlas & Gazetteer:* Page 16 H1; *DeLorme: Georgia Atlas & Gazetteer:* Page 16 C4

Finding the trailhead: *From the junction of US 76 and US 441 in Clayton, Georgia,* drive east on US 76 for 10.0 miles. Turn left onto Chattooga Ridge Road. Travel 2.0 miles. Turn left onto Fall Creek Road. Drive 0.3 mile. Turn left onto Fall Creek Road Extension (FS 722). Travel 0.5 mile to a small pull-off on the left, just after crossing a tiny stream. *From the junction of US 76 and the Chattooga River Bridge (Georgia–South Carolina state line),* drive east on US 76 for 2.0 miles. Turn left onto Chattooga Ridge Road. Follow directions above. *From the junction of US 76 and US 123,* drive west on US 76 for 15.2 miles. Turn right onto Chattooga Ridge Road. Follow directions above. The trailhead is in the middle of the pull-off. **GPS:** N34°49.362'/W83°15.047'

The Hike

The narrow path leads down into the forest and immediately bends right bringing you alongside the upper portion of the falls. Follow the rugged trail downhill and downstream to the base of Fall Creek Falls. A conveniently placed log helps you cross the creek to a sandbar on the opposite bank, giving you an even better view. Moss covers the stone as the water steeply flows over it, and a giant log to the left adds character. The base of this boisterous beauty has a shallow, golden brown pool that's just deep enough for you to sit in, or lounge out in the sun. The flow is healthy, but not overwhelming, so you can sit at the base and let the rushing water massage your back. These bonus features make this one worth the visit.

Gilled mushrooms are often poisonous.

Fall Creek Falls; Falls on Reedy Branch

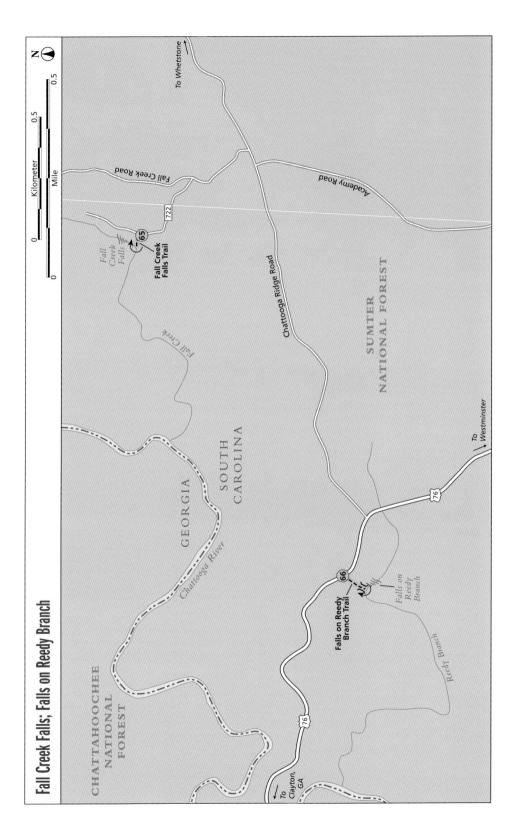

A short but steep scramble leads to Fall Creek Falls.

Aptly named, Fall Creek is home to not just one, but three cascades over a 1.0-mile stretch of creek. Each of these is more difficult and challenging to reach than the one before. For this reason, I have only showcased the first.

Miles and Directions

0.0 Hike southwest.

0.1 Arrive at Fall Creek Falls (N34°49.358'/W83°15.080'). Backtrack to trailhead.

0.2 Arrive at trailhead.

66 Falls on Reedy Branch

Mysterious! As you hike through the stone pillars at the trailhead, it feels as though you're trespassing, perhaps heading down the driveway to someone's dream home. Fortunately for us the Forest Service acquired the land, allowing public access.

See map on p. 181.
Height: 60 feet
Beauty rating: Very good
Distance: 0.4 mile
Difficulty: Easy to moderate
Surface: Wide old roadbed, narrow footpath
Hiking time: 20 minutes
Other trail users: None
Blazes: None

County: Oconee
Land status: Sumter National Forest–Andrew Pickens District
Contacts: (864) 638-9568; www.fs.usda.gov/scnfs
Maps: *DeLorme: South Carolina Atlas & Gazetteer:* Page 22 A1; *DeLorme: Georgia Atlas & Gazetteer:* Page 16 D4

Finding the trailhead: *From the junction of US 76 and US 441 in Clayton, Georgia,* drive east on US 76 for 9.8 miles to a pull-off on the right next to a low stone wall. This is the beginning of FS 2751. *From the junction of US 76 and the Chattooga River Bridge (Georgia–South Carolina state line),* drive east on US 76 for 1.7 miles to a pull-off on the right next to a low stone wall. *From the junction of US 76 and US 123,* drive west on US 76 for 15.5 miles to a pull-off on the left next to a low stone wall. The trailhead is the stone pillars south of the parking area. **GPS:** N34°48.435'/W83°16.853'

The Hike

Begin the hike by passing through the pillars and following the wide forest road FS 2751 downhill. At the bottom of the hill before you reach the creek, a side path heads off to the left and you can see the falls from here. Follow the path, cross a tiny footbridge, and you quickly arrive at the base of Falls on Reedy Branch. Rocks are strategically placed near the base so you can rock-hop across and enjoy a different perspective. The creek is shallow, but the falls stand tall and proud. There used to be a single gazebo sitting near the base of the falls, but time has taken its toll, so the gazebo has gone by the wayside. Regardless, this is one of those hidden local gems; easy to get to, easy to find, and worth the walk.

The area surrounding the falls was in the midst of a large development project when it was acquired by the Sumter National Forest. Lucky for us. Instead of this being off-limits on private property, we now have the good fortune to visit this one time and time again.

Falls on Reedy Branch: tall, just waiting for you to visit

Miles and Directions

0.0 Hike southwest, downhill on the forest road.

0.15 Go left (southwest) and cross a footbridge.

0.2 Arrive at Falls on Reedy Branch (N34° 48.309' W83° 16.895'). Backtrack to trailhead.

0.4 Arrive at trailhead.

67 Opossum Creek Falls

Stupendous! Brilliant, milky-white water flows freely over a wall of moss-covered stone enticing you to reach out and touch Opossum Creek Falls. Its mossy face and spongy touch make this waterfall a truly amazing thing to see and feel. Easily on the Author's Favorites list, this is one of my choice spots to spend a day.

Height: 120 feet
Beauty rating: Excellent
Distance: 4.7 miles
Difficulty: Moderate to strenuous
Surface: Hard-packed dirt
Hiking time: 2 hours, 30 minutes
Other trail users: None
Blazes: None

County: Oconee
Land status: Sumter National Forest–Andrew Pickens District
Contacts: (864) 638-9568; www.fs.usda.gov/scnfs
Maps: *DeLorme: South Carolina Atlas & Gazetteer:* Page 16 B1; *DeLorme: Georgia Atlas & Gazetteer:* Page 16 D4

Finding the trailhead: *From the junction of US 76 and US 441 in Clayton, Georgia,* drive east on US 76 for 12.4 miles. Turn right onto Damascus Church Road. Travel 0.8 mile to a fork. Go right onto Battle Creek Road. Drive 1.8 miles. Turn right onto Turkey Ridge Road (FS 755). Travel 2.1 miles to a pull-off on the left next to FS 755F. *From the junction of US 76 and the Chattooga River Bridge (Georgia–South Carolina state line),* drive east on US 76 for 4.4 miles. Turn right onto Damascus Church Road. Follow directions above. *From the junction of US 76 and US 123,* drive west on US 76 for 12.8 miles. Turn left onto Damascus Church Road. Follow directions above. The trailhead is on the west side of the road, about 200 feet south of the pull-off. **GPS:** N34°46.404'/W83°18.255'

The Hike

From where you parked, walk back down the road about 200 feet to reach the trailhead on your right (south), which you drove by on the way in. The first few tenths lead you downhill around some switchbacks. Once you reach the forest floor, it's a pleasant stroll in the forest alongside the passive but pretty Camp Branch creek. You'll cross a couple culverts over tributaries, but other than that, this is a fairly dry hike with no rock hops and no footbridges or fords. At least not until you reach the river. When you hit the 1.0-mile mark, you leave the forest floor and the trail begins to rise and fall. The creek also becomes livelier, and at 1.1 miles if you look over your left shoulder you may catch a glimpse of Camp Branch Falls in the distance, depending on the season. In general, the trail to Opossum Creek Falls is well groomed and easy to follow for the first 2.0 miles. At the 2.0-mile mark the trail seems to end at an open area where Opossum Creek flows out into the mighty Chattooga River. A downed tree acts as a natural log bridge crossing over the creek and leading out to an amazing sandy beach along the banks of the river. This makes a wonderful side trip along the

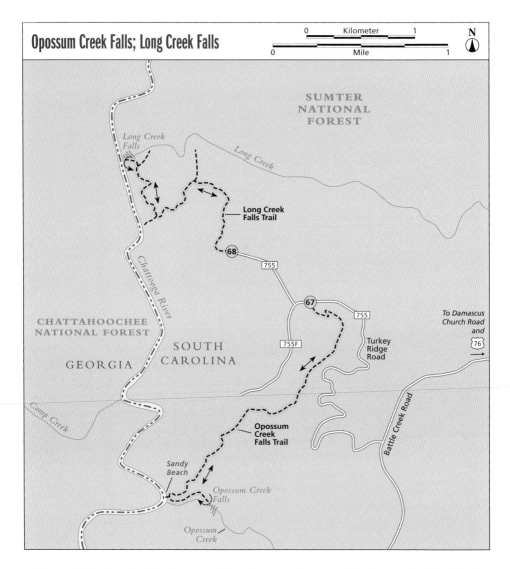

SUMTER
NATIONAL
FOREST

Long Creek Falls

Long Creek

Long Creek
Falls Trail

68

755

67

755

To Damascus
Church Road
and

76

CHATTAHOOCHEE
NATIONAL FOREST

SOUTH
CAROLINA

755F

GEORGIA

Turkey
Ridge
Road

Chattooga River

Battle Creek Road

Camp Creek

Opossum
Creek
Falls Trail

Sandy
Beach

Opossum Creek
Falls

Opossum
Creek

hike, and this beach is by far one of my favorite places to visit. To see the falls, don't cross the log bridge. Instead, when you first come down to the open area, make a U-turn to the left and follow the narrow footpath east and upstream. In contrast to the well-groomed trail that led you here, this part of the hike is an unmarked scramble upstream. Depending on the season it can be a bit overgrown as well, so zip-off pants may be useful. The "trail" follows Opossum Creek upstream for 0.35 mile until it ends at Opossum Creek Falls.

The forest surrounding the trail to Opossum Creek Falls provides an excellent habitat for wild turkey, bobcat, and black bear. While I've yet to see the latter two or any opossums, I have had the pleasure of seeing wild turkey here on many occasions.

Pull up a rock and enjoy the view at Opossum Creek Falls.

Miles and Directions

0.0 Hike generally south on the white-blazed trail.

2.0 Reach the creek where it flows out to the river. Make a U-turn to the left hiking east upstream on a narrow footpath.

OPPORTUNISTIC OPOSSUMS

Opossums are nocturnal creatures that are often misunderstood due to their frightening looks and mouth full of teeth. Typically slow-moving and passive animals, when cornered they'll usually just play dead, or "possum," as a defense mechanism.

People often fear them as carriers of rabies, but actually it's very rare for an opossum to be infected with the virus. You're far more likely to become infected by a cute and cuddly raccoon than by an ominous-looking opossum.

These marsupials are well adapted to a wide variety of habitats and are opportunistic omnivores, eating just about anything they can get their paws on.

2.2 Rock-hop the creek and continue upstream.

2.27 Rock-hop a tributary.

2.35 Arrive at Opossum Creek Falls (N34°45.826'/W83°17.963'). Backtrack to trailhead.

4.7 Arrive at trailhead.

Because they are cold-blooded, snakes often bask in the sun or linger on warm surfaces to help regulate their body temperature.

68 Long Creek Falls

Perfection! Long Creek Falls is like two ladies dancing under the moonlight, enticing you to cast your gaze upon them and then not allowing you to look away. On the Author's Favorites list, this hike is challenging, but the falls never disappoint.

See map on p. 186.
Height: 40 feet
Beauty rating: Excellent
Distance: 3.8 miles
Difficulty: Moderate to strenuous
Surface: Wide old roadbed, hard-packed dirt path
Hiking time: 2 hours
Other trail users: None

Blazes: None
County: Oconee
Land status: Sumter National Forest–Andrew Pickens District
Contacts: (864) 638-9568; www.fs.usda.gov/scnfs
Maps: *DeLorme: South Carolina Atlas & Gazetteer:* Page 16 B1; *DeLorme: Georgia Atlas & Gazetteer:* Page 16 D4

Finding the trailhead: *From the junction of US 76 and US 441 in Clayton, Georgia,* drive east on US 76 for 12.4 miles. Turn right onto Damascus Church Road. Travel 0.8 mile to a fork. Go right onto Battle Creek Road. Drive 1.8 miles. Turn right onto Turkey Ridge Road (FS 755). Travel 2.9 miles to where the road dead-ends. (**Note:** As you follow Turkey Ridge Road, bypass FS 755F on your left near the trailhead for Opossum Creek Falls.) *From the junction of US 76 and the Chattooga River Bridge (Georgia–South Carolina state line),* drive east on US 76 for 4.4 miles. Turn right onto Damascus Church Road. Follow directions above. *From the junction of US 76 and US 123,* drive west on US 76 for 12.8 miles. Turn left onto Damascus Church Road. Follow directions above. The trailhead is located where FS 755 continues into the woods on the right as a wide dirt path. **GPS:** N34°46.663'/W83°18.733'

The Hike

Follow the old roadbed of FS 755 west and downhill into the forest on a pretty decent grade. When you reach a fork at 0.15 mile, bypass FS 755B on the left and stay right continuing northeast along FS 755. The wide forest road undulates up and down as you descend and at 0.6 mile it ends at a turnaround. You'll see a narrow footpath on the right (southwest). Follow this footpath down into the forest and in about a tenth of a mile you'll come to a T. Go left (southwest), hiking farther downhill into the forest. As you do, you begin to feel a refreshing chill in the air, that familiar coolness of a creekside hike, although you haven't reached the creek yet. For now all you hear is birds singing, and the complete solitude of pure nature. The sounds of your footsteps and your own breath are the only things to interrupt the peace and pleasure of being outdoors. The narrow path is well trodden, which is surprising for as alone and isolated as this hike feels. At 1.15 miles you'll notice an obvious side path on the left (west) that is marked by an X formed from purposefully placed rock. Make sure you

Long Creek Falls flows directly into the Chattooga River.

bypass this path and continue straight (north) on the main trail. You'll continue for nearly another half a mile before the main trail peters out at 1.65 miles. Here you'll see another side path, which leads left (west) steeply downhill toward the sound of the falls. This part of the hike is a challenging, steep downhill trek to reach the river, but when you do, you'll arrive at the beautiful banks of the Wild and Scenic Chattooga

Left: Make sure you stay hydrated on your hike. Right: Indian pink is a rare and splendid find.

River. If that wasn't reward enough, you'll find yourself standing alongside Long Creek where it makes its confluence with the river. It's quite a treat. The waterfall sits just upstream from the confluence and is truly one of the most beautiful waterfalls in the area. As you return to the trailhead, that first part of the hike is one calf-burning quarter-mile. It makes the rest of the hike look like a cakewalk.

Long Creek Falls creates the perfect picture as it flows over the rocks and converges with Section IV of the Chattooga River. If you want these falls to yourself, avoid getting here at lunchtime; whitewater rafters often stop here for lunch daily. This is a popular landmark among the paddling community and a treat for all who visit.

The Chattooga River was also the setting of the 1972 Burt Reynolds–Ned Beatty film *Deliverance*. Some of its most famous scenes were filmed just over a mile downstream at Camp Creek.

Miles and Directions

0.0 Hike downhill and west into the forest on FS 755.

0.15 Bypass FS 755B on the left (northwest).

0.6 The forest road ends at a turnaround. Go right (west) on the narrow footpath.

0.72 Come to a T. Go left (southwest) and downhill.

FATHOM THIS

A fathom is a unit of measurement, length to be exact, equal to 6 feet. This nautical term is used to describe depth of water. So is the term *league*, as in *20,000 Leagues under the Sea*. A league is equal to 3 nautical miles. A nautical mile (a mile over sea) isn't the same as a statute mile (a mile over land) and is actually 1.15 times longer than a statute mile. So, by these terms, the average depth of the Wild and Scenic Chattooga River ranges from less than 1 fathom to over 2 fathoms, and its length of 57 statute miles translates to just under 50 nautical miles.

1.15 Bypass the side path on the left (west) marked by rocks with an X. Continue straight (north) on the main trail.

1.65 Follow the path on the left (west) steeply downhill toward the sound of the falls.

1.9 Arrive near the base of Long Creek Falls (N34°47.120'/W83°19.392'). Backtrack to trailhead.

3.8 Arrive at trailhead.

69 Upper, Middle, and Lower Brasstown Falls and Falls on Little Brasstown Creek

Stellar! Shining like the stars and heavens above, Brasstown Falls glimmers with excitement. Four incredible waterfalls greet you along this short but steep and rugged trail. With all four falls earning a beauty rating of excellent, this hike easily makes the Author's Favorites list.

Height: Upper: 35 feet; Middle: 25 feet; Lower: 20 feet; Falls on Little Brasstown Creek: 40 feet

Beauty rating: Excellent for all

Distance: 0.75 mile

Difficulty: Upper, Middle, and Lower Brasstown: moderate to strenuous; Little Brasstown Creek: easy

Surface: Hard-packed dirt

Other trail users: None

Hiking time: 30 minutes

Blazes: Yellow; Little Brasstown Creek, none

County: Oconee

Land status: Sumter National Forest–Andrew Pickens District

Contacts: (864) 638-9568; www.fs.usda.gov/scnfs

FYI: Upper, Middle, and Lower Brasstown Falls are not recommended for small children or dogs. Falls on Little Brasstown Creek is suitable for all hikers.

Maps: DeLorme: South Carolina Atlas & Gazetteer: Page 16 C1; DeLorme: Georgia Atlas & Gazetteer: Page 16 E4

Finding the trailhead: From the junction of US 76 and US 441 in Clayton, Georgia, drive east on US 76 for 13.6 miles. Turn right onto Brasstown Road. Travel 4.0 miles. Turn right onto FS 751 just before crossing a bridge. Follow FS 751 for 0.5 mile to the end. (**Note:** At 2.6 miles, Brasstown Road becomes a dirt road.) From the junction of US 76 and the Chattooga River Bridge (Georgia–South Carolina state line), drive east on US 76 for 5.6 miles. Turn right onto Brasstown Road. Follow directions above. From the junction of US 76 and US 123, drive west on US 76 for 11.6 miles. Turn left onto Brasstown Road. Follow directions above. The trailhead is at the southwest end of the parking area. **GPS:** N34°43.149'/W83°18.107'

The Hike

The trail leads southwest into the forest toward the sound of moving water. You'll pass a primitive campsite before coming to a fork. Left leads to Falls on Little Brasstown Creek. If you want to keep the hike easy, go left now. Otherwise, we'll come back here in a bit. For now, go straight (west) on the yellow-blazed trail toward Brasstown Falls. Please use caution along this hike. The narrow path closely passes by the brink of all three waterfalls as you follow the creek downstream. On top of that, the path is primarily a rooty, rocky, muddy scramble downstream from one waterfall to the next. It's exceptional that you get to see one extraordinary waterfall after the next, but the

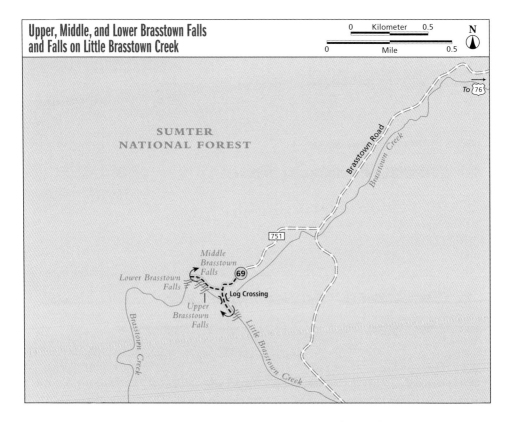

path is precipitous and recommended for experienced hikers only. The Upper Falls (Brasstown Cascades) is the tallest of the three as the creek tumbles down a staircase of stone. When you reach Middle Brasstown Falls (Brasstown Veil), you'll get a great view from the trail alongside the falls. The falls make a clean freefall that is simply flawless. If you're lucky you may catch a rainbow in the overspray from this one. The trail continues to scramble steeply down roots and rocks until you reach the base of Lower Brasstown Falls (Brasstown Sluice). The scenery set before you at the lower falls is unbeatable. A large pristine pool sits at the base and a cave on the opposite bank draws your attention. This cave is carved out of a tall wall of stone that stands watch over the creek. When you've had your fill, backtrack to the fork and now head right to see Falls on Little Brasstown Creek. The path leads to a primitive campsite. Look left, and you'll see some logs leading across the creek. Carefully cross here to keep your feet dry and you soon arrive at the base of Falls on Little Brasstown Creek.

Brass is an alloy made by mixing copper with zinc. This gold-colored metal is highly malleable, making it easy to cast into a wide variety of shapes. This attribute, combined with its acoustic properties, makes brass an ideal material for musical instruments, primarily horns such as trumpets, trombones, and tubas.

The Brasstown Valley was first explored by the Cherokee, who called it *Itseyi,* meaning "place of fresh green." Years later, white settlers confused *Itseyi* with another

Falls on Little Brasstown Creek brings a big bonus on this hike.

Cherokee word, *v-tsai-yi*, meaning "brass." Soon after, the area known as "Brass–town" came to be.

Miles and Directions

0.0   Hike southwest into the forest.

0.07 Come to a fork. Left leads south to Falls on Little Brasstown Creek. Go straight (west) toward Brasstown Falls.

0.18 Arrive at Upper Brasstown Falls (N34°43.113'/W83°18.265'). Continue downstream.

0.2   Rock-hop a tributary.

A pristine cove cradles Lower Brasstown Falls.

0.25 Arrive at Middle Brasstown Falls (N34°43.137'/W83°18.267'). Continue downstream.

0.3 Arrive at the base of Lower Brasstown Falls (N34°43.134'/W83°18.310'). Backtrack to the fork at 0.07 mile.

0.53 Arrive at the fork. Go right (south) toward Falls on Little Brasstown Creek.

0.6 Cross the creek.

0.65 Arrive at Falls on Little Brasstown Creek (N34°43.030'/W83°18.150'). Backtrack to the trailhead.

0.75 Arrive at trailhead.

70 Riley Moore Falls

Unmatched! The trail to Riley Moore Falls isn't the most entertaining, but when the trail ends and you reach the falls you'll be more than impressed with the scenery that unfolds before you. A long sandy beach lines the bank of the Chauga River, and the falls make a clean drop over a ledge that spans a breadth river wide. It really is unmatched.

Height: 15 feet
Beauty rating: Excellent
Distance: 2.2 miles
Difficulty: Moderate from the alternate trailhead. Easy to moderate from actual trailhead.
Surface: Hard-packed dirt
Hiking time: 1 hour, 10 minutes
Other trail users: 4-wheel-drive vehicles from alternate trailhead to actual trailhead

Blazes: Bluish purple
County: Oconee
Land status: Sumter National Forest–Andrew Pickens District
Contacts: (864) 638-9568; www.fs.usda.gov/scnfs
Maps: *DeLorme: South Carolina Atlas & Gazetteer:* Page 22 B2, *DeLorme: Georgia Atlas & Gazetteer:* Page 16 E5

Finding the trailhead: *From Walhalla,* follow SC 28. Turn left onto South Maple Street. Drive 0.1 mile to a stop sign. Continue straight ahead. Turn right onto Coffee Road. Drive 4.4 miles. Turn right onto Ramsay Creek Road. Travel 1.3 miles to a right on Cobb Bridge Road. Drive 2.3 miles. Turn right onto Spy Rock Road (FS 748). Drive 1.8 miles to FS 748C on the right. This is the alternate trailhead. If you have a high-clearance four-wheel-drive vehicle you can drive 0.5 mile down FS 748C to the official trailhead. *From the junction of US 76 and US 123 in Westminster,* drive west on US 76 for 7.1 miles. Turn right onto Cobb Bridge Road. Drive 1.3 miles. Turn left onto Spy Rock Road (FS 748). Follow directions above. *From the junction of US 76 and the Chattooga River Bridge (Georgia-South Carolina state line),* drive east on US 76 for 6.5 miles. Turn left onto Spy Rock Road (FS 748). Travel 4.0 miles to FS 748C. Trailhead **GPS:** N34°44.387'/W83°11.394'; Alternate trailhead **GPS:** N34°44.459'/W83°11.117'

The Hike

The type of vehicle you have will determine whether you begin this hike at the alternate trailhead, or at the actual trailhead. If you have a four-wheel-drive, high-clearance vehicle you can drive down FS 748C to reach the actual trailhead. This will shorten the hike by 0.5 mile. If you don't have four-wheel drive, park along FS 748 and hike down FS 748C to the trailhead. From the actual trailhead, the trail is to the left of the gate and leads east into the forest. Although you can't hear any water, you're in for a real treat even if you had to hike down the bumpy forest road.

If you visit during the week, you'll find this forest is extremely peaceful. Birds serenade as you follow a contour of the mountain. As you get closer to the falls the trail leaves the contour and descends to the creek. On weekends this trail sees a lot

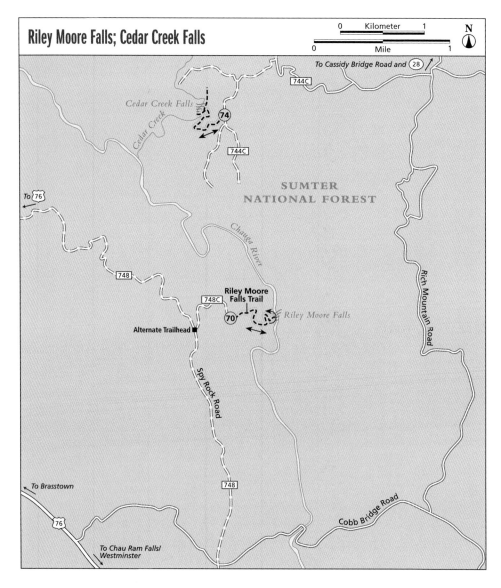

0   Kilometer   1

0   Mile   1

N

**SUMTER
NATIONAL FOREST**

Cedar Creek Falls

Cedar Creek

744C

74

744C

To Cassidy Bridge Road and 28

To 76

Chauga River

748

Riley Moore
Falls Trail

748C

70

Riley Moore Falls

Alternate Trailhead

Spy Rock Road

Rich Mountain Road

To Brasstown

748

76

Cobb Bridge Road

To Chau Ram Falls/
Westminster

of traffic, as it's a popular swim hole for the locals. When you reach the falls, it's easy to see why. A large beautiful sandy beach is accompanied by an amazing swim hole. Although this isn't a very tall waterfall, it's certainly one of the most scenic. It has a ton of character, and the falls form a shelf that spans the full width of the river.

Many years ago a miller named Riley Moore owned and operated a gristmill above the falls, which is how he became their namesake. Although the mill is long gone, the falls are a picture-perfect setting and the trail is one for all seasons. In spring and summer wildflowers welcome you with the full spectrum of colors, and the inviting swim hole is irresistible. Autumn brings a new array of colors as the forest

A sandy beach rests along the banks near Riley Moore Falls.

prepares itself for winter. Bring a blanket and a picnic lunch; you're going to want to stay awhile. But as always I implore you to "pack it in—pack it out."

Miles and Directions

0.0 Hike down FS 748C.

0.5 Reach the actual trailhead at the end of the road. Hike east into the forest.

1.1 Arrive at Riley Moore Falls (N34°44.461'/W83°10.762'). Backtrack to the trailhead.

2.2 Arrive at trailhead.

71 Chau Ram Falls

Sweet! This peaceful, stony-faced fall is located inside Chau Ram Park. A short walk from your vehicle takes you to the large, flat stones at the base of the falls. It's a great place for the whole family to enjoy. Bring a picnic and stay a spell.

Height: 30 feet
Beauty rating: Very good
Distance: Roadside
Difficulty: Easy
County: Oconee
Land status: Chau Ram Park
Contacts: (864) 888-1488; www.oconee
country.com/chaurampark.html

FYI: Fee required; 7 a.m.–dusk Mar to Nov 16; closed Martin Luther King Jr. Day, Thanksgiving, Christmas, New Year's Day
Maps: *DeLorme: South Carolina Atlas & Gazetteer:* Page 22 C2; *DeLorme: Georgia Atlas & Gazetteer:* Page 16 E5

Finding the trailhead: *From the junction of US 76 and US 441 in Clayton, Georgia,* drive east on US 76 for 22.8 miles. Turn right onto Chau Ram Park Road. Travel 0.3 mile to the main entrance to the park. Continue for 0.25 mile, going past the park office and around to the right. The road ends at the falls. *From the junction of US 76 and the Chattooga River Bridge (Georgia–South Carolina state line),* drive east on US 76 for 14.8 miles. Turn right onto Chau Ram Park Road. Follow directions above. *From the junction of US 76 and US 123,* drive west on US 76 for 2.3 miles. Turn left onto Chau Ram Park Road. Follow directions above. **GPS:** N34°40.931'/ W83°08.711'

The Hike

Chau Ram Falls can be viewed from the parking area as Ramsey Creek passes through this pleasant neighborhood park on its way to the Chauga River.

In addition to this lovely waterfall, Chau Ram Park has picnic shelters, a campground, and numerous hiking trails that offer great views of some of the rapids on this rowdy river. These rapids include telling names such as Can Opener, Surfing, and Lost Paddle rapids. Trail maps are available at the park office, and I definitely recommend branching out and exploring while you're here.

The trails can be reached by crossing a 175-foot-long "swinging bridge" over the Chauga River, which makes for yet another unique experience while visiting the park.

You can drive right up to Chau Ram Falls.

72 Yellow Branch Falls

Three-dimensional! Absolutely surreal, Yellow Branch Falls is like a Mayan village up on a hillside, with its many facets seeming to come to life. The depth of this waterfall is unlike anything I've ever seen before. This waterfall is highly recommended and squarely sits among my top five favorites.

Height: 60 feet
Beauty rating: Excellent × 3
Distance: 3.2 miles
Difficulty: Moderate to strenuous
Surface: Hard-packed dirt
Hiking time: 1 hour, 30 minutes
Other trail users: None
Blazes: None

County: Oconee
Land status: Sumter National Forest–Andrew Pickens District
Contacts: (864) 638-9568; www.fs.usda.gov/scnfs
Maps: *DeLorme: South Carolina Atlas & Gazetteer:* Page 22 A2; *DeLorme: Georgia Atlas & Gazetteer:* Page 16 D5

Finding the trailhead: *From the junction of SC 28 and SC 107,* drive south on SC 28 for 2.7 miles. Turn right at the sign into the Yellow Branch Picnic Ground. Bypass the road to your right and continue straight ahead for 0.2 mile to where the road ends. *From the junction of SC 28 and SC 183,* drive north on SC 28 for 5.3 miles. Turn left at the sign into the Yellow Branch Picnic Ground. Follow directions above. The trailhead is at the southwest side of the parking lot. **GPS:** N34°48.331'/W83°07.726'

The Hike

The trail leads south into the forest and quickly follows a small creek downstream. You'll rock-hop this creek three times before coming to a fork at the quarter-mile mark. Straight leads east 0.2 mile to an alternate trailhead on Yellow Branch Road, which you passed on the way in to the picnic area and primary trailhead. If the main parking lot is full you can park and hike from there, although I prefer the main path because it follows the creek.

From the above-mentioned fork, go right (south) and you quickly come to a footbridge over that same creek that you have been rock-hopping back and forth. Continue following the creek downstream through the forest on the flat footpath. You'll rock-hop the creek one more time before moving away from it. Bypass any game trails or side paths and stay on the heavily trodden unblazed trail. As you stroll through the forest, you can't help but notice the impressively large trees and lovely array of wildflowers.

You'll rock-hop the creek once more and it's barely a trickle at this point. Continue hiking generally south until you cross a footbridge. As the trail swings around the mountain, you'll cross a third and final footbridge, which passes over a gully.

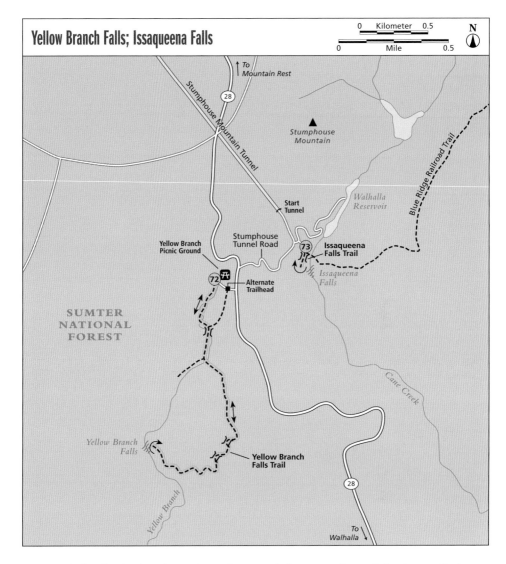

Yellow Branch Falls; Issaqueena Falls

0   Kilometer   0.5

0   Mile   0.5

N

To Mountain Rest

28

Stumphouse Mountain

Stumphouse Mountain Tunnel

Walhalla Reservoir

Blue Ridge Railroad Trail

Start Tunnel

Yellow Branch Picnic Ground

Stumphouse Tunnel Road

73

Issaqueena Falls Trail

72

Alternate Trailhead

Issaqueena Falls

SUMTER NATIONAL FOREST

Cane Creek

Yellow Branch Falls

Yellow Branch Falls Trail

28

Yellow Branch

To Walhalla

Beyond this footbridge the trail transforms and the rooty clay path begins to climb at a moderate pitch. The final half-mile leads you through the forest, and as you near the falls the sound of moving water becomes more and more intense. The final descent follows a narrow footpath to the base of the three-dimensional Yellow Branch Falls.

The Yellow Branch Picnic Ground has been around since at least the 1930s, with one of the original buildings still standing today. Oconee County, within which the picnic ground is located, has been around for hundreds of years longer. Many stories exist about how the county came to be named, most of which stem from Native American roots. The theory I prefer is that it takes its name from the Cherokee word *Uk-oo-na*, meaning "watery eyes of the hills." Take a peek at the abundance of creeks, lakes, and waterfalls around here and you'll understand why I prefer this one.

The three-dimensional Yellow Branch Falls is among my favorites.

Fire pink is a distinct red blossom that is unmistakable.

Miles and Directions

0.0 Hike south into the forest.

0.12 Rock-hop the creek.

0.15 Rock-hop the creek.

0.19 Rock-hop the creek.

0.25 Come to a fork. Go right (south).

0.27 Cross a footbridge.

0.43 Rock-hop the creek.

0.7 Rock-hop the creek.

0.92 Cross a footbridge.

1.07 Cross a footbridge.

1.6 Arrive at Yellow Branch Falls (N34°47.692'/W83°08.048'). Backtrack to trailhead.

3.2 Arrive at trailhead.

73 Issaqueena Falls

Captivating! The ecosystem that creates this waterfall is fantastic. It highlights the way that nature comes together and shows the unity of all living things needing one another to survive.

See map on p. 203.
Height: 100 feet
Beauty rating: Excellent
Distance: 0.2 mile
Difficulty: Easy
Surface: Wide mulch path
Hiking time: 10 minutes
Other trail users: None
Blazes: None

County: Oconee
Land status: Sumter National Forest–Andrew Pickens District
Contacts: (864) 638-9568; www.fs.usda.gov/scnfs
FYI: Fee required; 8 a.m.–8 p.m.
Maps: *DeLorme: South Carolina Atlas & Gazetteer:* Page 22 A2; *DeLorme: Georgia Atlas & Gazetteer:* Page 16 D5

Finding the trailhead: *From the junction of SC 28 and SC 107,* drive south on SC 28 for 2.6 miles. Turn left onto Stumphouse Tunnel Road. Drive 0.5 mile. At the bottom of the hill, turn right onto the narrow side road and immediately go right again into the picnic area. *From the junction of SC 28 and SC 183,* drive north on SC 28 for 5.4 miles. Turn right onto Stumphouse Tunnel Road. Follow directions above. The trailhead is at the south end of the parking area. **GPS:** N34°48.447'/W83°07.280'

The Hike

The falls are easy to get to, and found within a beautiful picnic area inside Stumphouse Tunnel Park. This area has grown in the last few years. Not only do you have the falls, you have the Stumphouse Tunnel, an old railroad trail, access to the Palmetto Trail, and now they've added a mountain bike park as well. That's a lot of bang for your buck. Which is a good thing, since they have also increased the entrance fee substantially.

An information signpost near the trailhead tells the tale of the Indian maiden for whom the falls were named. From the trailhead an obvious path leads you over two footbridges before coming to an observation deck overlooking Issaqueena Falls.

Issaqueena was an Indian maiden who fell in love with a white settler. Her lover was David Francis, a silversmith who lived in what is now the town of Ninety-six, South Carolina. Upon hearing that her tribe was planning to attack his town, Issaqueena rode on horseback some 92 miles to warn the settlers of the pending attack.

The settlers escaped, and David and Issaqueena fled to Stumphouse Mountain where they lived in a hollowed-out tree or "stump house." When her tribe finally tracked them down, Issaqueena fled to the falls, where she leapt from the brink. The

An observation deck gives you this view of Issaqueena Falls.

THE CURE FOR BLUE CHEESE

Clemson College purchased the Stumphouse Tunnel in 1951 because of its constant temperature and high humidity. Why, one might ask? To cure blue cheese, of course.

A professor in Clemson College's dairy department realized that the tunnel had the perfect climate to cure cheese. The college began in-depth studies, and the next thing you know, they were making the cheese on campus and then transporting it to the Stumphouse Mountain Tunnel for curing. This project continued with great success from 1951 until 1958, when the college was able to duplicate the tunnel's climate and began curing the cheese in special labs on campus called "cheese rooms."

Clemson University still uses the same ripening recipe for curing its world-famous blue cheese that it did back in the early 1950s in the Stumphouse Mountain Tunnel.

tribesmen thought her to be dead and gave up the chase, but she had landed in a small cave behind the falls. Hidden by the veil of water, she stayed there for days before rejoining her husband. The pair then fled to Alabama and lived happily ever after.

For an interesting side trip, visit the Stumphouse Mountain Tunnel. To get there, continue another 0.1 mile on Stumphouse Tunnel Road to where the road dead-ends at a parking area. From the parking area, head northeast up the hill to the entrance of this 1,600-foot-deep tunnel.

Miles and Directions

0.0 Hike south on the wide mulch path and cross two footbridges.

0.1 Arrive at the overlook for Issaqueena Falls (N34 48.390 / W83 07.308). Backtrack to trailhead.

0.2 Arrive at trailhead.

This old train car sits near the Stumphouse Tunnel.

74 Cedar Creek Falls

Symbiotic! As the waters of Cedar Creek flow past, I can't help but ponder the complex, yet simple, ways of nature. From the smallest stone in the creek to the bluest sky above, it's all so astonishing. The amazing link among all living things within an ecosystem always leaves me in awe.

See map on p. 198.
Height: 20 feet
Beauty rating: Good
Distance: 1.1 miles
Difficulty: Easy to moderate; steep scramble to the base
Surface: Wide forest road, wide gravel footpath
Hiking time: 40 minutes
Other trail users: None

Blazes: Blue
County: Oconee
Land status: Sumter National Forest-Andrew Pickens District
Contacts: (864) 638-9568; www.fs.usda.gov/scnfs
Maps: *DeLorme: South Carolina Atlas & Gazetteer:* Page 22 A2; *DeLorme: Georgia Atlas & Gazetteer:* Page 16 D5

Finding the trailhead: *From the junction of SC 28 and SC 107,* drive south on SC 28 for 1.9 miles. Turn right onto Whetstone Road. Travel 0.7 mile. Turn left onto Cassidy Bridge Road. Drive 0.85 mile. Turn left onto gravel FS 744 (Rich Mountain Road). Travel 3.2 miles. Turn right onto FS 744C. Drive 2.5 miles to FS 2658 on your right. *From the junction of SC 28 and SC 183,* drive north on SC 28 for 6.1 miles. Turn left onto Whetstone Road. Follow directions above. The trailhead is the gate for FS 2658. **GPS:** N34°45.712'/W83°11.179'

The Hike

The trail follows the wide gravel FS 2658 for nearly half the hike. Berries line the forest road and in summertime you can pick a plump juicy berry as a refreshing treat. After following the gravel road for a quarter-mile, you'll see a couple boulders and a blue-blazed footpath on the right leading off the road and into the forest. Follow this wide gravel footpath northeast toward the sound of moving water. Bypass any side paths until you've hiked half a mile and reach the creek. When you reach the creek, the main trail bends right (north) and a side path leads left (southwest) steeply downhill to the base of the falls. Cedar Creek Falls is a beautiful little rockslide. Although it's not a tall waterfall, there's a large pool at the base with flat rocks to relax upon and enjoy the clean mountain air. Another wonderful perk about this one is that it's well off the beaten path, so you're likely to have it to yourself.

Use caution at the base of Cedar Creek Falls, as it sits just upstream from the brink of South Carolina's Blue Hole Falls. (**Note:** Although Blue Hole Falls is just a stone's throw away, I have not included it in this guide because there's no safe way to reach it.)

A shallow, pristine pool gathers at the base of Cedar Creek Falls.

Cedar Creek is one of the many that feed into the Chauga River. The nearby Cassidy Bridge Campground offers primitive camping and is very popular among hunters during season. Between the campground and the National Forest Service Rifle Range off Cassidy Bridge Road, don't be surprised if you hear gunshots in the distance while hiking here.

Miles and Directions

0.0 Go around the gate and hike down FS 2658.

0.25 Go right (northeast) on the blue-blazed footpath.

0.5 Go left (southwest) on the side path hiking downstream.

0.55 Arrive at Cedar Creek Falls (N34°45.737'/W83°11.375'). Backtrack to trailhead.

1.1 Arrive at trailhead.

75 Chauga Narrows

Stormy! Chauga Narrows flows like freedom itself, carving its way through the bonds of the boulders and then dropping to the calm river below. The fierce force of the falls humbles you, and you can easily appreciate the power wielded by Mother Nature's might.

Height: 25 feet
Beauty rating: Excellent
Distance: 1.4 miles
Difficulty: Brink, easy to moderate; base, strenuous
Surface: Hard-packed dirt
Hiking time: 50 minutes
Other trail users: None
Blazes: None

County: Oconee
Land status: Sumter National Forest-Andrew Pickens District
Contacts: (864) 638-9568; www.fs.usda.gov/scnfs
Maps: *DeLorme: South Carolina Atlas & Gazetteer:* Page 16 H2; *DeLorme: Georgia Atlas & Gazetteer:* Page 16 C5

Finding the trailhead: *From the junction of US 76 and US 441 in Clayton, Georgia*, drive east on US 76 for 10.0 miles. Turn left onto Chattooga Ridge Road. Travel 5.7 miles. Turn right onto Whetstone Road. Drive 1.0 mile to a pull-off on the left just before crossing the bridge. *From the junction of US 76 and the Chattooga River Bridge (Georgia–South Carolina state line)*, drive east on US 76 for 2.0 miles. Turn left onto Chattooga Ridge Road. Follow directions above. *From the junction of US 76 and SC 123*, drive west on US 76 for 15.2 miles. Turn right onto Chattooga Ridge Road. Follow directions above. *From the junction of SC 28 and SC 107*, drive south on SC 28 for 1.9 miles. Turn right onto Whetstone Road. Travel 5.0 miles to a pull-off on the right just after crossing the bridge. The trailhead is located on the opposite (south) side of the road from the pull-off. **GPS:** N34°50.000'/W83°10.513'

The Hike

An old jeep road leads south past the iron remnants of the original Blackwell Bridge. Follow the jeep road as it shadows the Chauga River downstream. After just two-tenths of a mile the trail transforms into a narrow overgrown footpath. A brilliant green forest of ferns lines the path and you'll also enjoy rhododendron and mountain laurel, which are common along the water's edge. You'll pass through a tunnel formed by this flora before coming to a primitive campsite alongside the river. The river makes a wide sweeping bend to the right here, and you can picture yourself spending the night here with nothing but nature and serenity. Hike through the campsite and continue following the river downstream. In general, the trail leads primarily south

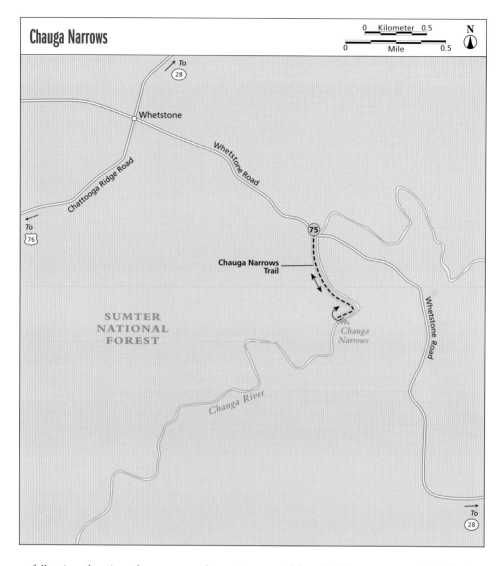

0   Kilometer   0.5

0   Mile   0.5

N

To
28

Whetstone

Whetstone Road

Chattooga Ridge Road

To
76

75

Chauga Narrows
Trail

SUMTER
NATIONAL
FOREST

Chauga
Narrows

Whetstone Road

Chauga River

To
28

following the river downstream the entire way. Although it's overgrown, the hike is fairly easy until you reach the primitive campsite. From the campsite to the falls the path is a strenuous full-on scramble over roots and rocks with precipitous dropoffs to the river. With that being said, this hike is for experienced hikers only, and certainly not for children or dogs. When you reach the falls, you're treated to a narrow chute of water that thunders through a stone passage with intense power and might. Please use extreme caution near the falls. This is not one to be trifled with.

In Cherokee, the word *Chauga* translates to "high and lifted up stream." It seems, however, that the Chauga River is just the opposite. The river drops an average of 60 to 80 feet per mile as it makes its way to its confluence with the Savannah River. A 9.8-mile stretch of the Chauga is very popular with whitewater rafters, and rightfully

Chauga Narrows carves through its stone cliff confines.

so. The river boasts Class I through V rapids that easily rival those on the famed Wild and Scenic Chattooga River.

Miles and Directions

0.0 Hike south on the old jeep road.

0.4 Hike through a primitive campsite.

0.7 Arrive at Chauga Narrows (N34°49.609'/W83°10.382'). Backtrack to trailhead.

1.4 Arrive at trailhead.

76 Pigpen and Licklog Falls

Ideal! This trail gives you two great waterfalls back to back. First, Pigpen Falls presents you with a magnificent place to picnic or camp. This is soon followed by a small sandy beach where Licklog Falls flow straight out into the Wild and Scenic Chattooga River.

Height: Pigpen: 10 feet; Licklog: 25 feet
Beauty rating: Very good
Distance: 2.0 miles (Pigpen only: 1.36 miles)
Difficulty: Easy to moderate
Surface: Hard-packed dirt
Hiking time: 1 hour, 10 minutes
Other trail users: None
Blazes: White

County: Oconee
Land status: Sumter National Forest–Andrew Pickens District
Contacts: (864) 638-9568; www.fs.usda.gov/scnfs
Maps: *DeLorme: South Carolina Atlas & Gazetteer:* Page 16 G2; *DeLorme: Georgia Atlas & Gazetteer:* Page 16 B5

Finding the trailhead: *From the junction of SC 107 and SC 28,* drive north on SC 107 for 3.3 miles. Turn left onto Village Creek Road. Travel 1.7 miles. Turn right onto Nicholson Ford Road just before the road makes a hard bend to the left (east). Drive 2.2 miles to the end. (**Note:** Along the way, Nicholson Ford Road becomes FS 2603.) *From the junction of SC 107 and SC 413 (Wiggington Road),* drive south on SC 107 for 10.5 miles. Turn right onto Village Creek Road. Follow directions above. **GPS:** N34°55.511'/W83°07.343'

The Hike

This hike begins by following the white-blazed Foothills Trail through the forest. A symphony of singing by the resident birds can be heard in the background. Woodpeckers drum on the trees keeping beat with the warblers as the trail makes a gentle descent. The path is well maintained and easy to follow thanks to the Foothills Trail Conservancy. This group does an amazing job maintaining the trail. It's always so well cared for, and always a pleasure to hike on no matter which section you venture out onto.

You'll cross a pair of footbridges with astonishment at how crystal clear the water is. Shortly after the second footbridge, you'll reach a fork. Left is the Chattooga River Trail (CRT) that leads southwest to Pigpen Falls. Straight ahead is the continuation of the Foothills Trail, which merges with the northbound Chattooga River Trail at this junction. Go left and you quickly come to the base of Pigpen Falls on your left. Large boulders at the base give you a perfect place to sit and enjoy the view of this

Pigpen Falls offers a rock with a view for all to enjoy.

small but beautiful waterfall. When you're ready to move on, continue hiking past the falls and immediately cross a footbridge. A variety of ferns line the path, creating a canvas of lush greenery that only Mother Nature could paint. As the sound of rushing water intensifies, you'll hike past the brink of Licklog Falls. In 0.2 mile from the footbridge, as the CRT bends left (west) moving away from Licklog Creek, you'll see a side path that follows the falls downstream (northeast). This path leads you on a steep scramble down to the Chattooga River near the base of Licklog Falls. The falls flow directly out to the river, and are far more impressive than they let on. From the base you can only see a small portion of the falls, but in its entirety it covers over 0.1 mile and makes one drop after the next as it rumbles down to meet the river. A very small sandy beach gives you marvelous views of the river, and you're likely to have it all to yourself.

Licklog Creek flows into Section 0 on the headwaters portion of the Wild and Scenic Chattooga River. The Chattooga is the crown jewel of Southern rivers. It is most famous for its whitewater rafting, but the treasure of this wonderful waterway also can be enjoyed by land. The Chattooga River Trail stretches a fabulous 40 miles along the river's glorious banks.

Licklog Falls flows right out to the Chattooga River.

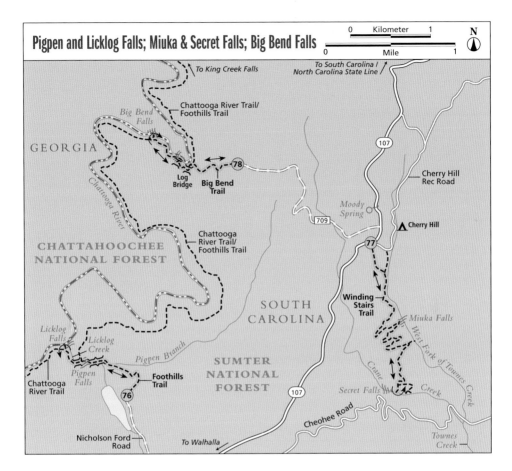

Pigpen and Licklog Falls; Miuka & Secret Falls; Big Bend Falls

Miles and Directions

0.0 Hike northeast.

0.5 Cross a footbridge.

0.56 Cross a footbridge.

0.65 Come to a fork. Go left (southwest).

0.68 Arrive at Pigpen Falls (N34°55.702'/W83°07.748'). Continue following the CRT west.

0.7 Cross a footbridge.

0.9 Go right (northeast) on the side path.

1.0 Arrive at the base of Licklog Falls (N34°55.824'/W83°07.868'). Backtrack to trailhead.

2.0 Arrive at trailhead.

77 Miuka and Secret Falls

Verdant! This hike leads to two tall waterfalls, but that's only part of the pleasure it imparts. A diverse forest offers an abundance of green hues, and an astounding array of colorful wildflowers rivals any trail in the area.

See map on p. 217.
Height: Miuka: 75 feet; Secret: 60 feet
Beauty rating: Miuka: good; Secret: fair
Distance: Miuka: 2.4 miles; Secret: 4.8 miles
Difficulty: Miuka: moderate; Secret: strenuous
Surface: Hard-packed dirt
Hiking time: Miuka: 1 hour, 10 minutes; Secret: 2 hours, 30 minutes
Other trail users: None

Blazes: Orange
County: Oconee
Land status: Sumter National Forest–Andrew Pickens District
Contacts: (864) 638-9568; www.fs.usda.gov/scnfs
Maps: *DeLorme: South Carolina Atlas & Gazetteer:* Page 16 G3

Finding the trailhead: *From the junction of SC 107 and Wiggington Road (SR 413),* drive south on SC 107 for 5.3 miles to a pull-off on the left just past Cherry Hill Rec Road. *From the junction of SC 107 and SC 28,* drive north on SC 107 for 8.4 miles to a pull-off on the right just before Cherry Hill Rec Road. The trailhead is at the southwest corner of the parking area, near the road. **GPS:** N34°56.474'/W83°05.394'

The Hike

Follow the well-groomed Winding Stair Trail south into a wonderfully diverse forest. Maple saplings stand alongside pines and hemlocks while patches of wildflowers add a splash of color to the greenery. Springtime brings an abundance of brilliant blue and gold dwarf iris, and a variety of velvety leaved violets accompany these beautiful bulbs. The twisted trunks of mountain laurel form an occasional tunnel over the trail, and that's just the first quarter-mile. When you reach the T, left is a spur trail leading north to the neighboring Cherry Hill Campground. Go right (south) heading deeper into the forest, and you soon begin to follow the creek downstream. Where the mountain laurel leaves off, the broad-leaved rhododendron picks up. Unique rock formations pique your curiosity, and you'll get glimpses of Lake Jocassee in the distance during winter and early spring.

At 1.15 miles as the trail makes a hard switchback to the right (southwest), take the spur trail to the left (northeast) toward the sound of the falls. The path ends at a stone platform where you'll get a view of Miuka Falls. Again it's best to visit in the winter and early spring before the foliage fills in and obscures the view.

Return to the Winding Stair Trail and continue hiking farther into the forest where pine needles begin to carpet the ground. As you make your way toward Secret

A natural overlook offers views of Miuka Falls.

Falls, you'll hike around several switchbacks. After making the final switchback, you'll rock-hop back-to-back tiny tributaries while the lush forest continues to amaze you with a multitude of green hues. At 2.35 miles as the main trail makes a bend to the left, you'll see an obvious side path to the right. Follow this well-trodden path south toward the sound of the falls. It leads steeply downhill, and the closer you get to the falls the steeper it becomes. You'll have to climb over some deadfall before reaching the base of Secret Falls. The beauty rating is "fair" mainly because you can't get a good view of the falls, despite their size. On top of that, the creek at the base is littered with logs.

While you are in the area, stop by to see Moody Spring. It sits just north of the pull-off on the west side of SC 107. The spring comprises a spring-fed spigot with stone and cement surrounding it. The words "Moody Spring" are etched into the concrete, and it's a popular watering hole for the locals. The water constantly flows, offering passersby a place to refill their water bottle, or dip their heads in the fresh mountain-fed spring water.

Miles and Directions

- **0.0** Hike south on the Winding Stair Trail.
- **0.23** Come to a T. Go right (south).
- **1.0** Step over a tiny tributary.

Dwarf crested iris decorate the trail to Miuka Falls in springtime.

1.15 As the trail makes a hard switchback to the right (southwest), follow the spur trail to the left (northeast) toward the sound of the falls.

1.2 Arrive at Miuka Falls (N34°55.971'/W83°05.152'). Backtrack to the main trail.

1.25 Arrive at the main trail; continue hiking southwest.

1.7 Cross a tiny tributary. The trail makes a hard switchback left (east) and you'll rock-hop the same tributary again.

1.9 Follow the main trail on a switchback to the right (south), bypassing a spur trail on the left (northeast).

2.08 Rock-hop a tributary.

2.1 Rock-hop a tributary.

2.35 As the main trail bends left (east), go right (south) on a spur trail.

2.45 Arrive at Secret Falls (N34°55.509'/W83°05.179'). Backtrack to trailhead.

4.8 Arrive at trailhead.

78 Big Bend Falls

Rowdy! Big Bend crashes down with the rage and fury one would expect from the famed Chattooga River. It's not easy to get a good view, but boy is it boisterous when you do.

See map on p. 217.
Height: 30 feet
Beauty rating: Good
Distance: 2.4 miles
Difficulty: Strenuous
Surface: Hard-packed dirt
Hiking time: 1 hour, 20 minutes
Other trail users: None

Blazes: White, green and white
County: Oconee
Land status: Sumter National Forest–Andrew Pickens District
Contacts: (864) 638-9568; www.fs.usda.gov/scnfs
Maps: *DeLorme: South Carolina Atlas & Gazetteer:* Page 16 F3

Finding the trailhead: *From the junction of SC 107 and Wiggington Road (SR 413),* drive south for 5.2 miles. Turn right onto an unmarked dirt road, FS 709, directly across the street from Cherry Hill Campground. Drive 1.7 miles to the end at a primitive campsite. *From the junction of SC 107 and SC 28,* drive north on SC 107 for 8.5 miles. Turn left onto an unmarked dirt road, FS 709, directly across the street from Cherry Hill Campground. Follow directions above. The trailhead is at the northwest end of the campsite. **GPS:** N34°56.990'/W83°06.471'

The Hike

The trail begins at the northwest end of the primitive campsite where you parked. It begins as a wide continuation of the forest road and swiftly makes a rapid descent into the forest. You can hear the roar of the river almost immediately as you enter the Chattooga River Wilderness. The trail follows the old clay bumpy roadbed for a tenth of a mile before it narrows to a footpath. There are no blazes as of yet, but it's easy to follow. You'll hike through a gully as the sound of the river urges you on. In less than a half-mile, you reach a T with the river in view down below. This is where the Big Bend Trail ends and you pick up the Chattooga River Trail/Foothills Trail. A hard right leads east a good ways to King Creek Falls. You want to go left (southwest) as you follow the Chattooga River downstream. At three-quarters of a mile you'll pass by an impressive rapid with an open area alongside it that offers a perfect view. Clear, green, clean, wild water greets you. It looks so inviting, you want to just jump right in, but you're wise enough to resist the temptation, as this river is untamed. Continue following the green- and white-blazed trail south as it loosely follows the river from high above. You'll follow some switchbacks back down to the river's edge before coming to a steep and dangerous side path that gives you a closer view of the fearsome power of Mother Nature. This path leads to a small, *steep* cliffside dropoff near

Big Bend rages after a heavy rain.

the falls. Use EXTREME CAUTION! NO CHILDREN, NO DOGS. The falls are formed as the Chattooga River forms a wall of whitewater that furiously rages down a drop of about 30 feet. If you look at a map you can easily see how this one earned its name. It sits on the southern half of a big deep bend in the river.

Although you only get a teaser view of Big Bend Falls, the views of the river in general are sheer perfection. As you hike back out you realize how steep the Big Bend Trail is. It follows a 9.9 percent grade, dropping nearly 500 feet of elevation in less than a half-mile.

Miles and Directions

0.0 Hike west down into the forest.

0.45 Come to a T. Go left (southwest).

0.5 Cross a log bridge.

0.65 Cross a footbridge.

0.75 Pass an impressive rapid. Continue hiking downstream.

1.15 A side path leads through a tunnel of rhododendron giving you a better view of the falls.

1.2 Arrive at Big Bend Falls (N34°57.201'/W83°07.141'). Backtrack to trailhead.

2.4 Arrive at trailhead.

79 King Creek Falls

Big, bold, and beautiful! A pristine swim hole awaits at the base of this big, bold, and beautiful waterfall. King Creek Falls stands proudly posed above the creek it feeds, like a fledgling taking its first flight shouting, "Hey, look at me!"

Height: 60 feet
Beauty rating: Excellent
Distance: 1.4 miles
Difficulty: Easy to moderate
Surface: Narrow rooty footpath
Hiking time: 40 minutes
Other trail users: None
Blazes: White, orange

County: Oconee
Land status: Sumter National Forest-Andrew Pickens District
Contacts: (864) 638-9568; www.fs.usda.gov/scnfs
Maps: DeLorme: South Carolina Atlas & Gazetteer: Page 16 F2–F3; DeLorme: Georgia Atlas & Gazetteer: Page 16 A5, 17 A6

Finding the trailhead: From the junction of SC 107 and SC 28, drive north on SC 107 for 10.0 miles. Turn left onto New Burrell's Ford Road (FS 708). Travel 2.2 miles. Turn left into the Burrell's Ford Campground parking lot. From the junction of SC 107 and SC 413 (Wiggington Road), drive south on SR 107 for 3.8 miles. Turn right onto New Burrell's Ford Road (FS 708). Follow directions above. The trailhead is at the southwest corner of the parking lot at the trail information signpost. **GPS:** N34°58.282'/W83°06.884'

The Hike

Follow the white-blazed Foothills Trail into the forest as you parallel the road you drove in on. You'll immediately bypass a set of steps on the left that lead across that same road. The trail leads you around some switchbacks as you hike on a slow winding descent into the valley. In less than a half-mile, you'll come to a fork. The right leg leads northwest back to Burrell's Ford Campground, and then up to the gate that you saw in the parking lot. Go left (south) and immediately cross a footbridge. As you follow King Creek southeast, you quickly come to another fork. Right is where the Foothills Trail makes a hard right west-northwest. You want to go left (southeast) and climb up the steps now following the orange-blazed King Creek Trail. The trail continues to loosely follow the creek upstream all the way to the falls. Colorful wildflowers and a variety of ferns greet you in springtime, and the cool air from the creek comforts you, even in the heat of summer. The trail climbs and dips and climbs again. When the falls come into view from afar, you realize how big this waterfall really is. The final tenth of a mile follows a damp rocky path to a perfect little cove housing King Creek Falls. A tall time-worn tree leans against the stone face of the falls, and a pristine swim hole awaits at the base of this big, bold, and beautiful waterfall.

King Creek Falls; Spoon Auger Falls

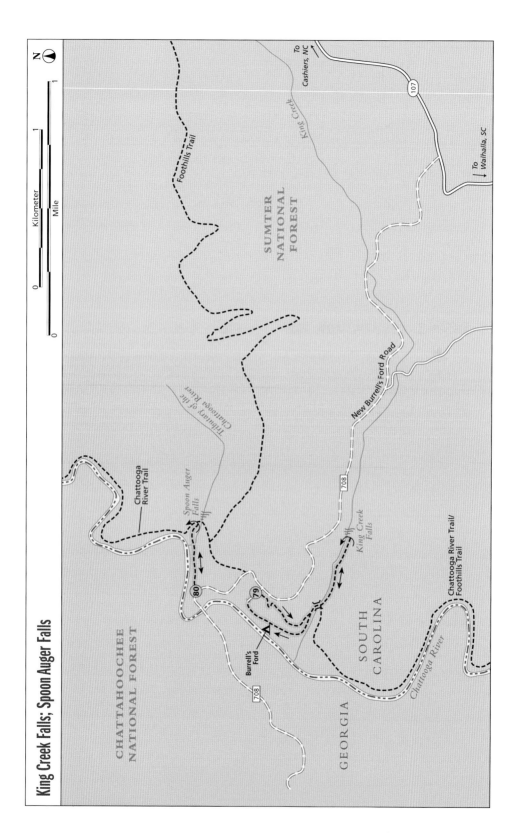

The large log leaning against the falls offers insight into its height.

The trail and surrounding area are best known for their splendid diversity of birdlife. The altitude is around 2,800 feet, yet bird species typical of elevations up to 4,000 feet are commonly found here. You may want to bring binoculars and do some birding on your way to the falls.

These round bales of hay can weigh more than 1,000 pounds each.

Note: Burrell's Ford Campground offers primitive camping only; there are no facilities available.

Miles and Directions

0.0 Hike south into the forest and bypass the steps on the left.

0.4 Come to a fork. Go left (south) and cross a footbridge.

0.45 Come to another fork. Go left (southeast) climbing the steps.

0.7 Arrive at King Creek Falls (N34°57.982'/W83°06.651'). Backtrack to trailhead.

1.4 Arrive at trailhead.

80 Spoon Auger Falls

Happy! Spoon Auger Falls smiles at you, as the sprinkles fly from her face to cool and comfort you in perfect tiny droplets.

See map on p. 224.
Height: 100 feet
Beauty rating: Good
Distance: 0.6 mile
Difficulty: Moderate
Surface: Hard-packed dirt
Hiking time: 25 minutes
Other trail users: None
Blazes: None

County: Oconee
Land status: Sumter National Forest–Andrew Pickens District
Contacts: (864) 638-9568; www.fs.usda.gov/scnfs
Maps: *DeLorme: South Carolina Atlas & Gazetteer:* Page 16 F2–F3; *DeLorme: Georgia Atlas & Gazetteer:* Page 16 A5, 17 A6

Finding the trailhead: *From the junction of SC 107 and SC 28,* drive north on SC 107 for 10.0 miles. Turn left onto New Burrell's Ford Road (FS 708). Travel 2.55 miles to a pull-off along the right side of the road next to the trail information sign. *From the junction of SC 107 and SC 413 (Wiggington Road),* drive south on SC 107 for 3.8 miles. Turn right onto New Burrell's Ford Road (FS 708). Follow directions above. The trailhead is located on the north side of the parking area next to the trail information sign. **GPS:** N34°58.487'/W83°06.887'

The Hike

The trailhead is on the northeast side of the road at the trail information sign. Begin by following the Chattooga River Trail east. The wide path meanders through the forest and within a tenth of a mile you'll cross a tributary and the Chattooga River comes into view. It's quite surprising how wide and fairly passive the river is, considering this is the mighty Chattooga River, which boasts rapids with ratings as high as Class VI. The trail leads into the Ellicott Rock Wilderness area of Sumter National Forest. At 0.2 mile you'll rock- and log-hop across Spoon Auger Creek. Just past this crossing, a side path follows the creek upstream to the falls. This path leads steeply uphill and around several short switchbacks. At the first of these switchbacks, you'll pass a lovely cascade, but this is a mere shadow in comparison to the main attraction. Although the hike is short, you'll get a workout in as the trail climbs steeply to reach Spoon Auger Falls. The falls drop over several sections, and the path dead-ends at the uppermost portion. Gold, brown, and tan rock shines through the crystal-clear water while a wave of white washes over the stone face forming the falls. This one drops from one ledge to the next like a staircase created by Mother Nature herself.

The falls are found at the south end of the Ellicott Rock Wilderness. Named for Andrew Ellicott, who surveyed the North Carolina–South Carolina borders around

Spoon Auger Falls drops from one stone step to the next as it flows out to the Chattooga River.

1811, the wilderness covers 8,274 acres within North Carolina, South Carolina, and Georgia.

In the center of it all, lying on the east bank of the Chattooga River, is the famed Ellicott Rock. Andrew Ellicott chiseled an inconspicuous mark on this boulder to

Busy at work

denote the junction of all three states. To this day, the rock marks the spot. Ellicott Rock was placed on the National Register of Historic Places in 1973.

Miles and Directions

0.0 Hike northeast on the Chattooga River Trail.

0.1 Cross a tributary.

0.2 Cross a tributary and immediately go right (south) on the Spoon Auger Falls trail.

0.3 Arrive at Spoon Auger Falls (N34°58.491'/W83°06.603'). Backtrack to trailhead.

0.6 Arrive at trailhead.

81 Upper and Lower Sloan Bridge Falls, and Hiker's Peril

Fresh! As you hike alongside the river, the cool, fresh water fills your heart with joy, enticing you to immerse yourself within the forest around you. This short enjoyable hike offers one waterfall after the next, but heavy brush obscures the view. Save this one for wintertime when you can see the falls through the trees as you hike along the famed Foothills Trail.

Height: Upper: 45 feet; Lower: 10 feet; Hiker's Peril: 100+ feet
Beauty rating: Upper: good; Lower: good; Hiker's Peril: fair
Distance: 1.4 miles
Difficulty: Mostly easy, with a steep and strenuous scramble
Surface: Hard-packed dirt
Hiking time: 1 hour
Other trail users: None
Blazes: White

County: Oconee
Land status: Sumter National Forest-Andrew Pickens District
Contacts: (864) 638-9568; www.fs.usda.gov/scnfs
FYI: Trash cans, restroom, trail information sign at parking area
Maps: DeLorme: South Carolina Atlas & Gazetteer: Page 16 E3; DeLorme: Georgia Atlas & Gazetteer: Page 17 A6

Finding the trailhead: *From the junction of SC 107 and the North Carolina–South Carolina state line,* drive south on SC 107 for 0.6 mile. Turn right into the Sloan Bridge parking area. *From the junction of SC 107 and SC 413 (Wiggington Road),* drive north on SC 107 for 0.15 mile. Turn left into the Sloan Bridge parking area. *From the junction of SC 107 and SC 28,* drive north on SC 107 for 14.0 miles. Turn left into the Sloan Bridge parking area. The trailhead is to the left, at the south end of the parking lot. **GPS:** N35°00.206'/W83°03.243'

The Hike

The hike begins at the south end of the small parking lot following the white-blazed Foothills Trail generally south. Although the path parallels a fairly busy road, you quickly lose the traffic as the river drowns out any sounds of civilization. It seems that many storms have passed through this area over the last decade, and it's now difficult to get a great view of any of the waterfalls along this stretch of trail. The first feature to greet you is at the 0.4-mile mark as you pass by Upper Sloan Bridge Falls. Although it stands at 45 feet, there's so much brush and blowdowns that it's hard to get a good visual of this lively three-tiered beauty. As you continue along the hike you'll reach the Lower Falls within a tenth of a mile. This one gives you a pretty good view from up above, and although it's only 10 feet tall, it certainly has enough flow to grab your attention. Less than a quarter-mile from the Lower Falls, you'll reach a footbridge

Sumter may be small, but it's full of natural wonders.

that crosses over Hiker's Peril, which doesn't appear to be too perilous even if the footbridge wasn't there. However, I imagine in times of heavy flow I might think otherwise. The falls are tall and narrow, dropping in tiers, but again there's so much overgrown brush that it's hard to get a good view of it in its entirety. In summertime this trail also can be a bit buggy; I'd reserve this one for the winter months when you can get a better view through the brush.

This section of the 77-mile Foothills Trail is shared with the Fork Mountain Trail, which starts streamside and makes its way to the top of Fork Mountain. At 3,294 feet, Fork Mountain is the tallest peak within the South Carolina tract of the Ellicott Rock Wilderness and the second-highest summit in South Carolina.

The Foothills Trail stretches through upstate South Carolina and into western North Carolina. This fabulous footpath leads past pristine preserves and wonderful waterfalls. As you make your way from the low country to the heights of Sassafras Mountain, a wealth of diversity awaits you.

Miles and Directions

0.0 Hike south and immediately cross a footbridge following the white blazes.

0.2 Cross a footbridge.

0.4 Arrive alongside Upper Sloan Bridge Falls (N35°00.027'/W83°03.349'). Continue downstream.

0.5 Arrive at Lower Sloan Bridge Falls (N34°59.942/W83°03.306). Continue downstream.

Upper and Lower Sloan Bridge Falls, and Hiker's Peril

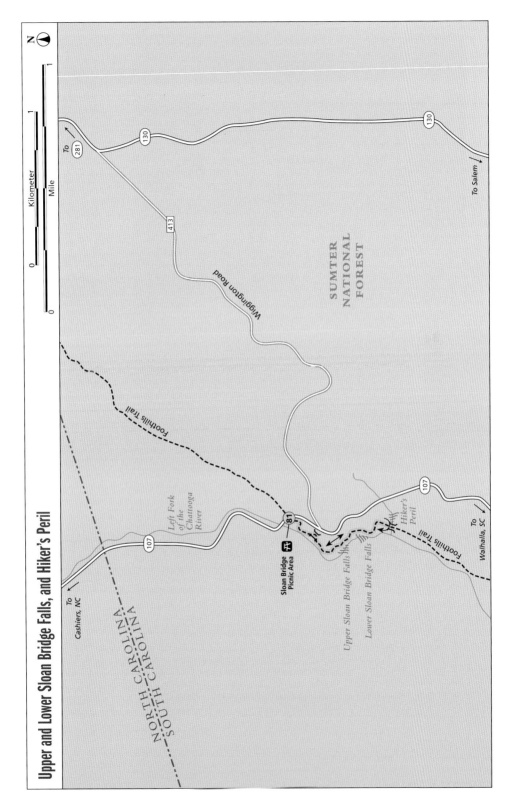

This massive downed tree now feeds the forest floor.

0.7 Arrive at the footbridge over Hiker's Peril (N34°59.840'/W83°03.286'). Backtrack to trailhead.

1.4 Arrive at trailhead.

82 Station Cove Falls

Unity! The water flows over each little section of the falls, working together to create the creek, all the while feeding the moss and plants upon it. A collection of tree trunks at the base give you insight into the size of this one, and large flat rocks offer a place to sit and take it all in.

Height: 80 feet
Beauty rating: Very good
Distance: 1.9 miles
Difficulty: Easy
Surface: Hard-packed dirt
Hiking time: 50 minutes
Other trail users: None
Blazes: Blue
County: Oconee

Land status: Sumter National Forest-Andrew Pickens District/Oconee Station State Historic Site
Contacts: (864) 638-9568; www.fs.usda.gov/scnfs/; (864) 638-0079; www.southcarolina parks.com
FYI: Oconee Station House is open on weekends 1 p.m.–5 p.m.
Maps: *DeLorme: South Carolina Atlas & Gazetteer:* Page 16 H3; *DeLorme: Georgia Atlas & Gazetteer:* Page 17 C6

Finding the trailhead: *From the junction of SC 11 and SC 183,* drive north on SC 11 for 1.9 miles. Go left onto Oconee Station Road. Travel 2.2 miles to a pull-off on the left. *From the junction of SC 11 and SC 130,* drive south on SC 11 for 6.6 miles. Turn right onto Oconee Station Road. Follow directions above. The trailhead is located next to the trail information sign. **GPS:** N34°50.932'/W83°04.469'

The Hike

Follow the wide clay trail down into the forest. Bypass any side paths and stay on the well-trodden, blue-blazed main trail. At 0.2 you'll come to a fork; go right. Over the next 0.45 mile, you'll cross four consecutive footbridges as you hike generally west. Although you can't hear any water yet, it leads you on a lovely stroll through the forest. After crossing your fourth and final footbridge, you'll come to a split rail fence across the trail. Go around the fence and continue straight ahead following the blue blazes. You'll rock-hop the creek a tenth of a mile before reaching the falls. You can use this, along with the number of footbridge crossings, to keep track of your progress. In just under a mile total, the trail ends at Station Cove Falls. The falls are multifaceted and very pretty, every time. It begins as narrow at the top, but as it drops, the falls widen with each stone ledge that it flows over. Large rocks near the base offer plenty of room for people to congregate at this popular place. Picnic, sunbathe, dip

The stoic Station Cove Falls proudly stands a full 80 feet tall.

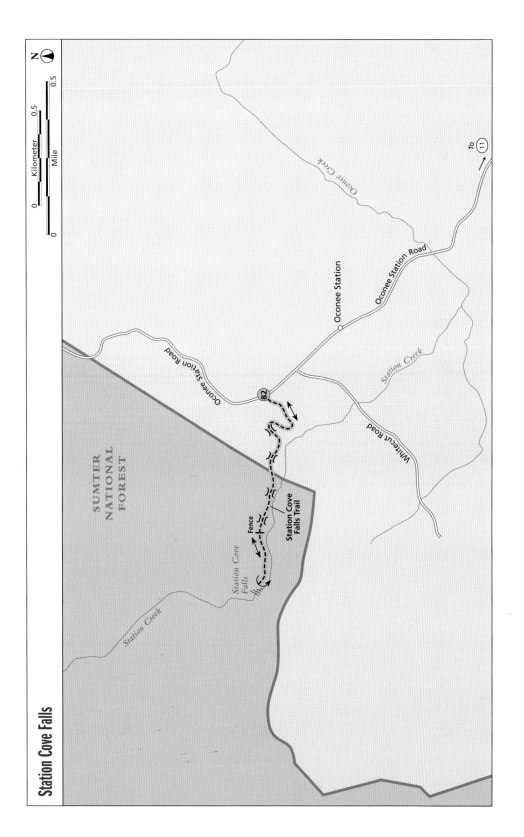

Station Cove Falls

your toes, or wade out farther to splash around in the refreshing water at the base of Station Cove Falls.

Located near the Oconee Station State Historic Site, Station Cove Falls was named for the historic Station House. Built in 1792, the Station House is the oldest structure in the South Carolina upcountry. This old stone building is the centerpiece of the park now, but in its day this was neither park nor picnic. The station was originally built as a military compound to protect against the Creek and Cherokee tribes. Ironically, it later became an Indian trading post and was used as such for many years.

Miles and Directions

0.0 Hike west into the forest.

0.2 Come to a fork. Go right (north).

0.3 Cross a footbridge.

0.45 Cross another footbridge.

0.57 Cross a footbridge.

0.65 Cross another footbridge.

0.68 Come to a split rail fence. Go around it and continue hiking west.

0.85 Rock-hop the creek.

0.95 Arrive at Station Cove Falls (N34°50.980'/ W83°05.126'). Backtrack to trailhead.

1.9 Arrive at trailhead.

Enormous root burls add to the scenery.

83 Lee Falls

Dramatic! This hike begins as a pleasant stroll across multiple open fields, but ends as a full-on boulder scramble upstream to the falls. Don't be dissuaded, it's worth the effort! Lee Falls is absolutely amazing! There's so much to this waterfall. So many facets. You could literally sit and stare at this one for hours. It's a blend of every type of falling water all put into one magnificent show. Little drops, and lovely cascades, mixed with freefall plunges. It certainly has more character than most, and is easily one of my favorites.

Height: 100 feet
Beauty rating: Excellent
Distance: 3.0 miles
Difficulty: Easy for the first 1.35 miles; strenuous for last 0.15 mile
Surface: Hard-packed dirt, boulder scramble
Hiking time: 1 hour, 30 minutes
Other trail users: None

Blazes: None
County: Oconee
Land status: Sumter National Forest–Andrew Pickens District
Contacts: (864) 638-9568; www.fs.usda.gov/scnfs
Maps: *DeLorme: South Carolina Atlas & Gazetteer: Page 16 G3*

Finding the trailhead: *From the junction of SC 11 and SC 130 in Salem,* drive south on SC 11 for 4.3 miles. Turn right onto Cheohee Valley Road. Drive 2.3 miles. Turn left onto Tamassee Knob Road. Travel 0.5 mile. Turn right onto Jumping Branch Road. Drive 1.5 miles. Turn left onto FS 715A. Travel 0.5 mile to a parking area on the right before crossing over Tamassee Creek. *From the junction of SC 11 and SC 183 near Walhalla,* drive north on SC 11 for 4.5 miles. Turn left onto Cheohee Valley Road. Follow directions above. The trailhead is the gate at the north end of the parking area. **GPS:** N34°53.631'/W83°04.901'

The Hike

Although on a map it looks very close to SC 107, Lee Falls is actually accessed from SC 11. From the trailhead, follow the narrow dirt path north across the large open field. As you do, a shallow rocky creek sits to your left, offering the familiar sweet flowing sound of moving water. At the far end of the field, you'll rock-hop the creek and hike across a second large open field bigger than the first. Again a water crossing greets you at the far end of the field, but this crossing is over a culvert. Beyond the culvert a third large open field awaits. Birdsong and a gentle breeze caress your senses as you hike across it. At the far end of this field, you'll rock-hop the creek once more before briefly following an old logging road through the forest. You quickly come out of the forest at your fourth and final field crossing. By three-quarters of a mile you're done crossing the open fields and enter the forest. The forest is filled with ferns, huckleberry, and hemlock, joined by a lovely array of immature maples and oak. It's quite a pleasant hike; even the portion that passes through the open fields offers serenity.

Lee Falls is one of the most impressive in the state.

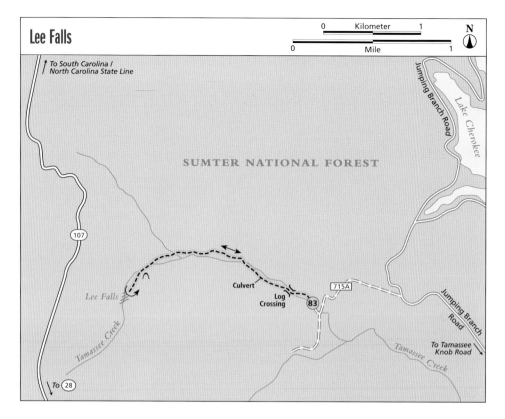

SUMTER NATIONAL FOREST

To South Carolina /
North Carolina State Line

Lee Falls

Culvert

Log
Crossing

83

715A

Tamassee Creek

To Tamassee
Knob Road

Jumping Branch Road

Lake Cherokee

Jumping Branch Road

To 28

107

At 1.25 miles you'll cross over the bold creek on a log. Bring a hiking stick to help with your balance and to keep your feet dry. Beyond this crossing the brush gets a little thicker, and you'll have to hop over the tattered trunks of several downed trees. A tenth of a mile past the log crossing the trail brings you out to the creek where it looks like a massive storm hit. Boulders and downed trees fill the area. From here, it's an unmarked boulder scramble upstream until you reach the base of the falls. Don't get me wrong, this is completely doable for the average adult with a moderate fitness level, but small children and dogs will definitely need assistance. Work your way upstream as best as you can. It's worth the effort! Lee Falls is phenomenal. The water makes a free-fall plunge at the top of the falls, before tumbling down over a multitude of stone. It's somewhat three-dimensional, and absolutely stunning. Bring an apple or a snack, and sit and stay awhile.

The falls are located on Tamassee Creek, which is one of the main waterways feeding into the Flat Shoals River near the town of Tamassee. The river consequently pushes forth to its confluence with Lake Keowee, which is undoubtedly one of the prettiest lakes in the region. If you stop in to Keowee-Toxaway State Park, you can rent a kayak and explore this clear green waterway surrounded by mountains in the South Carolina upcountry.

A narrow path leads from field to field on the way to Lee Falls.

Miles and Directions

0.0 Hike north across an open field.

0.17 Rock-hop the creek and cross a second field.

0.4 Cross over a culvert and cross a third field.

0.55 Rock-hop the creek and follow the road to a fourth field. Hike west across it.

0.7 Reach the end of the field. Hike west into the forest.

1.0 Rock-hop the creek and head right.

1.25 Cross a creek.

1.35 Reach the creek at an area littered with boulders and trees. Cross this area and follow the rugged path upstream.

1.5 Arrive at Lee Falls (N34°53.689'/W83°06.120'). Backtrack to trailhead.

3.0 Arrive at trailhead.

84 Lower Whitewater Falls

Immaculate! This hike showcases one of the tallest waterfalls in this book, with the bonus features of hiking on the Foothills Trail and crossing the Whitewater River. The forest is immaculate and untainted, which is a pleasant surprise since this trail sees a lot of traffic.

Height: 200 feet
Beauty rating: Excellent
Distance: 4.0 miles
Difficulty: Moderate to strenuous
Surface: Hard-packed dirt with rocky and rooty sections
Hiking time: 2 hours
Other trail users: None
Blazes: Blue, white

County: Oconee
Land status: Sumter National Forest-Andrew Pickens Ranger District; parking is on Duke Energy property at the Bad Creek Hydroelectric Station
Contacts: (864) 638-9568; www.fs.usda.gov/scnfs
Maps: *DeLorme: South Carolina Atlas & Gazetteer:* Page 16 E4

Finding the trailhead: *From the junction of NC 281 and the North Carolina/South Carolina state line,* drive south on NC 281 for 0.9 mile. Turn left and come to an automatic gate at the Bad Creek Hydroelectric Station. The gate opens as you approach. Follow Bad Creek Road for 2.15 miles. Turn left at the sign for the Foothills Trail. Drive 0.25 mile to the large parking lot. The trailhead is at the northwest end of the parking lot. **GPS:** N35°00.748'/W82°59.950'

The Hike

This hike is unique for a few reasons. First, it begins within the gated property of the Bad Creek Hydroelectric Station. Fortunately, it is open to the public, so you can enjoy one of the most impressive waterfalls in the area. The falls boldly stand at 200 feet, which is no surprise, since their upstream brother Upper Whitewater Falls is touted as the tallest waterfall east of the Mississippi. This beautiful behemoth is 411 feet tall and can be reached by driving north on SC 281 not far past the North Carolina state line.

Another unique and enjoyable thing about this hike is that it follows the famous Foothills Trail for half of the hike. The Foothills Trail leads you across the spectacular Whitewater River, where giant boulders mold the flow of water. On the opposite bank, stay straight at the fork and you'll immediately cross a footbridge over a small tributary. Just past the mile mark a blue-blazed spur trail leads you away from the Foothills Trail. As you follow this spur trail south, you are hiking through mountains

View Lower Whitewater Falls from an observation deck across the valley.

that form the northern shore of Lake Jocassee. If you've ever stood on the southern shore of this vast lake, you know exactly how spectacular and untainted these mountains appear. Now that you're hiking in the heart of them, you can confirm how sacred and pristine this ground really is. It's absolutely perfect virgin forest, undeveloped and un-intruded upon. Hiking along this peaceful trail you're exposed to a variety of trees, plants, wildflowers, creeks, and river. Holly, rhododendron, and mountain laurel are mixed with hardwoods like maple, oak, and poplar. These treasured trees cradle the trail offering shade and shelter from the elements. Tall pine trees add to the mix, and their sweet scent fills the air. The path is fairly rugged, yet well maintained and well marked.

At 1.12 miles the trail leads to a gate and parking area where people load and unload OHVs. Enter the parking area and immediately head out onto the gravel

Lower Whitewater Falls

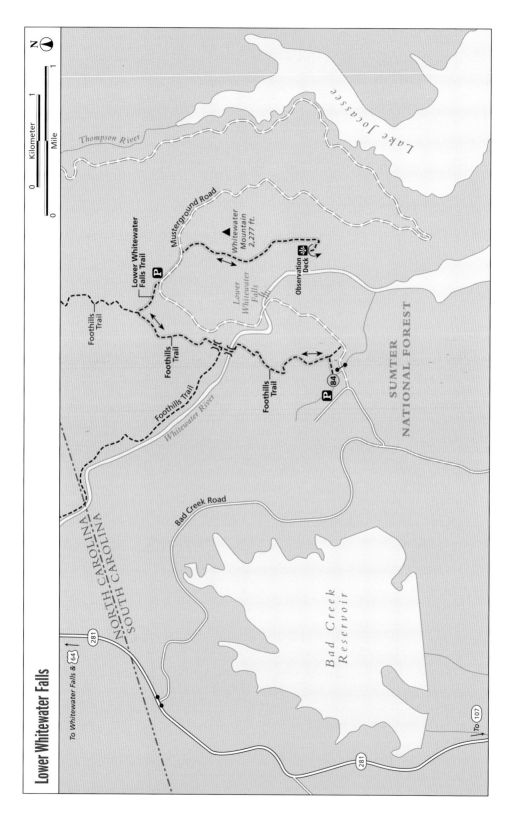

Musterground Road. Go left on the road, briefly following it southeast. Along the road blue blazes reassure you that you are on the right route. After 0.1 mile on the road, you return to the shade of the forest as a wide blue-blazed trail on the right leads southeast and climbs. The final leg of the hike makes a long slow descent to an observation deck overlooking Lower Whitewater Falls. The falls sit northwest across the valley, but the deck gives you a good vantage point, especially if you have a good zoom lens or a pair of binoculars.

The Duke Energy property also offers public access to another overlook, but this one you can drive right up to. The overlook is reached by driving on the main road of the property for 3.6 miles from the gate and following signs to the overlook (1.5 miles past the turn-off for the trailhead). This overlook

The spots on the head of this mushroom are a telltale sign that it's poisonous.

offers outstanding views of Lake Jocassee, and gives you glimpses of Wright Creek Falls to the left (northeast) in the distance. Although the view of this waterfall is no match for Lower Whitewater Falls, it's a pleasant addition to the day while you're in the area.

Miles and Directions

0.0 Hike east and uphill.

0.1 Come to a poorly marked fork. Right leads south toward Lake Jocassee. Go left north toward Whitewater River.

0.53 Cross a double bridge over the Whitewater River.

0.57 Come to a marked fork. Left (west) leads toward Whitewater Falls. Go straight (northeast) toward Lower Whitewater Falls.

0.59 Cross a footbridge.

1.0 Come to a T. Go right (east).

1.02 Come to a fork. Left is the Foothills Trail. Go right (east) on a blue-blazed spur trail toward Lower Whitewater Falls.

1.12 Arrive at a gate and a parking lot next to Musterground Road. Go out onto Musterground Road and turn left, following blue blazes southeast.

1.22 Go right (southeast) on the blue-blazed trail.

2.0 Arrive at the overlook for Lower Whitewater Falls (N35°00.846'/W82°59.401'). Backtrack to trailhead.

4.0 Arrive at trailhead.

85 Oconee Bells Nature Trail

Music to your ears! Although this waterfall is only 5 feet tall, the creek is lively at this location and the little drop that forms the falls is quite soothing: a melody with such perfect pitch, only Mother Nature could create it.

Height: 5 feet
Beauty rating: Fair
Distance: 0.96 mile
Difficulty: Easy to moderate
Surface: Hard-packed dirt
Hiking time: 20 minutes
Other trail users: None
Blazes: White
County: Oconee

Land status: Devils Fork State Park
Contacts: (864) 944-2639; www.southcarolina parks.com/devilsfork
FYI: Fee required; late spring to mid-fall 7 a.m.–9 p.m.; late fall to mid-spring 7 a.m.–6 p.m.
Maps: *DeLorme: South Carolina Atlas & Gazetteer:* Page 16 F4

Finding the trailhead: *From the junction of SC 11 and SC 130 near Salem,* drive east on SC 11 for 1.6 miles. Turn left onto Jocassee Lake Road. Travel 3.5 miles, following signs to the ranger station. Turn right onto Holcombe Circle. Drive 0.1 mile to the parking lot at the end of the road. *From the junction of SC 11 and SC 133 near Keowee-Toxaway State Park,* drive west on SC 11 for 4.5 miles. Turn right onto Jocassee Lake Road. Follow directions above. The trailhead is at the northeast corner of the parking lot. **GPS:** N34°57.126'/W82°56.708'

The Hike

Hike down the steps and you almost immediately come to a fork where the large loop begins. Go right following the footpath southeast into the forest. Interpretive signs educate you on such natural wonders as the chestnut oak, hickory, sassafras, and a variety of ferns. You'll cross a footbridge, and then a long boardwalk helps protect the local ecology from passersby. As you follow a tiny creek downstream, a second foot-bridge soon follows the first before the trail climbs to a spur. The path is white-blazed, but in reality they are not needed to stay on track. At 0.3 mile you'll pass a lovely little waterslide-style waterfall that makes a freefall at the very bottom. Although it's only about 5 feet tall in total, it's quite pretty. As you continue hiking you'll make two more footbridge crossings before reaching the second small waterfall where two slender creeks converge. This rockslide waterfall is about the same height as the first, but twice as long. In the world of waterfalls, these two are quite small, but the park and the trail are so fantastic I felt they were worth including.

This tiny waterfall is found along the Oconee Bells Nature Trail.

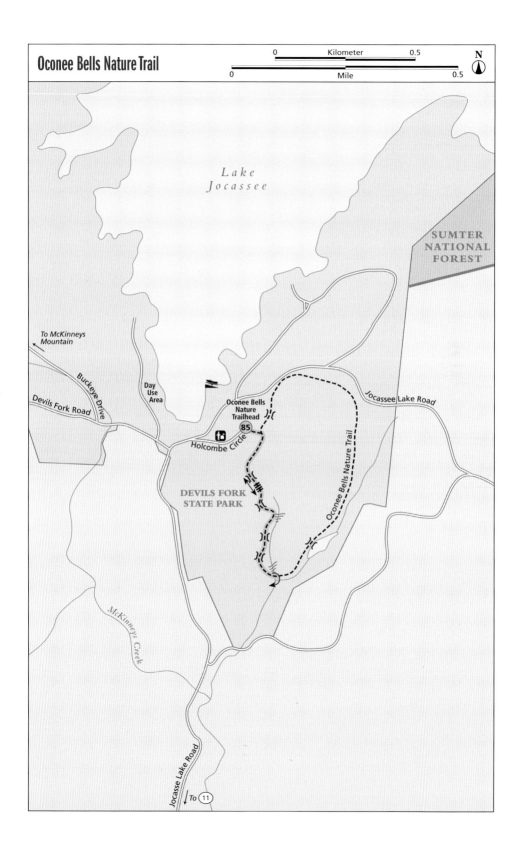

Oconee Bells Nature Trail

0   Kilometer   0.5

0   Mile   0.5

N

Lake Jocassee

SUMTER NATIONAL FOREST

To McKinneys Mountain

Buckeye Drive

Day Use Area

Devils Fork Road

Oconee Bells Nature Trailhead

85

Holcombe Circle

Jocassee Lake Road

Oconee Bells Nature Trail

DEVILS FORK STATE PARK

McKinneys Creek

Jocasse Lake Road

To 11

Devils Fork State Park offers extraordinary access to Lake Jocassee.

The forest that harbors this hike has a vast variety of plant life, and includes the rare plant species for which the trail was named, the Oconee bells. Please stay on the path to help protect these beautiful blossoms, which bloom in late spring. Devils Fork State Park is gorgeous. It sits along the southern shore of Lake Jocassee, which in and of itself makes this trail worth the visit. The lake is surrounded by mountains offering some of the most stunning views in the region. To make the most of Lake Jocassee the park has a busy boat ramp, kayak and paddleboard rentals, and a pristine sandy beach. To add to the list, they also have a campground and cabin rentals so you can stay awhile and take all of the beauty in.

Miles and Directions

0.0 Hike down the steps and come to a fork. Go right (southeast).

0.15 Cross a footbridge and then a long boardwalk next to the creek.

0.22 Cross a footbridge.

0.3 Hike past the first small waterfall (N34°56.951'/W82°56.676').

0.35 Cross a footbridge.

0.41 Cross a footbridge.

0.48 Arrive at the second falls (N34°56.848'/W82°56.663'). Backtrack to trailhead. (***Option:*** Complete the loop adding 0.92 mile to the hike.)

0.96 Arrive at trailhead.

86 Long Shoals

Rejuvenating! Although this is often overpopulated, you can't help but be impressed by the beauty of this long natural rockslide. Take a turn sliding down the rock yourself, and you're sure to be rejuvenated by the clear, crisp, chilly water when you make a splash at the base.

Height: 40 feet
Beauty rating: Very good
Distance: 0.2 mile
Difficulty: Easy
Surface: Wooden staircase, hard-packed dirt, rock face of the shoal
Hiking time: 10 minutes
Other trail users: None
Blazes: Blue

County: Pickens
Land status: Long Shoals Wayside Park within Poe Creek State Forest
Contacts: (864) 944-1104; www.visitpickenscounty.com/vendor/88/long-shoals-wayside-park/
FYI: 6 a.m.–10 p.m.; no camping, no alcohol
Maps: *DeLorme: South Carolina Atlas & Gazetteer:* Page 17 F6

Finding the trailhead: *From the junction of SC 11 and US 178 near Sunset,* drive south on SC 11 for 6.3 miles. Turn left into Long Shoals Wayside Park. Park in the upper lot. *From the junction of SC 11 and SC 133 near Keowee-Toxaway State Park,* drive north on SC 11 for 2.2 miles. Turn right into Long Shoals Wayside Park. **GPS:** N34°56.919'/W82°51.079'

The Hike

Holy cow this is gorgeous! The name says it all. A beautiful long shoal with a long, shallow sliding rock stands as the center of attention at this wonderful little "wayside" park. Locals flock to this popular swimming hole in summertime, and when you see it in person you'll understand why. Little Eastatoe Creek goes rushing by over smooth stone with a multitude of tan hues swirled within the rock. It's absolutely perfect. This brief hike begins by heading steeply down a wooden staircase. A narrow, blue-blazed path continues a steep trajectory toward the creek. In less than 0.1 mile, you're standing at the brink of Long Shoals. The falls are surrounded by large flat rocks that are easy to walk on, and there's no plummet or plunge at the brink. Looking upstream, massive boulders are propped up on the far side of the waterway, and a bed of smooth, sleek rock forms the creek itself. The rock is tan, beige, bronze, and brown, and the clear water running over it accentuates the rich tones of the stone. Glancing downstream, you'll see kids sliding down the rock, and hurrying back to the brink to do it all over again. The water at the base is deep enough for the whole family to take a swim. Downstream from the base, a pathway of rocks cuts directly across the creek. This adds to your options, giving you a place to sit out in the middle of the cool mountain water. This rudimentary rock walkway doubles as a good place to fish

Long Shoals

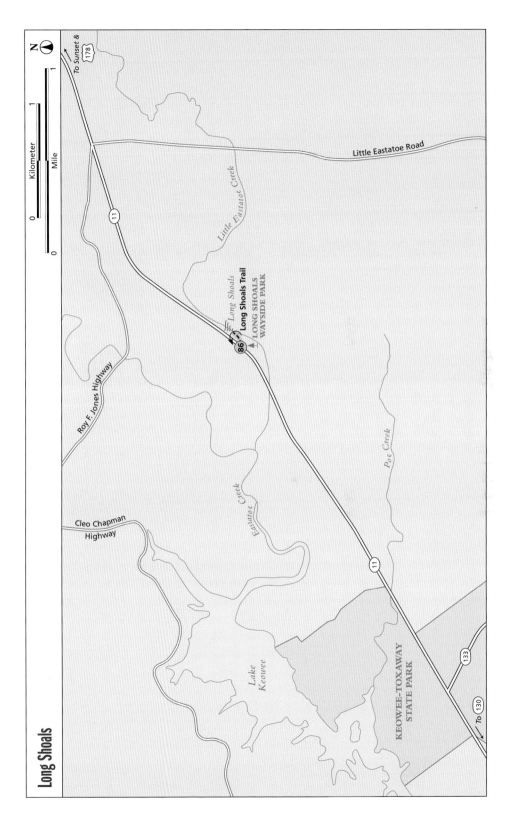

Large flat rocks line the banks of Long Shoals.

from as well, but you must have a state fishing license to do so. From the brink, you can walk up- or downstream on the large flat stone lining the banks. It's a fantastic place to explore, and an ideal place to lay a blanket out to sit a spell. The park has a picnic area between the upper and lower parking lots, but when you reach the creek, you won't want to leave its side. Please be respectful and bring a trash bag if you do picnic. It would be a shame to litter this fabulous little piece of paradise. And judging by the number of "pack it in, pack it out" signs at the trailhead, littering is clearly a problem here.

As the inviting waterway rushes by, you may find it hard to resist its allure. This is easily one of the best sliding rocks in the South. Laughter fills the air, and the sound of the water steadily coursing by beckons you back in to do it again. With Lake Jocassee to the west, the mountains to the north, and Greenville sitting to the south, this one has a perfect location for all your traveling needs.

Miles and Directions

0.0 Hike east down the steps.

0.1 Arrive at Long Shoals (N34°56.921'/W82°51.035'). Backtrack to trailhead.

0.2 Arrive at trailhead.

87 Twin Falls

Empowering! Twin Falls has so much to offer—from power and might to character and diversity—it easily lands on the Author's Favorites list. I highly recommend that you take the trip and embrace all the wonderful things this short hike has to offer.

Height: 100 feet
Beauty rating: Excellent
Distance: 0.6 mile
Difficulty: Easy
Surface: Wide dirt path
Hiking time: 20 minutes
Blazes: None
Other trail users: None

County: Pickens
Land status: Felburn Foundation nature preserve
Contacts: None
FYI: Dawn to dusk
Maps: *DeLorme: South Carolina Atlas & Gazetteer:* Page 17 E6; *DeLorme: Georgia Atlas & Gazetteer:* Page 17 A8

Finding the trailhead: *From the junction of US 178 and the North Carolina–South Carolina state line,* drive south on US 178 for 7.4 miles. Turn right onto Cleo Chapman Highway (SC 100). Drive 1.9 miles to a T. Go right onto Eastatoe Community Road. Drive 0.9 mile. Turn right onto Water Falls Road, which soon becomes gravel. Travel 0.4 mile to the gate at the end. *From the junction of US 178 and SC 11,* drive north on US 178 for 3.2 miles. Turn left onto Cleo Chapman Highway (SC 100). Follow directions above. The trailhead is at the northeast end of the parking area. **GPS:** N35°00.588'/W82°49.277'

The Hike

The hike begins by going around the gate and follows a wide roadlike trail generally northeast almost the entire way. As you hike upstream, bypass any side paths leading to the creek. Along the way you'll view several lovely cascades, and a small water wheel adds to the entertainment. From the water wheel the trail narrows and begins a slow ascent to an observation deck near the base of Twin Falls. The falls are spectacular! A pair of magnificent waterfalls plummet down, side by side, converging at the base to form one fabulous creek. Large flat rocks surround the base of the falls, tempting people to explore the area. I urge you to stay on the trail and on the observation deck! During mid-2020 there was a tragic waterfall death that happened here at Twin Falls. A young woman slipped and fell at the falls, leading to her death. I cannot stress enough the caution we all must take. Whether you're 22 or 72, your footing is no match for Mother Nature. The stones are slick and dangerous around this, and every

Twin Falls is one of South Carolina's finest falls.

Twin Falls

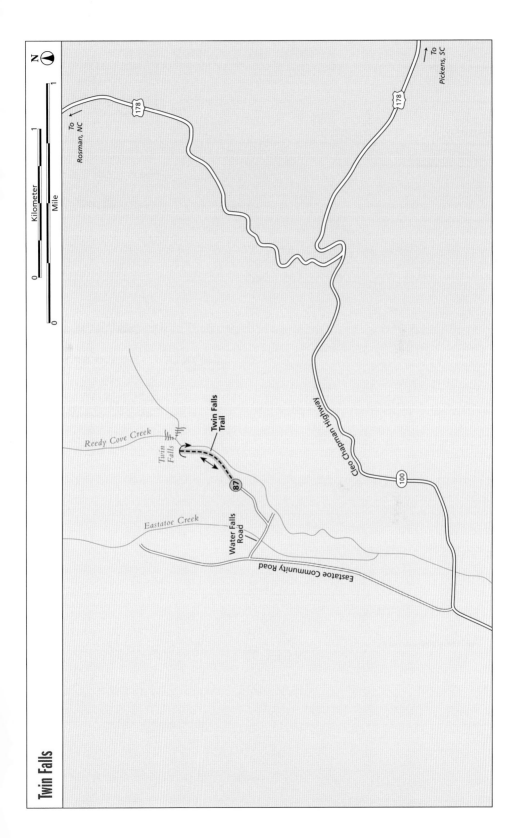

Billy goat is a term used to describe a male goat.

waterfall. PLEASE USE CAUTION and stay on the trail! For your own safety, and to protect the environment around you.

Located within the Felburn Foundation's nature preserve, Twin Falls has several aliases: Rock Falls, Reedy Cove Falls, and Eastatoe Falls, just to name a few.

Eastatoe is the Cherokee word for the Carolina parakeet (*Conuropsis carolinensis*). There was even an Eastatoe tribe known as the "Green Bird People." This parakeet once flourished in the Southeast, and was the only parrot species native to mainland North America. Its range covered as far north as the Ohio Valley and extended south to the Gulf of Mexico. The bird has been extinct since 1918, when the last one, named Incas, died in captivity at the Cincinnati Zoo.

Miles and Directions

0.0 Hike northeast on the wide path.

0.3 Arrive at Twin Falls (N35°00.789'/W82°49.115'). Backtrack to trailhead.

0.6 Arrive at trailhead.

88 Table Rock Lake Spillway

The splendid spillway at Table Rock State Park offers a lovely little bonus waterfall before you delve deeper into the park's trail system. The falls sit at the south end of Pinnacle Lake and are formed by a man-made wall of rock that drops from one shallow ledge to the next.

Height: 20 feet
Beauty rating: Fair
Distance: 0.2 mile
Difficulty: Easy to moderate
Surface: Hard-packed dirt
Hiking time: 10 minutes
Other trail users: None
Blazes: None
County: Pickens

Land status: Table Rock State Park
Contacts: (864) 878-9813; www.southcarolina parks.com/tablerock
FYI: Fee required; Sun–Thurs 7 a.m.–7 p.m., Fri–Sat 7 a.m.–9 p.m.; during Daylight Savings Time Sun–Thurs 7 a.m.–9 p.m., Fri–Sat 7 a.m.–10 p.m.
Maps: *DeLorme: Georgia Atlas & Gazetteer:* Page 17 E7

Finding the trailhead: *From the junction of SC 11 and SC 178 near Sunset,* drive east on SC 11 for 4.3 miles. Turn left onto Table Rock State Park Road at the East Gate of the park. Drive 0.3 mile to a small parking area on the left. *From the junction of SC 11 and SC 8 south,* drive west on SC 11 for 5.8 miles. Turn right onto Table Rock State Park Road at the East Gate of the park. Follow directions above. The trailhead is at the southwest end of the parking area. **GPS:** N35°01.591'/W82°41.801'

The Hike

This makes a nice little side trip as you travel through Table Rock State Park. Pinnacle Lake flows down over a spillway forming a lovely little waterfall. The water drops over a tall and narrow wall of stone as Carrick Creek continues through the south end of the park. You can view the spillway from the parking lot, but you'll get a better appreciation by taking a quick jaunt down to the base. A short, steep, rooty path leads down to the Lakeside Trail at the base of the Pinnacle Lake Spillway. Although the beauty rating of this man-made waterfall is fair, the scenery around it and the state park itself are excellent. The road beyond the spillway leads past the historic park lodge and gives you spectacular views

This spectacular view is obtained along the Lakeside Trail.

Table Rock Lake Spillway; Carrick Creek, Upper Carrick Creek, Spring Bluff, Mill Creek, and Green Creek Falls

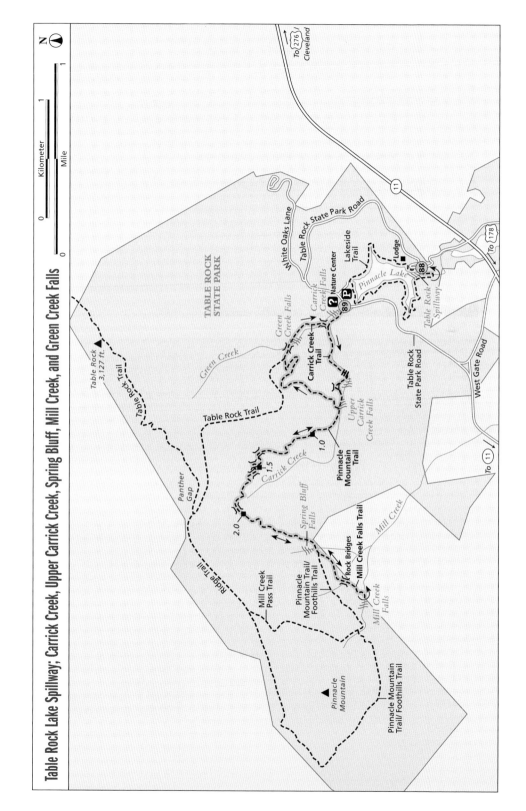

A quick little side trail leads to this spillway at the south end of Pinnacle Lake.

of Table Rock Mountain. While you're here in the park, I highly recommend that you hike the Carrick Creek Trail as well (Hike 89).

Miles and Directions

0.0 Hike southwest downhill toward the falls.

0.1 Arrive at Table Rock Lake Spillway (N35°01.575'/W82°41.837'). Backtrack to trailhead.

0.2 Arrive at trailhead.

89 Carrick Creek, Upper Carrick Creek, Spring Bluff, Mill Creek, and Green Creek Falls

Abstract! From easy to strenuous, short to long, clean to cluttered, this hike has it all. You can keep it simple and see Carrick Creek Falls, enjoy a moderate hike by looping around to Green Creek Falls, or challenge yourself by hiking up to Mill Creek Falls. The options are abundant and Table Rock Park is a real treat all the way around.

See map on p. 258.

Height: Carrick Creek: 15 feet; Upper Carrick Creek: 50 feet; Spring Bluff: 20 feet; Mill Creek: 25 feet; Green Creek Falls: 100+ feet

Beauty rating: Carrick Creek: very good; Upper Carrick Creek: good; Spring Bluff: fair; Mill Creek: fair; Green Creek Falls: good

Distance: 6.25-mile round-trip; shorter variations are possible, including a 0.1-mile hike to Carrick Creek Falls

Difficulty: Carrick Creek: easy; Mill Creek: strenuous; Upper Carrick Creek, Spring Bluff, Green Creek: moderate

Surface: Boardwalk, sidewalk, wide clay path, hard-packed dirt

Hiking time: 4 hours

Other trail users: None

Blazes: Green, white, yellow, pink

County: Pickens

Land status: Table Rock State Park

Contacts: (864) 878-9813; www.southcarolina parks.com/tablerock

FYI: Fee required; Sun–Thurs 7 a.m.–7 p.m., Fri–Sat 7 a.m.–9 p.m.; during Daylight Savings Time, Sun–Thurs 7 a.m.–9 p.m., Fri–Sat 7 a.m.–10 p.m.

Maps: *DeLorme: Georgia Atlas & Gazetteer:* Page 17 E7

Finding the trailhead: *From the junction of SC 11 and SC 178 near Sunset,* drive east on SC 11 for 4.3 miles. Turn left onto Table Rock State Park Road at the East Gate of the park. Drive 1.8 miles to the parking area on the left. *From the junction of SC 11 and SC 8 south,* drive west on SC 11 for 5.8 miles. Turn right onto Table Rock State Park Road at the East Gate of the park. Follow directions above. The trailhead is across the street at the nature center. **GPS:** N35°01.938'/ W82°42.035'

The Hike

A large trail map and hiker registration kiosk sits at the trailhead just outside of the nature center. You must register here before hiking. Follow the boardwalk and sidewalk northwest and you quickly arrive at Carrick Creek Falls. A well-built observation deck has benches built in giving parents a perfect place to perch on the platform while the kids splash around in the shallow water at the base of the falls. When you've had your fill, continue hiking northwest on the path. You'll quickly cross a footbridge and come to a fork. This is where the loop of the Carrick Creek Trail begins. Right

You'll hike past this pretty splash zone on the way to Mill Creek Falls.

leads northeast toward Green Creek Falls, left leads northwest to Upper Carrick Creek and Mill Creek Falls. Go left following the green, white, and yellow blazes. This part of the loop follows Carrick Creek upstream as it cascades down the mountain. The water puts on quite a show as it drops, swoops, and flows through chutes.

In less than a half-mile you're crossing a boardwalk near a super long, smooth, and silky rockslide. As the trail climbs steeper, the splendid creek keeps you distracted. At 0.65 mile you'll hike past Upper Carrick Creek Falls. This rockslide is longer than it is tall, and the water gleams as it passes over the beautiful golden brown rock. Continue hiking until you reach a T at 0.75 mile. Left (west) is the yellow-blazed Pinnacle Mountain Trail, which takes you on a long strenuous hike to Mill Creek Falls. Right is where the loop continues east leading past Green Creek Falls. If you're not up for a challenge, skip Mill Creek Falls and go right here. To see Mill Creek Falls, go left.

The trail makes a steady ascent and moves away from the creek. As you look around the forest, you can plainly see the impressive topography. Large boulders stand out from the scenery, some with trees growing out of them. Mile markers help keep track of your progress as you continue to climb steadily. Although you'll cross several footbridges, none are over water. It's not until you've gone nearly a mile from the T that you rock-hop your first trickle of clear mountain water. There's not a lot of shade, so make sure you bring lots of water, and a few snacks to keep you going. The trail climbs over 1,000 feet from the trailhead to the falls. Although it's an arduous trek, it's really quite peaceful. Wild berries, ferns, and flowers line the path, while giant pileated woodpeckers soar past. Their bright red heads and white-tipped wings help you spot these magnificent birds when in flight. At 2.4 miles the trail crosses a creek in front of a tall waterfall known as Spring Bluff Falls. The water splashes down directly onto the trail as you cross, and although there's not a lot of flow, it's a welcome sight. Not far from here another shower of water splashes down from giant cliffs that stand proudly beside the trail. This is another refreshing treat, and depending on the season you may want to lean your head under it to cool off. Just past the 2.5-mile marker you'll come to a fork where the Mill Creek Falls trail leads straight ahead (south) and the Pinnacle Mountain Trail heads up and to the right (north). Go straight, following pink blazes. This rocky overgrown footpath is clearly the path less traveled. Use caution as you cross back-to-back stone footbridges. Just below the bridges water flows over a rock ledge and plunges down the side of the mountain in a sheer drop. You'll get a good view of this on your way back to the trailhead. The rugged path ends at Mill Creek Falls, which is complete chaos. The area around the falls is littered with so much deadfall and overgrowth it's hard to appreciate the beauty. Of all the waterfalls on this hike, this is the hardest to reach, and the least scenic. Unless you're an avid hiker, I would skip this one.

Backtrack to the T at 0.75 mile and go left to finish the loop of the Carrick Creek Tail. The wide clay path moves away from Carrick Creek and climbs on a fairly steep grade. You'll make two rock-hop crossings before coming to another fork. Left (north) is the red-blazed Table Rock Trail. Go right (southeast) on the green-blazed

You'll get stunning views of Table Rock Mountain as you drive along SC 11.

Carrick Creek Trail. You quickly come to a footbridge over the brink of Green Creek Falls. The trail follows the creek downstream alongside the falls where the water cleanly drops from one smooth rock ledge to the next. Unfortunately, there's a bit of brush separating you from the creek, so this half of the loop is less intimate with the creek than the first. A footbridge crosses at the base of this long, steady waterfall, and the loop ends by leading you through a shaded tunnel of mountain laurel. Go left at the T passing Carrick Creek Falls once more before ending at the trailhead.

Table Rock State Park is at the foot of its namesake, and you're in for a fantastic treat when you visit. Not only do you get stunning views of Table Rock Mountain, the park offers an intricate trail system for all levels. You can wade into the water at Carrick Creek Falls, loop around Table Rock Lake, or hike all the way to the top of Pinnacle Mountain, which happens to be the highest mountain located entirely in the state of South Carolina. Other options include cabins, camping, swimming, or paddling. As a bonus waterfall, stop to get a roadside view of the Table Rock Lake Spillway (Hike 88).

Miles and Directions

0.0 Hike northwest on the man-made trail.

0.05 Arrive at Carrick Creek Falls (N35°01.962'/W82°42.072'). Continue hiking northwest.

0.13 Cross a footbridge and come to a fork. Right leads northeast to Green Creek Falls. Go left (northwest) to see Upper Carrick Creek and Mill Creek Falls.

0.27 Rock-hop Carrick Creek.

0.32 Rock-hop the creek.

0.46 Follow the boardwalk past a long rockslide.

0.55 Pass another small waterfall.

0.57 Cross back-to-back footbridges.

0.65 Hike past Upper Carrick Creek Falls (N35°01.943' W82°42.521').

0.75 Come to a T. Go left (west) on the Pinnacle Mountain Trail to see Spring Bluff and Mill Creek Falls.

1.35 Cross a trio of consecutive footbridges.

1.48 Cross a footbridge.

1.51 Cross a footbridge.

1.7 Rock-hop a tributary.

1.85 Cross a footbridge.

1.93 Rock-hop a tributary.

2.15 Rock-hop a trickle of water.

2.4 Cross the creek in front of Spring Bluff Falls (N35°02.135'/W82°43.280').

2.51 Come to a fork. Go left (south) on the pink-blazed Mill Creek Falls trail.

2.7 Cross back-to-back stone footbridges.

2.8 Rock-hop back-to-back tributaries.

2.9 Arrive at Mill Creek Falls (N35°01.843'/W82°43.596'). Backtrack to the T mentioned at 0.75 mile.

5.05 Arrive back at the T. Go left (east) to continue the loop of the Carrick Creek Trail.

5.2 Rock-hop a tributary.

5.37 Rock-hop a tributary.

5.75 Come to a fork. Go right (southeast) following the green blazes.

5.8 Cross a footbridge over the brink.

5.82 Hike downstream alongside Green Creek Falls (N35°02.180'/W82°42.220').

6.0 Cross a footbridge at the base of the falls.

6.12 Come to a T where the loop began. Go left (southeast) toward the trailhead.

6.25 Arrive at trailhead.

90 Raven Cliff Falls

Intense! Raven Cliff Falls flows with power, grace, and great intensity. All 420 feet of it! This is the tallest waterfall in South Carolina, and certainly one of the tallest waterfalls in the East in general.

Height: 420 feet
Beauty rating: Excellent
Distance: 4.4 miles
Difficulty: Moderate
Surface: Wide gravel path, hard-packed dirt
Hiking time: 2 hours, 30 minutes
Other trail users: None
Blazes: Red

County: Greenville
Land status: Caesars Head State Park
Contacts: (864) 836-6115; www.southcarolina parks.com
FYI: Fee required; pay at the ranger station or with exact change at the trailhead
Maps: *DeLorme: South Carolina Atlas & Gazetteer:* Page 17 D8

Finding the trailhead: *From the junction of US 276 and SC 11,* drive north on US 276 for 8.6 miles to a parking area on the right. *From the junction of US 276 and the North Carolina–South Carolina State Line,* drive south on US 276 for 2.1 miles to a parking area on the left. (If you miss the turn, the parking area is 1.0 mile north of the Caesars Head State Park Visitor Center.) The trailhead is located on the south/west side of US 276 (the opposite side from where you parked). **GPS:** N35°06.931/W82°38.303

The Hike

The Raven Cliff Falls Trail takes you downhill on a wide gravel path and into the forest. At the bottom of the hill, go right at the fork following the red blazes. You'll cross a tiny creek, and the well-maintained path then meanders up and down through the forest. Rhododendron and mountain laurel offer cool shade as you head deeper into the Mountain Bridge Wilderness. Stay with the red blazes and at 1.6 miles you come to a fork. Right (northwest) is the blue-blazed Gum Gap Trail. Go left continuing to follow the red-blazed Raven Cliff Falls Trail south. A half a mile farther another fork awaits where the Dismal Trail leads left (south). Go right here, following the wider Raven Cliff Falls Trail southwest as it begins to climb. Within a tenth of a mile, you quickly come to an observation deck overlooking Raven Cliff Falls in the distance. Bring binoculars or a good zoom lens to get the best view of this one, which sits far across the valley below.

Raven Cliff Falls is located within Caesars Head State Park in the Mountain Bridge Wilderness Area. Although it's popular for the falls, the park is more specifically

Raven Cliff Falls makes an impressive plunge, covering a full 420 feet from top to bottom.

known, and named, for Caesars Head, a rocky outcrop that is said to resemble the head of Caesar. An amazing overlook next to the park's visitor center offers dramatic views of the surrounding wilderness area. The visitor center is located a mile south of the Raven Cliff trailhead on US 276. Another unique feature within the park is the Devil's Kitchen, a narrow passageway leading down several slender stairways to give you a view from below the Caesars Head overlook.

While you're in the area, take a quick side trip down to Bald Rock. It too offers exceptional long-range views. This roadside, graffiti-covered bald rock sits just south of Caesars Head State Park. From here you'll enjoy splendid scenery and a wonderful view of Table Rock and the Table Rock Reservoir off in the distance.

Raven Cliff Falls: Cliff, Firewater, and Rock Cliff Falls

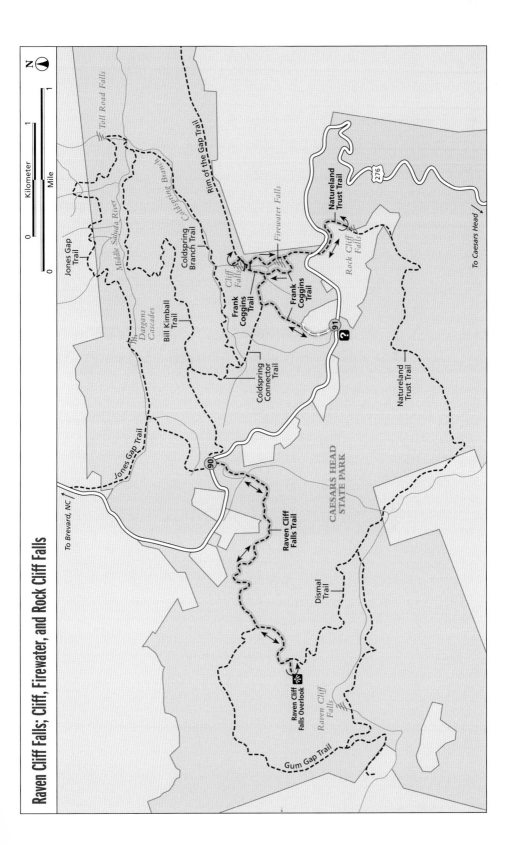

N

Kilometer

Mile

Jones Gap Trail

Toll Road Falls

Middle Saluda River

Coldspring Branch

Dargans Cascades

Bill Kimball Trail

Coldspring Branch Trail

Rim of the Gap Trail

Cliff Falls

Firewater Falls

Frank Coggins Trail

Frank Coggins Trail

Coldspring Connector Trail

Natureland Trust Trail

Rock Cliff Falls

276

To Caesars Head

91

Jones Gap Trail

To Brevard, NC

90

Raven Cliff Falls Trail

Natureland Trust Trail

CAESARS HEAD STATE PARK

Dismal Trail

Raven Cliff Falls Overlook

Raven Cliff Falls

Gum Gap Trail

Can you see the forest through the trees?

Miles and Directions

0.0 Hike south on the wide gravel path.

0.3 At the bottom of the hill go right at the fork, following the red-blazed trail southwest. Cross a tiny stream.

1.6 Come to a fork. The blue-blazed Gum Gap Trail heads right (northwest). Go left on the red-blazed Raven Cliff Falls Trail.

2.1 Come to another fork. The Dismal Trail leads left (south). Go right (southwest) on the Raven Cliff Falls Trail.

2.2 Arrive at an observation deck for Raven Cliff Falls (N35°06.554/W82°39.482). Back-track to trailhead.

4.4 Arrive at trailhead.

91 Cliff, Firewater, and Rock Cliff Falls

Courageous! Water clings courageously to the rock as it swiftly flows over all three of these waterfalls. With the force of gravity's pull beckoning it to the ground, the constant flow of water smooths the stone, shaping it like only Mother Nature can.

See map on p. 267.
Height: Cliff: 50 feet; Firewater: 20 feet; Rock Cliff: 40 feet
Beauty rating: Good for all
Distance: 3.0 miles
Difficulty: Strenuous
Surface: Gravel road, hard-packed dirt
Hiking time: 1 hour, 45 minutes
Other trail users: None
Blazes: Purple, yellow, pink

County: Greenville
Land status: Caesars Head State Park
Contacts: (864) 836-6115; www.southcarolina parks.com
FYI: Fee required; pay at the ranger station or with exact change at the trailhead; trail closes at 5 p.m. sharp.
Maps: *DeLorme: South Carolina Atlas & Gazetteer:* Page 17 D8

Finding the trailhead: *From the junction of US 276 and SC 11,* drive north on US 276 for 7.6 miles to the Caesars Head State Park Visitor Center. *From the junction of US 276 and the North Carolina–South Carolina State Line,* drive south on US 276 for 3.1 miles to the Caesars Head State Park Visitor Center. Park at the south end of the parking lot. The trailhead is across the street on the east side of US 276. **GPS:** N35°06.371'/W82°37.547'

The Hike

Be advised, this trail closes at 5 p.m. You must be off the trail and back to your car before closing time or they may end up locking your vehicle inside the gate. Begin by following the Frank Coggins Trail north and down into the forest on a wide, gravel road. In less than 0.2 mile, you come to a fork where the gravel road goes up to the right (east) and a trail leads left (northeast) into the forest. Go left, following the purple-blazed footpath on a steady descent. Just under the half-mile mark you come to another fork. Left (west) is the blue-blazed Coldspring Connector Trail. Go right (east), staying on the Frank Coggins Trail. The forks are well marked, but there's no substitute for having a map. I suggest buying the Mountain Bridge Wilderness trail map sold in the visitor center. It's a fantastic map, and definitely worth having here. When you reach the next fork at 0.65 mile, right leads south over a log bridge. Go straight (east) and within a tenth of a mile you're crossing a footbridge over the brink of Cliff Falls. Immediately after crossing this footbridge you come to a T. Left is the yellow-blazed Rim of the Gap Trail, and right continues the lollipop loop portion of the Frank Coggins Trail. Go left (north) for now and you almost immediately see a side trail on the left (west) that scrambles down to the base of Cliff Falls. The water rolls down over staggered stone steps forming this tall and narrow waterfall. Backtrack to the T on the Rim of the Gap Trail and go straight as you continue around the lollipop loop portion of the Frank Coggins Trail. The shaded path rises and falls as you meander through the forest. Although you are following a mere trickle of a stream, it's enough to cool the air and bring the common creekside flora of rhododendron and mountain laurel. One mile into the hike you'll pass Firewater Falls, which is basically a large boulder with a stream of water trickling down. It looks like Mother Nature's shower bath. Beyond the falls you soon come to another T where the Natureland Trust Trail goes left (east) and the Frank Coggins Trail goes right (west). Go left, following pink blazes. You'll hike for nearly 0.2 mile before carefully crossing US 276. On the other side the footpath heads into the forest but stays fairly close to the road leading you southeast. At 1.4 miles into the hike you will cross a private driveway. Please respect that this is private property. As the trail heads back into the forest, it begins to make a fairly steep descent. At 1.6 miles you reach Rock Cliff Falls. Although the flow is slight, there's something about this falls that draws you in. A perfect groove is carved into the center of the stone where the water gently pours down. It's unique and completely mesmerizing. When you snap out of the spell, backtrack to the T that you reached at 1.07 miles and go left on the Frank Coggins Trail. Within 0.2 mile you're back at the fork where the loop began at 0.65 mile. Backtrack to the trailhead from here.

Kudos must go out to Caesars Head State Park. They do such a wonderful job as the guardians and keepers of the Mountain Bridge Wilderness. Because of their efforts, this trail system is well marked, and well blazed. While you're here, a visit to the Caesars Head overlook is an absolute must. The overlook is accessed from the parking lot just 200 feet north of the visitor center. The long-range views are spectacular!

Miles and Directions

0.0   Follow the wide gravel road north into the forest.

0.17 Come to a fork. Go left (northeast) on the purple-blazed trail.

0.45 Come to a fork. Left is the Coldspring Connector Trail. Go right (east) following the Frank Coggins Trail.

0.65 Come to a fork. Go straight (east).

0.75 Cross a footbridge over the brink of Cliff Falls.

0.76 Come to a T at the Rim of the Gap Trail. Go left.

0.77 Go left (west) on a side path and scramble steeply down to the base of Cliff Falls (N35°06.801'/W82°37.220'). Backtrack to the Rim of the Gap Trail and go right (south) back toward the fork.

0.8   Arrive back at the fork. Bypass the trail to the right where you came from. Go straight (south) returning to the Frank Coggins Trail.

1.0   Hike past Firewater Falls (N35°06.638'/W82°37.180').

1.07 Come to a T. Go left (east) on the Natureland Trust Trail.

1.25 Carefully cross US 276; the trail continues on the west side of the road.

1.4   Hike across a private driveway.

Cliff Falls clings to the sheer rock face.

1.6 Arrive at Rock Cliff Falls (N35°06.321'/W82°37.011'). Backtrack to the T at 1.07.

2.13 Reach the T. Go left (west) on the Frank Coggins Trail.

2.35 Come to the T where the Frank Coggins loop began (see 0.65). Go left (west); backtrack to the trailhead.

3.0 Arrive at trailhead.

92 Lower, Middle, and Upper Wildcat Branch Falls

Proud! With three waterfalls on a trail that covers a tad more than a mile, Wildcat Branch greets you with beaming pride and pure joy. The Lower and Middle Falls can be seen from the trailhead, so if a mile seems too long for your taste, don't fret. Two out of three ain't bad.

Height: Lower: 30 feet; Middle: 10 feet; Upper Wildcat Branch: 200 feet
Beauty rating: Lower: excellent; Middle: very good; Upper Wildcat Branch: fair
Distance: 1.02 miles
Difficulty: Easy to moderate
Surface: Hard-packed dirt
Hiking time: 30 minutes

Other trail users: None
Blazes: Yellow
County: Greenville
Land status: Mountain Bridge Wilderness
Contacts: (864) 836-6115; www.southcarolina parks.com/caesarshead/introduction.aspx
Maps: DeLorme: South Carolina Atlas & Gazetteer: Page 17 D9

Finding the trailhead: From the junction of US 276 and SC 11 south, drive south on SC 11/US 276 for 0.5 mile to the parking area on the left. From the junction of US 276 and SC 11 north, drive north on SC 11/US 276 for 4.9 miles to the parking area on the right. **GPS:** N35°04.427'/W82°35.813'

The Hike

Lower Falls literally sits right next to the trailhead. A beautiful, shallow pool at the base makes this a popular summertime destination for the locals. Stone steps quickly lead up the left side of the creek bringing you to the Middle Falls. This one has a smaller splash zone, but the water makes a freefall that you can stand under. Use caution if you allow Mother Nature to shower down on you as the rocks are super slippery. After crossing the creek in front of the Middle Falls, you'll hike past the remnants of an old chimney. Fifty years ago if you hiked this trail you would be passing by a splendid picnic shelter with a fireplace built into it at one end. With the creek flowing by, this was an ideal location for a family outing. Hike past the chimney and you'll immediately come to a fork at the creek where the loop portion of the hike begins and ends. Straight leads north across the creek, and right follows the creek upstream (east). While you can go either way, I am describing it here in a clockwise fashion. Go straight, rock–hop the creek, and begin to follow it upstream. The peaceful path is lined with rhododendron and mountain laurel, and best of all you're likely to have it to yourself. It's a lovely stroll through the forest with the birds softly singing in the background.

As you follow the shallow creek upstream, the farther you go, the more alive the creek becomes. When you reach a rocky creek crossing at 0.4 mile, the trail leads

Easy access and a shallow pool at the base make Lower Wildcat Branch Falls a fun stop for the family.

across the base of Upper Falls. A giant steep wall of stone forms the face of the falls. Although there's not a lot of flow here, there's enough to distinguish it as a waterfall. The base is filled with impressive boulders resting one on top of the other. If you choose to explore this area, use extreme caution!

To finish the loop, the trail leads back south to where it began. Along the way you'll rock-hop a tributary in front of another small waterfall. This one also makes a steep rockslide, but it's minute in comparison to Upper Falls. When the loop ends you'll happily backtrack past Middle and Lower Falls once more, before the hike ends at the trailhead where you began.

This area off of SC 11 really packs a punch and includes some serious heavy hitters in the bunch. You've got the grand slam of state parks with Devils Fork, Table Rock, Caesars Head, Lake Keowee-Toxaway, and Jones Gap to top it off. These spectacular parks offer plenty of hiking, waterfalls, amazing natural features, and tons of beautiful scenery for you to marvel at.

Miles and Directions

0.0   The trail begins to the left of Lower Wildcat Branch Falls (N35°04.433'/W82°35.810'). Hike upstream.

0.05 Arrive at Middle Wildcat Branch Falls (N35°04.452'/W82°35.816'). Rock-hop the creek and continue upstream.

0.1   Hike past the old chimney.

Lower, Middle, and Upper Wildcat Branch Falls

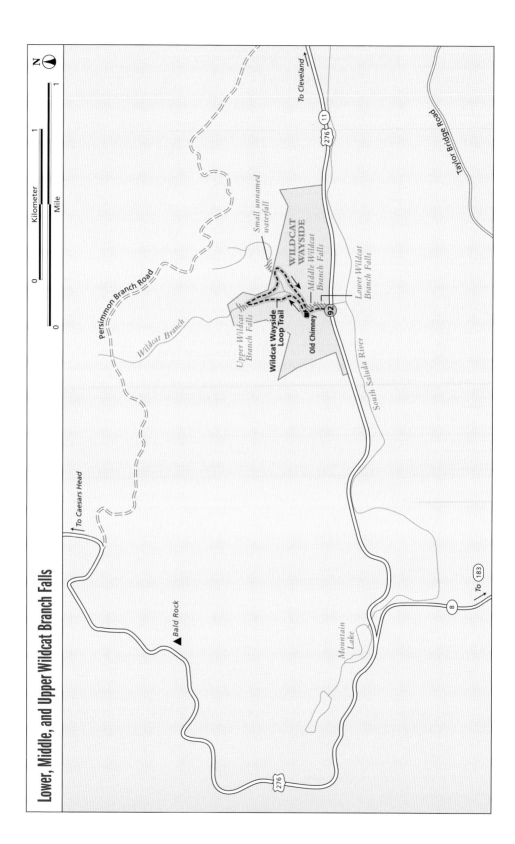

N

Kilometer
0   1

Mile
0   1

To Caesars Head

Bald Rock

Persimmon Branch Road

Wildcat Branch

Small unnamed waterfall

Upper Wildcat Branch Falls

Wildcat Wayside Loop Trail

WILDCAT WAYSIDE

Middle Wildcat Branch Falls

Old Chimney

Lower Wildcat Branch Falls

South Saluda River

Mountain Lake

To Cleveland

276
11

92

276

8

To 183

Taylor Bridge Road

A short uphill jaunt puts you right at the base of Middle Wildcat Branch Falls.

0.12 Come to a fork at the creek. Go straight (north) crossing the creek. Follow the trail upstream.

0.4 Arrive at Upper Wildcat Branch Falls (N35°04.731'/W82°35.786'). Cross the creek in front of the falls and follow the loop south.

0.6 Rock-hop a tributary in front of a small waterfall (N35°04.624'/W82°35.665').

0.9 Come to the fork where the loop began. Go left toward the trailhead.

1.02 Arrive at trailhead.

93 Falls off Jones Gap Trail

Energetic! Holy smokes this hike is heaven. Waterfall after waterfall greet you as you follow the marvelous Middle Saluda River upstream. The river is full of life, with rocks and rapids, cascades and crescendos keeping you enthralled over the full length of the hike. If the river wasn't entertaining enough, a pair of side trails offer two bonus waterfalls to boot.

Height: Rainbow: 100 feet; Jones Gap: 50 feet; Ben's Sluice: 25 feet; Toll Road: 25 feet; Dargan's Cascades: 25 feet
Beauty rating: Rainbow: excellent; Jones Gap: very good; Ben's Sluice: very good; Toll Road: good; Dargan's Cascades: very good
Distance: 11.4 miles; shorter options are available
Difficulty: Moderate
Surface: Wide rocky trail, hard-packed dirt
Hiking time: 7 hours

Other trail users: None
Blazes: Blue, red
County: Greenville
Land status: Jones Gap State Park
Contacts: (864) 836-3647; www.southcarolina parks.com/jonesgap
FYI: Fee required; 9 a.m.–9 p.m. during daylight savings time; 9 a.m.–6 p.m. the remainder of the year
Maps: *DeLorme: South Carolina Atlas & Gazetteer:* Page 17 C9

Finding the trailhead: *From the junction of US 276 and SC 11 east near Cleveland,* drive north on US 276 for 1.4 miles. Turn right onto River Falls Road. Travel 3.8 miles. Turn left onto Jones Gap Road. Drive 1.9 miles to the park at the end of the road. *From the junction of US 276 and SC 11 west,* near Caesars Head, drive south on US 276 for 3.4 miles. Turn left onto River Falls Road. Follow directions above. The trailhead is at the southwest end of the road near the large trail information kiosk. **GPS:** N35°07.518'/W82°34.450'

The Hike

Before I even begin to delve into this exceptional hike, there are a few important reminders that the rangers at Jones Gap State Park have asked me to share.

First off, the park requests that you check with a park ranger prior to hiking. Although trail information may be posted online, it's not always up to date. It's important to confirm with a ranger that there are no hazards or trail closures before you begin the hike. Next, this is a long hike into a rugged and remote section of the Mountain Bridge Wilderness Area. Before heading into the backcountry wilderness you must register at the kiosk near the trailhead.

If you visit all of the waterfalls along this hike, you'll be covering a lot of ground on nearly 12 miles of trails. Plan to start early in the morning and spend the entire day enjoying all that each waterfall has to offer. There are five of them in total, and each has a unique beauty all unto itself.

A strenuous hike leads to the rewarding and remarkable Rainbow Falls.

Follow the wide rocky "road" west into the forest. This portion of the Jones Gap Trail (JGT) is also part of the much longer Palmetto Trail, which is the longest hiking trail in South Carolina, spanning diagonally across the state over a full 500 miles.

A perfect sandy beach sits at the base of Dargan's Cascades.

The JGT follows the Middle Saluda River upstream nearly the entire way. The river is stunning and was the first state-designated scenic river in South Carolina. As you hike alongside it, it's easy to see why. This river is full of life, forming one cascade after the next with eager enthusiasm. Early on you'll hike past some primitive campsites, and you can imagine spending the night here with the sounds of nature and solitude all around you.

Many years ago this trail was actually a road known as "Solomon's Road," named for Solomon Jones, who cut the old toll road back in the mid-1800s. Just past the half-mile point you'll come to a fork. Left (southwest) is the continuation of the JGT. Right (west) is the Rainbow Falls trail. If you're not up for a strenuous uphill trek, stay on the JGT. Otherwise, head right following the red-blazed path toward Rainbow Falls. You'll cross three footbridges before the trail begins a steep ascent all the way to the falls. This portion of the hike is a strenuous trek leading over rugged rocks and roots and is a full-on butt burner. The reward is hard earned, but well worth the arduous journey. That being said, bring lots of water. You'll need it even in the cooler months. The trail leads past pretty cascades and impressive cliffs before ending at the grand finale of Rainbow Falls. This waterfall is spectacular. It makes a free-falling plunge from high above, and within the rock you'll see a kaleidoscope of color. Gold and red and brown and green all garnish the stone across the full spectrum. Without a doubt, this one was aptly named. Not only is the rocky face of the falls full of color, but when the light hits the water just right, the water offers a beautiful rainbow alongside the falls. Large rocks at the bottom of the drop give you plenty of places to sit and enjoy the magnificent view. Return to the JGT and continue following the blue blazes deeper into the wilderness.

The trail is easy to follow and leads you across a sturdy bridge over the river. Not far from this crossing you'll rock-hop a creek and immediately come to a second fork. Again, the right leads to a splendid waterfall, but this side trail is much easier than the last. A quick jaunt of less than 0.1 mile leads to the base of Jones Gap Falls. The top of the falls flows over rock ledges, while the bottom fans out over bright orange–colored rock with gold, brown, and tan hues blended into it. Gray swirls add to the amazing array. The stone is simply astonishing, and you could easily sit and stare at this one for a while. Large rocks give you a spot to sit and dangle your feet in the small but pleasant little pool at the base. After enjoying the falls, backtrack to the JGT and continue following the impressive river upstream.

You'll make one more rock hop before arriving at Ben's Sluice. This one is on the river itself, and is a lovely little waterfall with a sandy beach at the base. It's a perfect place for a picnic, with the river rapidly running by. When you're ready to move on, continue hiking upstream. The grandeur of this river is absolutely amazing. It's as though Mother Nature handpicked each boulder and placed it perfectly in the riverbed to form one extraordinary cascade after another.

It's easy to see how alive this river is when you look at the topography. From the trailhead to the turnaround point at Dargan's Cascades, the JGT makes a slow and steady ascent of over 1,000 feet of elevation. As gravity carries the water downstream, it brings with it a magnificence that is only found within the Mountain Bridge Wilderness.

Beyond Ben Sluice you'll rock-hop several tributaries before coming to another fork. Left (west) is the orange-blazed Coldspring Branch Trail, right (north) is the JGT. Go right, and within 0.1 mile you'll cross a footbridge over the base of Toll Road Falls. Giant boulders form the banks of the falls as it drops over deep ledges. The water is so clear and the breeze that it generates is delightful. As you continue hiking past the falls on the JGT, you'll rock-hop several tributaries over the next 2.0 miles. When you reach the point where the JGT heads right (east) around a switchback, you'll see a spur trail leading straight ahead (west). Follow this spur trail as it leads directly to the base of the final falls on this hike, Dargan's Cascades. The water rolls down a smooth ledge of stone, resembling a small sliding rock. A beautiful brownish gold swimming hole sits at the base, with a sandy beach joining it as the perfect accompaniment. From the switchback the JGT continues on to its western terminus along US 276, but there are no more waterfalls along this stretch of trail. For this reason, I recommend that you return to the trailhead after enjoying the tranquil serenity of Dargan's Cascades.

Miles and Directions

0.0 Hike west into the forest.

0.05 Bypass the Rim of the Gap Trail on the left (south).

Falls off Jones Gap Trail; Falls Creek Falls (Jones Gap State Park)

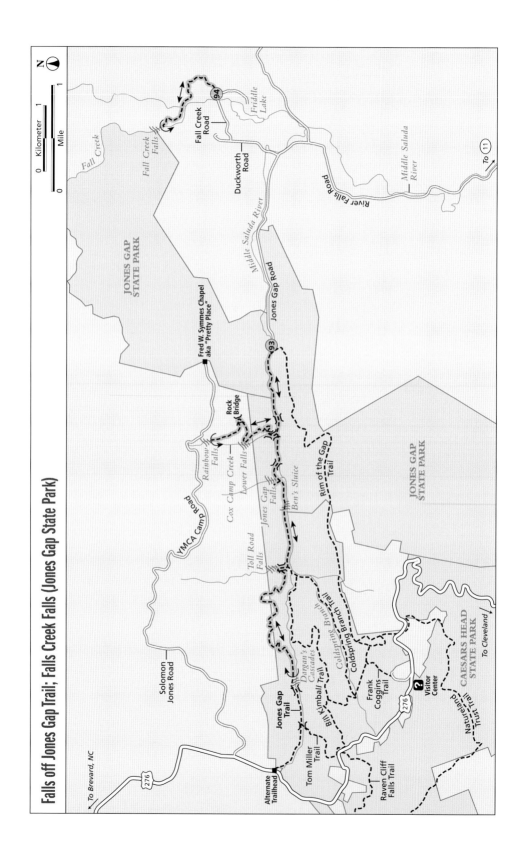

0.55 Come to a fork. Go right (west) on the Rainbow Falls trail. (***Option:*** Bypass Rainbow Falls and stay southwest on the JGT.)

0.62 Cross a footbridge.

0.77 Cross a footbridge; follow the red blazes.

0.85 Cross another footbridge.

1.2 Hike past a pretty sliding rock waterfall (N35°07.716'/W82°35.312').

1.6 Cross a stone bridge over a tributary.

1.65 Step over a small tributary alongside the cliffs.

1.8 Rock-hop a tributary.

2.1 Rock-hop the creek near the base of Rainbow Falls. Hike upstream.

2.15 Reach the base of Rainbow Falls (N35°08.004'/W82°35.280'). Backtrack to JGT.

3.7 Arrive back at JGT. Go right (southwest) deeper into the forest. (***Option:*** Backtrack to the trailhead.)

3.83 Rock-hop back-to-back tributaries.

4.25 Cross a footbridge over the river.

4.35 Rock-hop Jones Gap Creek and immediately come to a fork. Go right toward Jones Gap Falls.

4.4 Arrive at Jones Gap Falls (N35°07.490'/W82°35.632'). Backtrack to JGT.

4.45 Arrive back at JGT. Go right (southwest).

4.6 Rock-hop a tributary.

4.75 Arrive at Ben's Sluice (N35°07.372'/W82°35.926'). Continue hiking farther into the forest. (***Option:*** Backtrack to the trailhead.)

4.85 Rock-hop a tributary.

4.91 Rock-hop a tributary.

5.05 Rock-hop another tributary.

5.26 Hike across a tributary.

5.3 Come to a fork. Left (west) is the Coldspring Branch Connector Trail. Go right (north) staying on the JGT.

5.4 Cross a footbridge at the base of Toll Road Falls (N35°07.433'/W82°36.525'). Continue hiking on the JGT.

5.98 Rock-hop a tributary.

6.35 Rock-hop a tributary.

6.42 Rock-hop another tributary.

6.7 Rock-hop a tributary.

6.85 Rock-hop another tributary.

7.32 Follow the spur trail straight (west) toward the falls.

7.35 Arrive at Dargan's Cascades (N35°07.309'/W82°37.631'). Backtrack to the trailhead, staying on the JGT the entire way.

11.4 Arrive at trailhead.

94 Fall Creek Falls (Jones Gap State Park)

Good God, you're in for a treat! The hike is challenging, but worth every step. Luckily, that challenge is only 1.1 miles to reach one of the most impressive waterfalls in the state. It goes without saying: This is a favorite.

See map on p. 280.
Height: 125 feet
Beauty rating: Excellent
Distance: 2.2 miles
Difficulty: Very strenuous
Surface: Wide clay path
Hiking time: 2 hours
Other trail users: None
Blazes: Purple

County: Greenville
Land status: Jones Gap State Park
Contacts: (864) 836-3647; www.southcaro
linaparks.com/jonesgap
FYI: Fee required; 9 a.m.–9 p.m. during daylight savings time; 9 a.m.–6 p.m. the remainder
of the year. Register at the trailhead.
Maps: *DeLorme: South Carolina Atlas & Gazetteer:* Page 17 C9–C10

Finding the trailhead: *From the junction of US 276 and SC 11 east near Cleveland,* drive north on US 276 for 1.4 miles. Turn right onto River Falls Road. Travel 4.0 miles. Turn right onto Duckworth Road. Drive 0.4 mile. Turn right onto Fall Creek Road. Travel 0.4 mile to a small parking area on the left. *From the junction of US 276 and SC 11 west,* near Caesars Head, drive south on US 276 for 3.4 miles. Turn left onto River Falls Road. Follow directions above. The marked trailhead is at the northeast corner of the parking area. **GPS:** N35°07.953'/W82°31.939'

The Hike

This hike is not for the faint of heart. Although the Miles and Directions are fairly simple, the terrain is the hardest hike in this book. The first half follows a wide trail on a steep ascent until you rock-hop a creek. The second half is a challenging scramble. The wide clay path steeply climbs for a solid 0.3 mile before giving you a reprieve. There are no signs of water yet, but a variety of birdsongs fill the air. By a half-mile you finally hear the reassuring sound of water and appreciate the cool air that comes with it. You'll rock-hop a creek, and the trail climbs even steeper than before through a root-covered gully. Stay with the purple blazes as you climb steeply over roots and rocks. At 1.0 mile as you come around a bend the falls come into view, and what a welcome sight they are. You may even shout "hallelujah" after the strenuous climb it took to get here. Follow the rock scramble that leads down alongside the falls to the base. As you make this scramble you think, *Wow, this is beautiful.* But when you reach the base and look up, you realize how astonishing it really is. It's easily three times as big as what you can see from the scramble, and it is filled with character. It truly has exceptional beauty. Fortunately, this isn't a very long hike, and the falls are worth every step. This hike isn't for everyone, but those who are capable and willing to make the trek won't be disappointed.

The hardest hike in this book leads to the fantastic Fall Creek Falls.

Miles and Directions

0.0 Hike steeply uphill northeast on the clay path.

0.6 Rock-hop the creek.

1.0 Follow the rocky scramble downhill alongside the falls.

1.1 Arrive at the base of Fall Creek Falls (N35°08.371'/W82°32.256'). Backtrack to trailhead.

2.2 Arrive at trailhead.

95 Reedy River Falls

What a view! You have two winning options here. The Liberty Bridge crosses over the Reedy River right above the falls giving you an exceptional vantage point with a perspective that's not often seen, unless you have a drone that is. After appreciating the aerial aspect, head down to the river's edge for a view that's equally as awesome.

Height: 30 feet
Beauty rating: Very good
Distance: 0.1 mile
Difficulty: Easy
Surface: Cement steps, sidewalk
Hiking time: 5 minutes
Other trail users: Bicyclists
Blazes: None

County: Greenville
Land status: Greenville County Parks and Recreation
Contacts: (864) 288-6470; www.greenvillerec .com/ghs-swamp-rabbit-trail/
Maps: *DeLorme: South Carolina Atlas & Gazetteer:* Page 18 H1

Finding the trailhead: *From the junction of US 276 (Laurens Road) and SC 291 in Greenville,* drive north on US 276 for 1.1 miles. Turn left onto East Washington Street. Travel 0.6 mile and veer left at the stoplight. You'll now follow East McBee Avenue for 0.5 mile. Turn left onto Main Street. Travel 0.3 mile to the entrance to the park on the left. ***Note:*** Parking is street side. **GPS:** N34°50.703'/W82°24.117'

The Hike

A set of steps lead down into the park directly to the Liberty Bridge, which crosses over the falls. The railings of the bridge are see-through, giving you a fantastic view from up above. If you're afraid of heights, you may want to skip this vantage point and instead enjoy the falls from the riverside paved path below. But the best option is to do both! They give you different perspectives and both are equally pleasing.

The paved path is part of the famous Swamp Rabbit Trail. This trail covers 20 miles and weaves from park to park all around the city. Follow it as far as you feel. Greenville has done an amazing job developing a number of "green spaces" and Falls Park is certainly one of them. The park is surrounded by activity, with businesses and traffic steadily at work. But honestly, once you get next to this river the hustle and bustle quickly fades away. There are a few lovely cafes on the outskirts of the park. After enjoying your recreational respite, stop in for a bite and support the local restaurateurs.

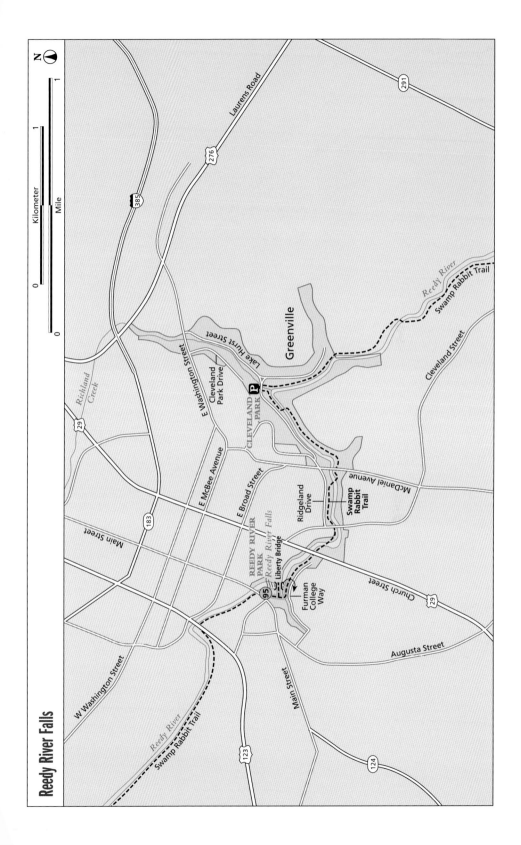

Reedy River Falls

Sitting in the heart of the city, Reedy River Falls is Greenville's crown jewel.

Miles and Directions

0.0 Hike down the steps into Falls Park on the Reedy River.

0.05 View the falls from the path or the Liberty Bridge (N34°50.673'/W82°24.056'). Backtrack to the park entrance.

0.1 Arrive at the park entrance.

96 Horseshoe Falls

Joyful! Not only does the waterfall have a joyful air about it, but the sound of laughter and delight fills the air as the many visitors splash about in the passive Enoree River.

Height: 8 feet
Beauty rating: Very good
Distance: 0.2 mile
Difficulty: Easy
Surface: Sidewalk, hard-packed dirt
Hiking time: 10 minutes
Other trail users: None

Blazes: None
County: Spartanburg
Land status: Musgrove Mill State Park
Contacts: (864) 938-0100; www.southcarolina parks.com/musgrovemill
Maps: *DeLorme: South Carolina Atlas & Gazetteer:* Page 25 D8

Finding the trailhead: *From SC 56 and SC 49 in Cross Anchor,* drive south on SC 56 for 2.1 miles. Turn right onto Horseshoe Falls Road. Drive 1.4 miles to the parking area on the right. *From I-26 near Clinton (from the south),* get off at exit 52. Drive north on SC 56 for 7.6 miles. Turn left onto Horseshoe Falls Road. Follow directions above. The trailhead is across the street from the parking area on the east side of Horseshoe Falls Road. *Note:* The waterfall is in a remote part of the park on the north side of the river. **GPS:** N34°35.815'/W81°51.317'

Daisies line the bank upstream from Horseshoe Falls in springtime.

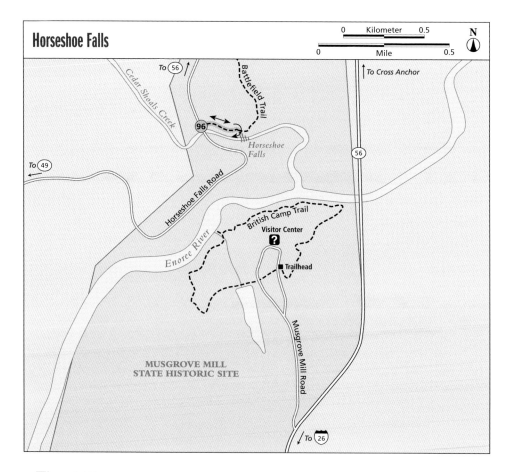

In the map:

0   Kilometer   0.5

0   Mile   0.5

N

To 56

Battlefield Trail

To Cross Anchor

Cedar Shoals Creek

96

Horseshoe Falls

56

To 49

Horseshoe Falls Road

British Camp Trail

Visitor Center

Enoree River

Trailhead

Musgrove Mill Road

MUSGROVE MILL
STATE HISTORIC SITE

To 26

The Hike

The trail begins on the northeast side of the bridge and follows a paved path nearly due east along the Enoree River. You quickly arrive at a flat sandy area at the base of Horseshoe Falls. At 8 feet, this is one of the smallest waterfalls in this book, but it really has a lovely personality about it. The water is shallow and perfect for wading, and depending on the water levels, flat stones jut up out of the water giving you a perfect place to sun yourself. Don't expect any privacy though. This waterfall nearly always has someone sitting peacefully by it.

If you want to take a longer hike, two other trails are found within the confines of Musgrove Mill State Historic Site. The Battlefield Trail shares the same parking lot as Horseshoe Falls, while the British Camp Trail is on the south side of the river in the main body of the park. Both trails are steeped in history, and interpretive signs offer insight into that rich and patriotic history. The park hosts an annual Living History Festival each spring. Hundreds participate, dressing in period attire and reliving a

Slight of size but just as pretty as the rest

time that forged our country. For more information on the festival, contact the park directly.

Miles and Directions

0.0 Follow the sidewalk east.

0.1 Arrive at Horseshoe Falls (N34°35.800'/W81°51.244'). Backtrack to trailhead.

0.2 Arrive at trailhead.

Hike Index

About the Author

Waterfall hunter, nature enthusiast, tree hugger, and avid hiker
Melissa Watson is truly at her
best when she's in the forest. Her
passion for waterfalls and nature in
general stems back to childhood,
and she continues to fulfill that
passion to this day. For the past 30
years Melissa has been exploring
the forests of Georgia and South

Carolina—hiking by day and camping by night continuing her quest for new trails
and new waterfalls. Whether searching for new waterfalls or revisiting old favorites,
she has come to be known as a local expert in the field.

Melissa is a career firefighter and paramedic, with 29 years on the job. She has
been adventure racing since 2000 and continues to master her skills as a navigator and
mountaineer. She is also the author of several other FalconGuides, including *Hiking
Waterfalls North Carolina, Camping North Carolina, Camping North Carolina, Camping
South Carolina, Best Dog Hikes North Carolina, Best Dog Hikes South Carolina,* and *Tour-
ing the Springs of Florida.*

THE TEN ESSENTIALS OF HIKING

American Hiking Society

American Hiking Society recommends you pack the "Ten Essentials" every time you head out for a hike. Whether you plan to be gone for a couple of hours or several months, make sure to pack these items. Become familiar with these items and know how to use them.

1. Appropriate Footwear
Happy feet make for pleasant hiking. Think about traction, support, and protection when selecting well-fitting shoes or boots.

2. Navigation
While phones and GPS units are handy, they aren't always reliable in the backcountry; consider carrying a paper map and compass as a backup and know how to use them.

3. Water (and a way to purify it)
As a guideline, plan for half a liter of water per hour in moderate temperatures/terrain. Carry enough water for your trip and know where and how to treat water while you're out on the trail.

4. Food
Pack calorie-dense foods to help fuel your hike, and carry an extra portion in case you are out longer than expected.

5. Rain Gear & Dry-Fast Layers
The weatherman is not always right. Dress in layers to adjust to changing weather and activity levels. Wear moisture-wicking cloths and carry a warm hat.

6. Safety Items (light, fire, and a whistle)
Have means to start an emergency fire, signal for help, and see the trail and your map in the dark.

7. First Aid Kit

Supplies to treat illness or injury are only as helpful as your knowledge of how to use them. Take a class to gain the skills needed to administer first aid and CPR.

8. Knife or Multi-Tool

With countless uses, a multi-tool can help with gear repair and first aid.

9. Sun Protection

Sunscreen, sunglasses, and sun-protective clothing should be used in every season regardless of temperature or cloud cover.

10. Shelter

Protection from the elements in the event you are injured or stranded is necessary. A lightweight, inexpensive space blanket is a great option.

Find other helpful resources at AmericanHiking.org/hiking-resources

PROTECT THE PLACES YOU LOVE TO HIKE.

Become a member today and take $5 off an annual membership using the code **Falcon5**.

AmericanHiking.org/join

American Hiking Society is the only national nonprofit organization dedicated to empowering all to enjoy, share, and preserve the hiking experience.

American Hiking Society